EBURY PRESS

# THE GOOD HEALTH ALWAYS COOKBOOK

**Charmaine D'Souza** is an Indian dietician, clinical nutritionist, health consultant and author. She has three decades of experience in guiding her clients to good nutrition and healthcare. She is the author of *Kitchen Clinic* and *Blood Sugar and Spice*, published by Penguin Random House India.

**Charlyene D'Souza** has studied naturopathy and has a diploma in nutrition and health education. She has also done a course in culinary nutrition from George Brown College, Toronto.

**Savlyene D'Souza** has studied sport~ ~ ~ied yoga instructor. She has diplom~ ~s well as in food and nutrition.

ADVANCE

'I have been using Charmaine's spice mixes for years now. They literally are my oxygen. Charmaine has the insight, expertise and wisdom to heal even the most difficult and complex health issues. She inspires such confidence in me that I trust her more than any medical doctor or anyone else. Charmaine's empathy and compassion help me remain calm and grounded, even when the going gets really tough. I am so overjoyed that she has shared her unlimited knowledge and experience in *The Good Health Always Cookbook*, which is a must-have on every bookshelf. With this treasure of herbs, spices and vegan recipes, one can easily create and concoct delicious meals with a twist. That too with zero food wastage, healthy choices and, most importantly, by taking full charge of one's own well-being.'—Nadya A. Rahimtoola, author of *Invisible Ties*, psychotherapist and motivational speaker

'I wholeheartedly endorse Charmaine's book, *The Good Health Always Cookbook*. I have been a client of Charmaine's for many many years, and benefitted greatly from her diets, especially in controlling thyroid, diabetes and cholesterol. She is truly gifted and knowledgeable, and I wish her great success with this new book.'—Kirron Kher, member of Parliament, BJP, and Bollywood, theatre and TV actor

'I feel so proud of Charmaine as I was one of her first clients. She has been with my family for over a decade as her treatment is safe and cures any ailment. Her knowledge of the human body is tremendous! Thank you, Charmaine D'Souza, for taking care of my family.'—Neetu Kapoor, Bollywood actor

'Congratulations, Charmaine, for the 30 years of untiring service to humanity. Double congratulations to you as Charlyene and Savlyene have co-authored the third book, *The Good Health Always Cookbook*. All praise to our awesome and living God for gifting you with talents that help you as a family to be at the service of humanity at large. It is God's desire that we care for our bodies and eat nutritive foods to remain healthy. God bless you all abundantly.'—Fr Anthony Rebello, Botswana, Africa

'Charmaine is a health magician. Her simple, easy-to-put-together healing recipes are super effective. You feel the benefits immediately—less bloating, more energy and a feeling of vitality. Within a few days the weight comes off, your skin becomes brighter and your organs are totally revitalized. And the best part, all the ingredients are so easily available. Charmaine rocks!'—Hanut Singh, contemporary jewellery designer

'Charmaine has truly been a delight. She not only positively influences your body with the simple, easy-to-make plans for you to heal, but also makes you look at good health as something natural and necessary.'—Priyanjili Goel, fashion designer, Delhi

'Charmaine Ma'am has been looking after our family's health for some time now. Her recipes have always been effective and doable . . . With Charmaine Ma'am's new book, I am sure we are in for a wonderful surprise, finding bits and pieces which can be used in our stocks, dips, sauces and many more! She introduces us to not only Indian but to a world of different cuisines.'—Michelle Seo, restaurateur, Delhi

# THE
# good health always
## COOKBOOK

*recipes and*
*nutrition secrets for a better you*

## Charmaine, Charlyene and Savlyene D'Souza

EBURY
PRESS

An imprint of Penguin Random House

EBURY PRESS

USA | Canada | UK | Ireland | Australia
New Zealand | India | South Africa | China

Ebury Press is part of the Penguin Random House group of companies
whose addresses can be found at global.penguinrandomhouse.com

Published by Penguin Random House India Pvt. Ltd
7th Floor, Infinity Tower C, DLF Cyber City,
Gurgaon 122 002, Haryana, India

First published in Ebury Press by Penguin Random House India 2021

Copyright © Charmaine, Charlyene and Savlyene D'Souza 2021

ISBN 9780143452904

Typeset in Sabon by Manipal Technologies Limited, Manipal
Printed at Manipal Technologies Limited, Manipal

www.penguin.co.in

# Contents

## MILK, MILK PRODUCTS

## PLANT-BASED MILK/MYLK

# Foreword

Our earliest and fondest memories are of food. We would wake up early in the morning to the aroma of oatmeal, besan chila, uttapams, ragi dosa, chole, khichdi, pulau or omelettes wafting up to our bedroom upstairs, while Mum cooked in the kitchen downstairs. School was a 30-minute drive from home and we had a working mum, so mornings were pretty frenetic in the kitchen. Breakfast, mid-morning snack, lunch and evening snack had to be prepared and packed before we all set out.

On the mornings our favourite mung dal khichdi would be prepared, we would run down to try and grab a spoonful at six in the morning, just before it was packed into our lunch boxes. However, it would take a lot of coaxing to get us to get ready for school if an unfamiliar vegetable or cereal was being prepared.

Did we mention that we would only eat what Mum (or Dad, whenever he was in town) cooked? Poor Mum tried hiring a cook once to ease her workload. But spoilt brats that we were, we would hide our tiffin boxes in the refrigerator, much to Mum's chagrin. In our defence, the cook was useless. She would use our traditional east Indian bottle masala in each and every one of the sabjis she would prepare for us. Realizing that the meals all tasted the same, Mum decided to keep her precious bottle masala locked away one day. What did the smart cook do? She found a box of Gujarati chai masala, which was a gift from one of Mum's Gujju patients, and used it liberally in our mattar palak! Needless to say, she was very kindly relieved of her duties the very next day.

Our Mum says she knew exactly what was in store for her right from the time her first-born (Charlyene) was nine months old. Mum would have to spend most nights playing with Charlyene, who was super excited to be playing with a 'kitchen set' that some well-meaning relative had gifted her. So, at two in the morning, there would be a lot of cooking in our bedroom! By the time the second child (Savlyene) was ready to play, three-year-old Charlyene was an expert at frying 'plastic' eggs, making copious 'empty' cups of tea, burning 'invisible' toast and, of course, using the rolling pin to roll out maps of countries that no one knew of!

Since Mum is a nutritionist, Charlyene was expertly weaned off breastmilk at fifteen months of age. No salt, no packaged food, no commercial infant formula, no sugar, no additives and no preservatives. A mix of cereals and pulses was methodically washed, sprouted, sun-dried and ground to a fine powder. Then a 'secret' spice combination was added for gut health, immunity, mental acuity and calmness. This weaning mix was used to make gruels, porridges, kanjis and, later, rotis, dosas, pancakes, crepes, etc., which Charlyene loved and ate in abundance!

Three years later, our 'well-experienced' Mum made the same weaning mix for Savlyene, expecting her to devour it just like her older sister had. To her utter surprise, Savlyene would howl and cry at the sight of a bowl of 'pap'. Once Savlyene had calmed down, she would turn her little nose away and mutter 'feesh, feesh'. Detective Charmaine just had to get to the bottom of this. Why was her timid tot screaming like a banshee at mealtimes? The perplexing case was soon solved. Our kind house help had once tasted the porridge and found it inedible. So Savlyene's developing taste buds were introduced to a local Goan delicacy—spicy, salty, crunchy, fried mandeli (a tiny fish) that the house help had an affinity for! How can you expect a baby to eat bland, healthy 'pap' after a bowlful of fish? This time around, the house help could not be let go of and was sternly told that, in this case, sharing was NOT caring.

So now, both us children were on the right track and delicious, healthy, nourishing vegetarian meals were what we craved for. East Indian vegetarians? Yes, you read that right! Here we must share that as a child, our dad would only eat rice, dal and dahi, much to the annoyance of his non-vegetarian-loving family. He was nicknamed 'Bhatji'. It was only after he started working on the oil rigs that he started eating meat to avoid facing ridicule from his colleagues and bosses. He was most happy to know that the girl of his dreams loved rice, dal and dahi as much as, if not more, than him. It was her happy meal.

Our childhood was filled with happy, wholesome and delicious meals made at home, made with love, and made by Mum and Dad. If you've been reading intently, you will know that Dad, too, can cook. His onion-chopping skills will make the neighbourhood bhel puri vendor hang his head in shame. However, there is a major difference in the way our parents cook. Mum gets into the kitchen, delves into the pantry, refrigerator, spice cabinet and veggie basket, puts stuff on the chopping board and, a few minutes later, she is done with preparing a meal. A few seconds later, we polish off her healthy concoction. She is a no-fuss cook and, by that, we mean that she does not stress if she is running short on jeera for a jeera pulao or carrots for a jalfrezi. She is the type of person who will find a dhokla mix, add some chopped spinach, grated corn and carrots, pour the mix into cupcake moulds and, 20 minutes later, we will be savouring mouth-watering vegetable muffins. Muffins that we've never tasted before—and will probably never taste again!

But when Dad dons his chef's cap, his entire persona changes. While there is a method to his madness and mess in regular life, he is a stickler for recipe rules in the kitchen. Till date, Mum has to tell him, and us, to keep things in their proper places, because 'meticulous' is her middle name. This rule is almost never adhered to until it comes to the kitchen! Chef Dad will look up a recipe, make a list of ingredients, neatly weigh and measure them, go to the market to buy whatever is not available at home and then start cooking. If the recipe calls for dry-roasting the spices for 3 minutes, Dad will set a timer! Poor Mum starts palpitating and has to take a walk outside to maintain her sanity. Three hours later, the most delicious feast, fit for a king—no, his princesses, us—is ready.

So, growing up in the D'Souza household has been a win-win for us, especially in terms of good food. As we approached our teenage years, we started experimenting in the kitchen. Dad would be away on work assignments for weeks, and sometimes months. By that time, Mum, too, had started consultations in other cities. Her short weekend work trips gave us ample time to try our hand at some weird but memorable meals. If Mum had cooked rajma for us, we would put it into a baking dish with some boiled pasta, smother it in grated cheese and broil it. Sounds good till now, right? However, once it was out of the oven, ingenuity would creep into our very being. This yummy bake would then be slathered in whatever sauce we found in the refrigerator, including a caramel glaze!

Thankfully, better sense has since prevailed. The dawn of adulthood saw us move away from home to study nutrition.

Toronto is a city for foodies. We were introduced to funnel cakes, butter tarts, Nanaimo bars, beaver tails, Timbits, iced capps, poutines, pickled eggs, croque monsieurs, croque madames, cretons, pierogi, pastrami sandwiches and a whole lot of other gastronomical delights. We spent time in the kitchens of our Mum's chef brother and his French-Canadian wife, as well as Mum's sister and her Mangalorean husband. Each of them is a culinary expert in their own right. Uncle Chelston Fernandes or Chelly is a professional chef, who cooks restaurant-style as well as homestyle meals with ease, and Aunty Alley bakes the most amazing French pies, cookies, flans, etc. Aunty Laraine Pinto or Lane loves to make healthy soups, breads, cakes and desserts, while Uncle Allwyn Pinto or O is a wiz at Goan sausages, Mangalorean bafat, vindaloo, Mughlai biryani and butter chicken. So could we be blamed for packing in the pounds while in Toronto?

While our studies in the field of natural and sports nutrition continue, at that time, we also started looking at yoga to improve our flexibility and general well-being. This led to in-depth studies and training at the Yoga Institute, Mumbai. What a cultural change that was from Toronto in terms of food, environment, and the attitudes of the teachers and students towards one another and life in general. It was here that we learnt that the principles of yoga and Ayurveda are like the intertwined branches of the Vedic wisdom tree. Yoga and Ayurveda cannot exist on their own—they must be connected to maintain balance for not just living happily but abundantly as well. Harmony should be prevalent in all aspects of our being—the way we breathe, sleep, eat, drink, walk, talk, act, think and live. Only when this happens will we truly be in a state of good health.

Yoga teaches us that food is sacred and helps balance our mind, body and spirit. These three entities exist as one and cannot be separated. According to Ayurvedic principles, sattvic foods are the purest types of foods that you can consume. These foods help in organ growth and function, increase physical and mental strength, and boost cognitive ability. They also help you achieve a state of good health and increase your lifespan. Good health is not merely an absence of disease and infirmity but a state of physical, mental, emotional, spiritual and social well-being.

At the Yoga Institute, we thrived on a sattvic diet, cooked and eaten with love, gratitude and awareness. The light, easily digestible diet included seasonal fruits and vegetables that were freshly harvested and abundantly available, whole grains, pulses and sprouts, dried nuts, honey, the freshest herbs from their kitchen garden, milk and rennet-free dairy products. The food was cooked in a hygienic open kitchen and the dishes were prepared using minimal oil. They were extremely tasty, despite the fact that no onion, garlic or spices were used in any of the preparations. In Ayurveda, onion, garlic and spices are considered rajasic foods, which deplete your body of energy in the long run. Needless to say, tamasic foods such as eggs, meat, fish, poultry, alcohol and processed foods were never served there because of their ability to make people dull, careless and lacking in motivation. We ate our meals in a calm, serene environment. To say that we thrived there would be an understatement.

Strenuous yogic asana classes, the practice of kriyas, meditation classes, public-speaking sessions, lectures on anatomy, physiology, yogic philosophies and sutras, yogic AVAV—*ahar*, *vihar*, *achar* and *vichar*—and PTS, or practice teaching sessions, culminated in us receiving our yoga training certification.

Apart from this, we launched our entrepreneurial venture, SaCha's TheraSpice, in 2018. We manufacture hot and cold compresses, shoulder wraps, knee wraps, neck compresses, massage stone *potlis*, herbal oils, shampoo and conditioner packs, and have recently started a line of handmade artisan soaps. All our products are filled with the therapeutic benefits of herbs and spices. The venture is a small one and profit margins are meagre, but the pleasure and pride we derive from our clients' positive testimonials is immense.

Coming back to our culinary skills, we've realized that we have embarked on a remarkable but endless journey. Like our dad, we love following recipes right down to the last instruction. Fortunately, like our mum, we also like to innovate, experiment, tweak and elevate a humble dish to another level of deliciousness. Flexitarians, a term we learnt in nutrition school, is what we label ourselves. We are partial to plant-based foods but will occasionally eat fish, chicken and lamb.

*The Good Health Always Cookbook* is our way of saying thank you to God and to the universe.

Charlyene and Savlyene D'Souza

# Introduction

The 'where do I begin?' part of my culinary journey started way, way back in childhood, culminating in an offer to write a cookbook after my first health book, *Kitchen Clinic: Good Health Always with Charmaine*, was published in August 2013. Then, in 2014, once I had finished writing *Blood Sugar & Spice: Living with Diabetes*, I thought I would set a deadline for completing the cookbook but couldn't do that—that is, until now, when the coronavirus pandemic and the subsequent lockdown forced me to rethink the way I looked at life in general and food in particular. *In His Time* is a lovely hymn by Diane Ball that encourages us to trust God's timing for every situation in life. This has been my go-to hymn to listen to every so often. Afterall, He makes all things beautiful, in His time.

Preparing a meal for someone is a significant act of love, especially when the meal is also good for health. The way to a man's heart is through his stomach and the way to increasing his lifespan is by preparing meals that protect his heart and his gut. The world over, dietary guidelines are encouraging us to eat food that has more nutritive value, with little or no added sugar, lesser sodium, lesser fat and more protein, rich in antioxidants, minimally processed and with no additives or preservatives. Science teaches us that the Mediterranean diet—low in fat, high in protein from nuts and seeds, and including plenty of fresh fruits and vegetables, healthy fats from avocados and olive oil, and some artery-friendly red wine—should be made a model diet. But our Indian Ayurvedic diets incorporate therapeutic herbs, spices and condiments in chutneys, gravies, pickles and other dishes to make our food truly medicinal.

Bad food habits, just like old habits, die hard. Changing old food habits for the better involves four important steps. Over time, these bad food habits give way to new, healthier habits that can protect you from a host of health conditions, such as obesity, hypercholesterolemia, hypertension, diabetes, cancer, renal disease and liver cirrhosis, to name a few. The first of the four steps is the contemplation stage, during which you start thinking about incorporating changes in your diet and exercise schedule. Next comes the preparation step, where you make up your mind about following a particular food and activity regimen. This is followed by the action step, in which you start making realistic changes in your lifestyle. These three steps lead to the last step of maintenance, where you stick to your new routine and come to terms with the fact that good health is dependent on lifelong behavioural events and is not just a one-time change.

Now that you've decided to embark on your 'good health always' journey with us, you need to give priority to certain things. Grocery shopping for good health should always be first. My advice here is that whenever you shop for groceries, you must learn to treat your grocery cart as your stomach. Fill it with the best and freshest produce. Your body deserves it. Good nutrition starts with the smart food choices you make in the grocery aisles of your local grocery store or while shopping online. Buying healthy, fresh produce will also ensure that the meals you cook nurture both your and your family's body and mind. Luckily, good, nourishing, nutrient-dense food is not expensive, and shopping for it needn't be complicated. I would like to share some grocery-shopping tips with you. They work very well for me, and I'm sure they would also stand you in good stead.

- Never shop when you are hungry, or you might end up buying in larger quantities, much more than you need. You could also end up buying food products that might not be healthy for you.
- Make a detailed shopping list before you set out, and try your very best to stick to it.
- Head first to the fruit and vegetable section, and shop for fresh fruits and vegetables that add as many colours to your cart as possible. The more varied the colours, the more superfoods and nutrients you will end up with.
- We all get tempted by price markdowns. Discounts are good, but always keep in mind that, more often than not, it's the unhealthier options that are discounted or offered as 'buy one get one free'.
- Add variety to your cart by choosing one item that your family hasn't eaten before or rarely eats, such as red rice poha, green tomatoes or bitter gourd. In this cookbook you will find a recipe for bitter gourd chips, which you should try to make.
- Read food labels carefully, not only for dates of manufacture and expiry but also for nutrient content, especially for salt, artificial colours and sweeteners.
- Avoid buying tinned, canned, bottled or packaged sauces and dips as far as possible. Most commercial brands have a very high salt and sugar content, apart from the fact that they have artificial colours and many non-nutritive elements.
- Shop for leaner cuts of meat, fresh fish and poultry, and for eggs that have clean and intact shells.

- When you return home, make sure the perishable items are washed, prepped and refrigerated first. Food hygiene is extremely important.
- Lentils and other pulses have high protein and low fat content. So make them a priority.
- Always buy small amounts of fresh and dried herbs. Buying in larger quantities may be economical but they will lose their freshness and therapeutic benefits.
- Avoid buying packaged fruit and vegetable juices. It is always better to eat fresh fruits and vegetables. A small amount of freshly squeezed juice extracted at home is better for your health and that of your family members.

The fresh herbs and dried spices that you have purchased on your grocery rounds will be amply made use of to prepare meals using recipes that you will find in this cookbook. They not only make the food taste brilliant, but also have nutritional powers and therapeutic benefits. If you do not believe me, please check the section on 'The Magic of Herbs and Spices'. I have been prescribing herb and spice combinations in our GHA Spice Mix recipes as an essential part of diet therapy, along with spice-infused therapeutic waters. Our clients draw up a list of their ailments, their dietary recall, personal and family health history of major issues such as cancer, cardiovascular disease and diabetes. They also let us know about allopathic, Ayurvedic or homoeopathic medicines and supplements they may be taking. This is just so we can have a better understanding of nutrient-drug interaction. Based on this information, we formulate case-specific herb and spice recipes, which have helped our clients achieve a state of balance in their physical and mental health.

Once you've shopped for your groceries, menu planning should be your next priority when it comes to preparing meals that are simple, easy to make, nutritious and, most importantly, relished by your family members without a fuss. I've been blessed with a family that does not kick up a fuss at the dining table. Rajma burgers, tofu sliders, bajra pizza base with beet-and-carrot-based pizza sauce, methi, karela and every veggie in sight in our pav bhaji, soya keema pav, cucumber cake, black rice salad, broccoli and chana dal soup, spinach brownies— you name it and I've cooked it, and they've asked for more! However, I do consult parents of 'picky eaters'. Hence, I am always on the lookout for healthier food alternatives. I tell mums to give their kids' meals a nutritional boost by sneaking in healthy ingredients or by making a few substitutions to the original recipe. Be judicious with key ingredients, add sufficient spices and condiments, and no one will know that your pasta sauce has doodhi in it or that your gajar ka halwa has paneer. You can always sneak in pureed doodhi, karela, beetroot and other vegetables in soups, sauces and gravies. Our cookbook will offer you ample ideas. You are cooking with love, keeping their health in mind. And the reward for this loving deception is good health always!

When you get into the kitchen to prepare meals for yourself and your family, you may not notice just how much edible food 'scraps' end up in the bin. You wash fruits and vegetables, and even before you chop them you remove the peels and put them in the garbage bin designated for wet waste. You are segregating your waste, and you are happy that you are doing your bit to save the environment. But take a minute here to understand that maximum nutrients are found in the tissues just beneath the peel and by discarding these 'scraps', you are losing out on key nutrients. If you are worried about the pesticide residues on non-organic fruits and vegetables, you can either soak them in salt water for 20–30 minutes or clean them with vinegar and baking soda. If you want to keep track of just how much edible food is going into the bin, keep a bowl on the kitchen counter right next to your chopping board. Put the 'scraps' there. This will give you a clearer idea of how much you are wasting. When my children were younger and they had just begun their experiments in the kitchen, they would be rewarded for having 'scrap' bowls with lesser waste. Hopefully after reading our section on 'Reduction of Food Waste', you will never toss out stems, pulp, pith or seeds again.

Inculcating good food habits in children right from the time they are very young is important. I would like to address all parents here. If you are a working parent, I'm sure you have experienced working-parent guilt, just as my husband and I have (and continue to)—the guilt of keeping your children in day care, missing play dates, PTA meetings, coffee mornings or bar nights with other parents, or important milestones in the life of your child (especially if your work involves a lot of travel). The list is endless. It can really stress you out, hijack your thoughts and stop you in your tracks. My husband has been extremely involved in the upbringing of our children, despite having oilfield job assignments in different parts of the world when our girls were younger. He is a great cook and some of the girls' most memorable meals have been prepared by him! So here are some tips that have worked for my husband and me:

- Do not compare yourselves to other parents.
- Do not compare your children to others'.
- Make detailed to-do lists—for yourself, your children and your spouse.
- Go easy on yourself and your children sometimes.
- Delegate work and keep reminding yourself that you are not a superhuman being.

- Breathe deeply, especially before you turn apoplectic with rage.
- Nourish yourself and your family with healthy home-cooked meals.
- Eat well.
- Pray every day.
- Love.

I do hope these tips help you enjoy the journey. Very soon, your little ones will grow up to be independent, resourceful, well-rounded, gloriously IMPERFECT adults, just like you!

You need to look at the food you eat with gratitude and learn to eat intuitively from a place of positivity. Your current food choices should not be viewed as a punishment for previous dietary transgressions. It is important that you feel good while eating a meal and also after it. In today's age of fad diets, detox diets, clean eating and food phobias, there is an increasingly long list of foods that health-conscious people feel guilty about eating. When eaten in the privacy of their homes, they carry the guilt inside them. If they eat them in public, they apologize with every bite, as if in atonement of a great sin. As long as 'not-so-healthy' food is eaten 'not-so-regularly', there should be no guilt associated with its occasional consumption. Food is not a reward—it is a source of fuel. Period. So if you are really craving something that is not on your list of healthy dishes, eat a small portion of it and move on with life.

Your health is your greatest asset and armed with *The Good Health Always Cookbook,* I do hope you will be able to make your greatest asset your greatest benefit.

Stay blessed with good health . . . Always!

# The Miracle of Herbs and Spices

Exotic, aromatic and exciting, herbs and spices play a stellar role in almost every culinary delight. They stimulate the appetite and heighten the anticipation of what is to come, even before you have eaten that first morsel of food. Apart from adding to our enjoyment of food, they are invaluable ingredients in folk medicines as well as in modern medications. The phytochemicals derived from herbs and spices interrupt the damaging path of a variety of diseases. There are hundreds of research programmes conducted by medical authorities that verify the inclusion of these super substances in healing protocols for practically every ailment.

The antioxidant values of foods are expressed as ORAC (oxygen radical absorbance capacity) units per 100 gm of food. The spices we use in our daily cooking, such as the ones listed below, have the potential to prevent diseases such as cancer, diabetes, cardiovascular disease, psoriasis, asthma and even Aids. Foods that have a higher ORAC score may be more effective in negating the effects of free radical damage that contributes to degeneration and disease. Each of our GHA Spice Mix Therapy recipes and GHA Therapeutic Water recipes that we prescribe for our clients makes use of these miraculous herbs and spices. Almost all the recipes in this cookbook incorporate fresh herbs and dried spices that account for a significant part of the antioxidant property of the dish.

**ASAFOETIDA (HING)** is used as a carminative and cures various digestive disorders such as colic and stomach spasms, acidity, intestinal worms and digestive weakness. The strong, unpleasant smell of hing has earned it the names 'stinking gum' and 'devil's dung'. It has been used to treat mood swings and depression, to calm hysteria and epilepsy, to heal painful menstrual cramps and to be an opium antidote to opium addicts. **ORAC value: 18,967**

**BAY LEAF (TEJ PATTA)** is effective in treating migraines, diabetes, gastric ulcers, bacterial and fungal infections, rheumatism, amenorrhea, colic, maintaining blood sugar levels, pulse rate and blood pressure, and improving the immune system. Bay leaf is also used as an antidote to poison. **ORAC value: 289**

**BISHOP'S WEED (AJWAIN)** stimulates the appetite and enhances digestion. The aroma from crushed ajwain seeds provides respite in heavy colds and migraines. Its oil is used in ear drops for earache. The seeds relax the uterus and provide relief from menstrual cramps. This herb contains several chemicals that used to make prescription medications. **ORAC value: 52,133**

**CARDAMOM (ELAICHI)**(green) helps treat infections in the teeth, gums, throat, lungs, eyelids and the digestive system. It has been used as an antidote for scorpion and snake bites. Black cardamom relieves stomach-gas formation, soothes the mucus membranes, improves vision, treats abnormal appetite increase, reduces ulcers and inflammations, acts as a mild aphrodisiac and is used to treat a variety of male health issues. **ORAC value: 2764**

**CINNAMON (DALCHINI/TAAJ)** is an excellent fat burner. It stops vomiting, relieves flatulence and, when consumed with steamed rice, helps control diarrhoea and haemorrhage in the womb. It is also the magic ingredient for an apple pie. **ORAC value: 131,420**

**CLOVES (LAUNG)** provide relief from toothaches, sore gums, oral ulcers, abdominal gas and bloating, peptic ulcers, nausea, hiccups, motion sickness and vomiting. It also purifies the blood, stabilizes blood sugar levels and augments disease resistance. Clove oil is an antiseptic and antifungal, excellent for skin disorders such as acne. It relaxes the mind, reduces mental exhaustion, insomnia, fatigue, depression, anxiety and memory loss. **ORAC value: 290,283**

**CORIANDER (DHANIYA)** is used to decrease gas, manage bowel movements, ease nervousness, reduce fevers and increase appetite. The seed and leaf help treat dysentery, flu, vomiting, chicken pox, glandular enlargement, measles, hernia, insomnia, haemorrhoids, nausea, thirst, cold and coughs, piles, stomach ache, swellings, anxiety and gastritis. **ORAC value: 5141**

**CUMIN (JEERA)** reduces superficial inflammation and pain, soothes skin itchiness, purifies the blood, kindles the appetite, improves digestion, and reduces indigestion, flatulence and stomach heaviness. It also reduces inflammation of the uterus and increases milk production in lactating mothers. **ORAC value: 50,372**

**CURRY LEAVES (KADIPATTA)** are rich in iron, calcium, vitamin A and amino acids. The leaves tend to excite the taste buds, relieve stomach ulcers caused due to excessive acid secretion and control diarrhoea. Curry leaves are known to be effective in treating premature greying. **ORAC value: 39,208**

**FENNEL (SAUNF)** benefits the stomach and intestines, aids in digestion, stimulates metabolism, helps improve and cure problems related to irritable bowel syndrome (IBS) and the spleen, improves liver and kidney function, and protects against cardiovascular disease and cancers (especially oestrogen-dependent cancer). Fennel tea is used to treat respiratory congestion, cough, bronchitis, sore throat and hoarseness of voice. **ORAC value: 30,289**

**FENUGREEK (METHI)** improves digestive-tract function, acts as a cleansing agent, heals ulcers in the digestive tract, acts as a mild laxative, helps remove toxins from the body and, most importantly, helps diabetics manage their blood sugars. **ORAC value: 2090**

**GARLIC (LASAN)** has anti-parasitic, antiseptic and fungicidal properties to treat vaginitis, candida and ringworm. It helps lower blood pressure and cholesterol, aids digestion and prevents flatulence. Externally, garlic juice is an excellent antiseptic for treating wounds while internally, it helps alleviate asthma. Let its strong smell not be a deterrent. **ORAC value: 6665**

**GINGER (ADRAK)** is a classic tonic for the digestive tract that stimulates digestion, prevents vomiting, boosts the pumping action of the heart, protects the stomach from the damaging effects of alcohol and non-steroidal, anti-inflammatory drugs, and may help prevent ulcers. It is also used as relief for sore throats if added to warm water and used to gargle with. **ORAC value: 14,840**

**LIME (NIMBU)** prevents urinary and respiratory disorders, and constipation. It also helps with weight loss, skin and eye care, and digestion, and heals scurvy, piles, peptic ulcers, gout and gum inflammation. It is a good appetizer and digestive. It helps cure arthritis, rheumatism, early-stage prostate and colon cancer, cholera, arteriosclerosis, diabetes, fatigue, heart diseases and even very high fever. **ORAC value: 823**

**MACE (JAVITRI)** is the outer lacy orange-red cover of nutmeg. It takes 400 pounds of nutmeg to produce 1 pound of mace. Mace is used to cure gastrointestinal disorders, malaria and measles. It is also used in combination with other herbs as an aphrodisiac and galactagogue (lactation stimulant). Mace can also be chewed to prevent halitosis. **ORAC value: 82,103**

**MANGO POWDER (AMCHUR)** is acidic, astringent and antiscorbutic in nature. It has a high iron content, which is good for pregnant women and people suffering from anaemia. It fights acidity, improves digestion and unclogs skin pores. It is a superior source of vitamins A and E, which helps the hormone system function proficiently. **ORAC value: 102,190**

**MINT (PUDINA)** acts as an analgesic, helps dissolve gallstones, eliminates heartburn, improves bile acid and lecithin levels in the gallbladder, kills microorganisms (*Candida albicans*, *Herpes simplex*, influenza A viruses and the mumps virus), inhibits constipation and diarrhoea, and serves as a mild anaesthetic to the stomach wall. It also normalizes gastrointestinal activity, prevents congestion of blood in the brain, reduces cholesterol levels and stimulates circulation. **ORAC value: 13,978**

**NUTMEG (JAIPHAL)** has antibacterial properties and kills cavity-causing bacteria in the mouth. Alzheimer's is promoted by a certain enzyme in the brain. Myristicin in nutmeg inhibits production of that enzyme, preventing Alzheimer's and improving memory. In small doses, nutmeg reduces flatulence, aids digestion, improves appetite, combats asthma and relaxes muscles. However, when taken in large quantities (more than 10 gm), it has hallucinogenic effects, so be careful. **ORAC value: 69,640**

**ONION SEEDS (KALONJI)** are used to treat asthma, rheumatism and other inflammatory diseases. Its oil is used to treat eczema and boils, colds and diabetes. It normalizes secretions of the stomach and the pancreas. It removes mucus obstruction in the lungs, expels gases and strengthens the stomach. **ORAC value: 4728**

**OREGANO**, a favourite pizza topping with many, is used to treat indigestion, bloating, flatulence, coughs, urinary problems, bronchial problems, headaches and swollen glands, and to promote menstruation. It has also been used to relieve fevers, diarrhoea, vomiting, jaundice, pain from rheumatism, swelling, itching, aching muscles and sores. **ORAC value: 175,295**

**PAPRIKA** is used for relieving sore throats, coughs, colds, nasal congestion, fever and headaches. Paprika is useful for treating obesity and boosting immunity. It helps the breakdown of carbohydrates in one's diet, keeping blood sugar levels from fluctuating widely after meals. It is beneficial in controlling diabetes. **ORAC value: 21,932**

**PARSLEY** is a natural cure for bladder, prostate and kidney issues. Parsley root is a diuretic used for dropsy (abnormal accumulation of fluid in body tissues or a body cavity), decongestion of abdominal viscera and for lowering blood pressure. It helps bring down fever, improves blood circulation, helps toxin elimination, stimulates blood flow in the pelvic area and the uterus, checks menstrual problems such as amenorrhoea and dysmenorrhoea, purifies the digestive system, urinary tract, bladder and the uterus. **ORAC value: 1301**

**PEPPERCORNS (KALI MIRCH)** have been used to treat colds and upper-respiratory-tract infections, indigestion, vomiting, diarrhoea, flatulence, constipation, earache, gangrene, heart disease, hernia, insect bites, insomnia, joint pain, liver and lung disease, sunburn and toothache. They promote proper urination and sweating that helps get rid of harmful toxins from the body. They should not be used by patients who are going to have or have recently had abdominal surgery. **ORAC value: 27,618**

**POMEGRANATE SEEDS (ANARDANA)** have natural oestrogenic, antioxidant, antimicrobial and anti-inflammatory properties. They improve skin elasticity, provide relief from minor skin irritations and inflammation, including dry skin, eczema, psoriasis and sunburnt skin. They are rich in polyphenols such as tannins, quercetin and anthocyanins, which offer heart health and anti-cancer benefits. **ORAC value: 4479**

**POPPY SEEDS (KHUS KHUS)** have anti-inflammatory and antiseptic effects that provide relief from inflammations in the circulatory and nervous systems. They help check gout, arthritis, rheumatism and other bone-related diseases. Khus khus oil has a sedative effect and helps in the treatment of insomnia, anger, anxiety, epileptic and hysteria attacks, restlessness and nervousness. **ORAC value: 481**

**PUMPKIN SEEDS (KADDU KE BEEJ)** promote overall prostate health and alleviate difficult urination associated with an enlarged prostate. They help treat depression too. They are high in zinc and protect against osteoporosis. They lower blood pressure and cholesterol, and are a natural cure for tapeworms and intestinal parasites. **ORAC value: 526**

**SAFFRON (KESAR)** is used to treat mild or moderate depression. Saffron is taken at bedtime, usually in tea or milk, to treat insomnia. It is also helpful in treating asthma by clearing the airways to aid breathing. Saffron acts as an antioxidant and stimulates blood circulation, which prevents hardening of the arteries. Carotenoids in saffron help fight cancers such as leukaemia and sarcoma. Women use saffron to induce menstruation and take care of painful periods. **ORAC value: 20,580**

**STAR ANISE (STAR PHOOL)** improves memory, prevents flatulence, gets rid of oily skin, boosts milk production for nursing mothers, acts as a natural antacid, cures coughs, bronchitis and asthma, relieves menopausal discomfort, treats prostate cancer in men and is a potential treatment for hepatitis and cirrhosis. **ORAC value: 11,300**

**TAMARIND (IMLI)** is used for treating colds, constipation, liver problems, gall bladder ailments, fever, nausea during pregnancy, intestinal parasites and stomach complaints. It is applied to the skin as a dense paste to make a cast for broken bones. Tamarind-seed extract is also used in eye solutions to treat symptoms of dry eyes. **ORAC value: 3500**

**TURMERIC (HALDI)** has a range of benefits, which make use of its powerful anti-inflammatory abilities that researchers believe make it a cure for arthritis and joint stiffness, and even Alzheimer's. Turmeric is extremely helpful in curing common cold, healing wounds, infections of the liver and is even used as a blood purifier. It acts as an antiseptic for small scratches and burns, as it has the ability to fight bacteria. This spice is useful in aiding digestive-tract and circulatory-system problems, along with being an antioxidant. **ORAC value: 159,277**

# The Reduction of Food Waste

Long before the coronavirus pandemic and its subsequent lockdown forced us all to rethink the way we look at and deal with food ingredients, food wastage has been on the top of the minds of many conscientious meal makers. Food 'scraps', those edible but unused parts of vegetables, fruits, meat, fish and poultry, do not have to find their way into the garbage bin. Putting them there is really a waste of some of the nutritive value of the food as well as tonnes of flavour. If used intelligently, these 'scraps' have the potential to be converted into great dishes, filled with taste-bud-tantalizing flavours as well as nourishment. Top chefs from around the world, including the late Anthony Bourdain, have created inspiring dishes from food 'scraps' that would have otherwise sadly gone to waste. *Wasted! The Story of Food Waste* has greatly inspired us and helped us take on the challenge of eliminating food waste and reducing our expenditure on various artificial nutraceuticals.

So what comes to mind when you see cauliflower stalks, coriander stems, melon seeds, celery roots, red pumpkin peels, the bones and skin of meat, fish and poultry lying around on your kitchen countertop, chopping board or sink? We hope it's not the garbage bin. Please remember that these are not just bits to be discarded. If used well, food 'scraps' can be used as important bases for dishes that provide varied layers of texture and flavour to a meal. In current times, when produce is difficult to come by, not because of scarcity but because we are making fewer grocery rounds, reduction of food waste is very important. Understanding this and learning how to safely cook with food 'scraps' prolongs the use of the different food groups and stretches to the maximum every rupee we spend on our food. There are the added benefits of diverting these foods from garbage bins and teaching us to value each and every part of our food and create sustainable, environment-protecting, healthy habits in the process.

To learn that more than 70 per cent of household food waste could have actually been incorporated into recipes and eaten is a crying shame, especially in our country, where thousands of people go to bed hungry. Imagine hundreds and thousands of ripened bananas that could have been part of a mid-morning snack; tonnes of melon and pumpkin seeds that could have been toasted and added to a salad or bhel; kilos and kilos of mint and coriander stems that could have gone into making soups, chutneys, gravies and pachadis; large amounts of filleted-fish skin that could have been cured and crisped and used in salads; meat bones that could have been used to make soup stock and bone broth—all ending up in the garbage bin. A colossal waste of money and resources! All the food waste that ends up in the garbage bin and subsequently in a landfill is damaging to our environment because of the greenhouse gases it produces. To prevent this from happening, we have listed some easy hacks for you to use up all those food 'scraps' in your kitchen. Most of our recipes also make use of these 'scraps'. This is 'root-to-stem' cooking at its simplest and best.

SEEDS of white pumpkin, red pumpkin, cucumber, winter melon, musk melon, watermelon, sunflower, etc., can be washed, dried and roasted until crisp. They make for crunchy snacks and healthy additions to soups, salads, breakfast cereals, granola bars, muffins, seed butters and chikkis. Jackfruit seeds can be boiled and eaten plain or added to gravies, dals, kadhis and smoothies, or made into jackfruit-seed butter. Jackfruit-seed atta can also be used in baking and for making rotis.

**ROOTS AND TOPS** of root vegetables such as yams, beets, turmeric, ginger, radishes, carrots, potatoes, sweet potatoes and turnips may not be the main parts of the vegetables but are still delicious, edible and high in nutritive value. Since these root vegetables grow under the soil, they absorb a large amount of nutrients from it. So you are wasting nutrients if you throw away the roots and tops. Collect them in a freezer bag or box, and use them in soups, sauces, juices, green smoothies and gravies. Beet greens are a perfect addition to Russian borscht. You can also blend them together and use them when you are making cutlets, kebabs, falafel and burgers. When cooked well, they also make a great addition to stuffed parathas, pulaos and chilas.

**STALKS AND STEMS** of broccoli, cauliflower, spinach, mint, coriander, parsley and oregano should definitely not be discarded. Some of the stalks are tough and many stems can be bland or bitter. Just cook the tough stalks well and add them to the main dish or to a side dish, along with some crumbled cheese or paneer, lemon juice, vinegar, pepper, sea salt, olive oil, nuts and dried herbs. If you use only the whites of spring onions, please continue chopping the greens too, else you will have lost out on 50 per cent of its nutritive value. Leek tops can be chopped into bits and cooked until tender. We like to add them to omelettes, vegetable pulaos, stews and soups, or simply use them in place of onions. Broccoli and cauliflower stalks can be sliced and added to stir-fried vegetables, or grated and used to make fritters, frittatas and broccoli/cauliflower rice, or even spiralized just like you would courgettes, zucchini and carrots. The chopped-up stems of herbs and leafy vegetables will add so much more flavour to chutneys, raitas, pestos, hummus, sauces and dips. When used as garnish, they will provide that appealing look and satisfying crunch. When muddled, they will even uplift the flavour of your favourite cocktail and mocktail!

**LEAVES** of broccoli and cauliflower are another source of good nutrients. Wash them well, tear them into smaller pieces, toss them in a little oil, along with some sea salt and chaat masala or cracked pepper, and place them in a hot oven. Move them around occasionally, and 30 minutes later, you will have a bowlful of crispy chips.

**PEELS** of citrus fruits such as oranges and lemons have natural essential oils, and a citrusy flavour and aroma. When you are done with extracting citrus fruit juice, you can zest the peels and use this in a variety of salads and bakery products. After that, you can try to incorporate bits of the peel into cold-pressed oils or vinegars to make amazing salad dressings and vinaigrettes that will provide a flavoursome punch to simple vegetables, steamed quinoa, thuli, lapsi or couscous. Else you can use the citrus peels along with the fruit pulp in marmalades, murabbas, compotes, sherbets, pickles and chutneys. Peels of apples and pears can be placed on a baking tray and allowed to oven-dry. Adding some oil or butter will ensure that they do not burn. They make a crisp, crunchy addition to stodgy oatmeal. Apple and pear peels can also be boiled in water to make delicious caffeine-free fruit teas. Candied citrus orange and lemon peels placed in a cup of hot water right before you place your tea bag will give you an amazing infusion to clear blocked sinusoids. Overripe fruits can be pureed and frozen to save them from ending up in the garbage bin. A scoopful of this puree can then be added to a pancake mix, cake/muffin batter or even to your morning smoothie.

If you put lemon peels in a bowl of water, along with your kitchen dusters, sponges and scourers and scrub pads, and bring this to a boil on the stovetop or in the oven, not only will they get sanitized and disinfected, but your oven as well as your entire kitchen will smell divine!

The inner whitish portions of watermelon peels can be grated and made into a yummy side dish when tempered with mustard seeds and kadipatta. Else discard the outer dark-green skin, grate the whitish rind and make a sweet pickle, much like mango chunda. Or cut the rind into small pieces, place in a clean glass jar along with some cloves of garlic, sea salt, green chillies and oregano, top with water and allow the fermentation process to occur over the next few days. The tangy, spicy pickle that results should be kept in the refrigerator to retard further fermentation. Do try it for its probiotic benefits. Your gut will thank you for it.

Vegetable peels are another excellent source of vitamins and minerals. Nearly half the nutritive value of the food is in the layer just beneath the peel. So if you are sure that your produce is not laden with pesticide residues, please go ahead and use the peels. If not, you can immerse food produce in salt water or a baking soda solution or a vinegar solution. Grated and, in some cases, subsequently steamed peels are a great addition to raitas, kachumbers, halwas, sheeras and phirnis. Beetroots, potatoes and sweet potatoes should ideally be cooked with their peels, provided that they are scrubbed well to ensure that they are free of soil. If, however, you must peel them, save the peels. Spread these in single, even layers over a lightly oiled baking tray. Add a drizzle of vegetable oil, some sea salt, herbs, chilli flakes and/or pepper and bake until crisp in a hot oven. These homemade crisps/chips are a healthy alternative to ready-made preservative- and additive-laden snacks.

**LENTIL, RICE AND VEGETABLE WATERS** should also never be discarded. Use them to make the gravies of the main dish, add them to knead the dough for chapatis, rotis and parathas, or incorporate them in soups, broths and shorbas. Aquafaba is the viscous water in which chickpeas have been cooked. Save this water in a clean container and keep it in the refrigerator. Aquafaba can be used as an egg-white replacement in dishes such as meringues, mousses, macaroons, brownies, pavlovas and marshmallows. The viscous aquafaba mimics the functional and stabilizing properties of egg whites.

If you love eating pickled gherkins, dill, green peppers and cucumbers preserved in brine, what do you do with the fermented brine? We encourage you to save it to add flavour to soups, liven up a bland hummus or salad, marinate meat or poultry or even drink a shot of it daily to improve the health of your gut. When meat is grilled over very high heat, a number of cancer-causing/carcinogenic compounds called HCAs are produced. Marinating meat in this fermented brine for a few hours before grilling it will reduce the amount of HCAs produced.

# Weights and Measures

## WEIGHT

| | | | |
|---|---|---|---|
| 7 gm | ¼ ounce | 200 gm | 7 ounces |
| 20 gm | ¾ ounce | 220–225 gm | 8 ounces |
| 25–30 gm | 1 ounce | 250–260 gm | 9 ounces |
| 40 gm | 1 ½ ounces | 300 gm | 10-½ ounces |
| 50 gm | 1-¾ ounces | 325 gm | 11-½ ounces |
| 60–65 gm | 2-¼ ounces | 350 gm | 12 ounces |
| 70–75 gm | 2-½ ounces | 400 gm | 14 ounces |
| 80 gm | 2-¾ ounces | 450 gm | 1 pound |
| 90 gm | 3-¼ ounces | 500 gm | 1 pound, 2 ounces |
| 100 gm | 3-½ ounces | 600 gm | 1 pound, 5 ounces |
| 110–115 gm | 4 ounces | 700 gm | 1 pound, 9 ounces |
| 120–130 gm | 4-½ ounces | 750 gm | 1 pound, 10 ounces |
| 140 gm | 5 ounces | 800 gm | 1-¾ pounds |
| 150 gm | 5-½ ounces | 900 gm | 2 pounds |
| 175–180 gm | 6 ounces | 1 kg | 2-¼ pounds |

# VOLUME

| | | | |
|---|---|---|---|
| 50 ml | 1-¾ fl oz | 300 ml | 10 fl oz |
| 60 ml | 2 fl oz (4 tbs/¼ cup) | 350 ml | 12 fl oz |
| 75 ml | 2-½ fl oz (5 tbs) | 400 ml | 14 fl oz |
| 90 ml | 3 fl oz (3/8 cup) | 450 ml | 15 fl oz |
| 100 ml | 3-½ fl oz | 475 ml | 16 fl oz (2 cups) |
| 125 ml | 4 fl oz (½ cup) | 500 ml | 18 fl oz |
| 150 ml | 5 fl oz (2/3 cup) | 600 ml | 20 fl oz |
| 175 ml | 6 fl oz | 800 ml | 28 fl oz |
| 200 ml | 7 fl oz | 850 ml | 30 fl oz |
| 250 ml | 8 fl oz (1 cup) | 1 l | 35 fl oz (4 cups) |

# LENGTH

| | | | |
|---|---|---|---|
| 5 mm | ¼ in | 8 cm | 3 -¼ in |
| 1 cm | ½ in | 9 cm | 3-½ in |
| 2 cm | ¾ in | 10 cm | 4 in |
| 2.5 cm | 1 in | 12 cm | 4-½ in |
| 3 cm | 1-½ in | 14 cm | 5-½ in |
| 4 cm | 1-½ in | 20 cm | 8 in |
| 5 cm | 2 in | 24 cm | 9-½ in |
| 6 cm | 2-½ in | 30 cm | 12 in |

# CEREALS AND PSEUDOGRAINS

For hundreds of years, cereal grains from the grass family—such as wheat, rice, sorghum, oats, millets and barley—have played a major role in meeting the nutritional and caloric needs of human beings. They have high carbohydrate, starch, fibre and B-complex-vitamin content, such as thiamine, riboflavin, niacin and pantothenic acid. However, they naturally lack other vitamins, minerals and phytonutrients. Hence, the fortification of cereal grains is essential to prevent micronutrient deficiency in a large percentage of the world's population. The number of foods that can be prepared using cereals as the main base is the largest food group in the world. Cereals are cultivated in large amounts all around the world and are a food staple for many regions.

Pseudograins, or pseudocereals, such as amaranth, buckwheat and quinoa, are not from the grass family. They are rich in micronutrients and phytonutrients. When compared to staple cereals, pseudocereals are richer in minerals such as magnesium, potassium, phosphorus, calcium, iron and zinc. They have more B1 and B2 vitamins, folate and vitamin E than cereals. Most importantly, they are gluten-free. Even though they can be used in place of whole grains to provide excellent nutritional benefits, their use is underutilized by a large section of the population. Their usage is limited to breakfast cereals, snacks and salads.

When cereals and pseudocereals are combined in the diet, they provide an ideal amino acid composition.

1

# BARLEY (JAU)

Barley is a whole cereal grain that has been used in cooking since ancient times. It is readily available in two forms. Hulled barley has an intact germ along with the bran. It is minimally processed to only remove the hard, inedible outer shell. Pearl barley, on the other hand, has neither hull nor bran. Barley is rich in vitamin B6 and folate, both of which are necessary to reduce the levels of homocysteine, a cardiac risk marker. Beta-glucans in barley are a type of fibre that can help lower both LDL cholesterol and blood sugar levels. When you eat barley, its betaine content gets converted to choline in your body. Choline is needed for proper sleep, memory, learning and cognitive ability, reducing inflammation in the body and for fat absorption. Barley also contains lysine, an amino acid necessary for the production of the most abundant protein in the body—collagen. Collagen is found in each and every cell of the body and it gives skin its structure, suppleness and elasticity.

*Pro-tip:* Barley contains gluten, a protein that can cause inflammation in the small intestine of some people. So you will have to avoid it if you have been medically diagnosed with celiac disease, have gluten or wheat allergy, or non-celiac sensitivity to gluten. Read food labels carefully. Barley is found in beer, brewer's yeast, malted milk, milkshakes, malt vinegar and many other food products. The food label could say 'malt extract', 'flavouring', 'syrup', 'maltose' (malt sugar), 'dextrimaltose' or even some types of caramel colouring—all referring to barley.

## LEMON BARLEY

This is an excellent diuretic, which helps prevent the occurrence of urinary tract infections as well as kidney stones. Apart from this, this cooling drink helps balance electrolytes in the body, making it a good choice for people with gastrointestinal disturbances, heat exhaustion and dehydration. It also acts as a marathon runner's saviour. Our summer-beverage list always includes a mandatory bottle of home-made lemon barley.—*Charmaine*

*Preparation time* 10 minutes, plus 8 hours overnight soaking
*Cooking time* 20 minutes
*Serves* 8

*Ingredients*

- 200 gm pearl barley
- 30 mint leaves with stalks
- 4 limes with the peel, deseeded and chopped into pieces
- Salt to taste
- Honey or jaggery sugar (optional)

*Method*

- Wash and soak the pearl barley overnight in about 2 litres of water.
- The next morning, discard the water and boil the barley grains in 4 litres of water for 15 minutes.

- Cool completely, add the mint leaves with the stalks and lime pieces, and set aside for an hour.
- Strain and pour into glass bottles after adding salt to taste and the sweetener (optional).
- Reserve the lime pieces for a pickle or a chutney, or infuse them in a bottle of water to drink through the day.
- Refrigerate and consume 1 litre through the day to derive its health benefits.
- Do not discard the barley grains. Use them to make a delicious Mediterranean barley pilaf (p. 6).

*Nutritive value per serving*

- Energy: 88.33 kcal
- Carbohydrates (CHO) 17.01 gm
- Protein: 3 gm
- Fat: 0.56 gm
- Sodium: 2.31 mg
- Potassium: 80.47 mg
- Calcium: 25.78 mg
- Iron: 0.64 mg
- Vitamin A: 19.93 mcg
- Vitamin C: 9.87 mg

'Charmaine had shared this recipe with me some time ago and I regularly make lemon barley water at home. Both my husband and I had kidney stones; I also used to have urinary infections frequently. But since using this simple home-made lemon barley, we are fine'

—Reema Kare, Nashik

## MEDITERRANEAN BARLEY PILAF

If you make lemon barley a couple of times a week in summer, you will end up with a lot of cooked barley. Please do not waste it. There are so many great dishes you can prepare with it—our Mediterranean barley pilaf is just one of them. The best thing about the recipe is that you do not have to stick to the roasted veggies used here—simply add what you have in stock and you will always end up with a winning dish.—*Charmaine*

*Preparation time* 10 minutes
*Cooking time* 35 minutes
*Serves* 4

*Ingredients*

- 200 gm barley, cooked
- 200 gm mixed vegetables (corn, carrots with the peel, zucchini with the peel, red and yellow bell peppers with the seeds)
- 1 bunch spring onions with green stems, finely chopped
- 8 cloves garlic, minced
- 4 tbs coriander or parsley with the stalks, freshly chopped
- 1 tsp paprika powder
- 4 tbs lemon juice (reserve the zest for dips, salads and bakery products; the lemons for relishes, pickles, chutneys, etc., or infuse them in a bottle of water to drink through the day)
- 1 tbs olive oil for cooking
- 1 tbs extra-virgin olive oil
- Salt to taste

## *Method*

- Dice the vegetables and roast them on a greased baking tray in a hot oven, along with the corn kernels for around 20 minutes.
- Once roasted, bring the baking tray out of the oven, season the roasted veggies with salt and paprika, and set aside.
- Heat 1 tablespoon olive oil in a large pan and sauté the garlic, along with the spring onions.
- Add the boiled barley and cook for 3 minutes.
- Toss the roasted vegetables in with the barley, making sure to add the roasted veggie juice from the baking tray.
- Season with salt and remove the pan from the stovetop.
- Add the extra-virgin olive oil, chopped coriander or parsley, and the lemon juice, and give it a good stir.
- Serve hot.

## *Nutritive value per serving*

- Energy: 208.68 kcal
- CHO: 34.57 gm
- Protein: 6.85 gm
- Fat: 4.78 gm
- Sodium: 13.24 mg
- Potassium: 311.41 mg
- Calcium: 37.33 mg
- Iron: 1.60 mg
- Vitamin A: 135.34 mcg
- Vitamin C: 21.85 mg

'I have often made lemon barley and looked for recipes to use the barley kernels rather than throw them away. This Mediterranean barley pilaf comes as a welcome relief from my regular barley salads. The roasted vegetables, along with the pan juices, provide so much more flavour to the dish. Great taste, great flavour, great recipe'

—Megha Phull, Mumbai

# FINGER MILLET (RAGI)

*Eleusine coracana*, or finger millet, originated in Africa and is a staple in Karnataka, Maharashtra and Tamil Nadu in India. Since it does not contain gluten, it can be safely consumed by even those with celiac disease, wheat or gluten allergy, and non-celiac gluten sensitivity. It is easy to digest, does not form acids and makes for an excellent malted weaning food. It is high in fibre, calcium, iron, potassium, amino acids such as tryptophan and methionine, antioxidants and phytochemicals, and low in fat. Its regular consumption can lower the risk of diabetes mellitus. Finger millet has the highest calcium content among all cereals. In short, finger millet is a functional food and a wonder grain. People with kidney stones should watch their consumption of this grain because of its oxalate content.

*Pro-tip:* Roast ragi flour before you use it in bakery products such as cakes, cookies and muffins. Roasting helps it exude a lovely nutty flavour. Your cake batter will be naturally brown when you use ragi flour, so you can decrease the amount of chocolate the recipe calls for (or omit it completely). Be sure to use a natural sweetener such as jaggery sugar or agave nectar to get a deeper brown colour.

## FINGER MILLET BREAD

If you are looking for healthy grains to make bread with, your search should end here. This loaf of bread slices well and has a good crumb. It tastes good plain and even better when toasted and served with a smidgen of butter as an accompaniment to a bowl of hot soup or crunchy salad. Leftover ragi bread slices can be used to make bread upma or bread pudding.—*Savlyene*

*Preparation time* 20 minutes, plus 2 hours rising time
*Cooking time* 35 minutes
*Serves* 10

*Ingredients*

- 200 gm finger millet flour
- 150 gm wheat flour
- 50 gm oat flour
- 250 ml milk
- 50 ml vegetable oil
- 3 tbs dry yeast
- 2 tbs sugar
- 1 tsp salt

*Method*

- Take a glass bowl and dissolve yeast in 3 tablespoons of lukewarm water.
- Add sugar to the yeast and keep aside for 15 minutes.
- Gradually add spoonfuls of the finger millet flour, wheat flour and oat flour to the yeast mixture.
- Add milk, oil and salt, and knead to form a soft, smooth dough.
- Cover the dough with a damp cloth and keep the bowl in a warm place to allow the bread dough to rise for approximately 2 hours.
- Preheat the oven to 180 degrees Celsius.

- Once the bread dough has risen to double its size, knock it down.
- Place the dough in a greased loaf pan and allow it to rise once again.
- Brush with milk and bake for approximately 30 minutes, until it gets a golden crust.
- Remove from the oven, unmould and allow the bread to cool on a wire rack.
- Once cool, cut the bread into slices with a serrated knife.
- Serve warm.

*Nutritive value per serving*

- Energy: 201 kcal
- CHO: 31.30 gm
- Protein: 5.5 gm
- Fat: 6.03 gm
- Sodium: 1.25 mg
- Potassium: 135.25 mg
- Calcium: 871.41 mg
- Iron: 1.764 mg
- Vitamin A: 0.11 mcg
- Vitamin C: 0.26 mg

'I am always on the lookout for healthier bread recipes. It's a good way to put my breadmaker to good use! This is a nice, dense loaf, which cuts well and has a nutty taste because of the ragi flour. Great with a little butter and some bruschetta. I did add a bit more milk'

—Laraine Pinto, Toronto

## FINGER MILLET PORRIDGE

My earliest food memory is of ragi porridge. I'm told it was part of my weaning food regimen. All the tasty gruels were ragi-based. In fact, growing up, I would always ask for—and readily eat—my 'chocolate' pudding. When I finally tasted chocolate at a classmate's birthday party, I was left wondering why it tasted so different from the 'chocolate' pudding my mum made. Nearly twenty years later, I reserve the right to remain silent on this one, because anything I say will be promptly deleted by the proofreader (MUM)!—*Charlyene*

*Preparation time* 2 minutes
*Cooking time* 10 minutes
*Serves* 4

*Ingredients*

- 120 gm ragi flour, roasted
- 1 tbs pumpkin or sunflower seeds, powdered
- 150 ml coconut milk (reserve the coconut meal for cookies, chutneys or to thicken gravies)
- 2 tbs Goan black jaggery or organic jaggery, grated
- 2 tsp ghee
- 1/2 tsp fennel powder
- 1/4 tsp cardamom powder
- Salt to taste

*Method*

- Mix the roasted ragi flour and pumpkin seed powder with 1/2 cup cold water and stir well, so there are no lumps formed.

- Add 1 cup water and bring to a gentle boil.
- Cook for 5 minutes, stirring all the time.
- Add the fennel powder and cardamom powder along with the coconut milk, and cook for another 2 minutes.
- Just before turning off the flame, add a pinch of salt, the jaggery and the ghee.
- Serve warm.

*Nutritive value per serving*

- Energy: 187.77 kcal
- CHO: 28.49 gm
- Protein: 4.41 gm
- Fat: 6.24 gm
- Sodium: 14 mg
- Potassium: 212.5 mg
- Calcium: 161.47 mg
- Iron: 1.95 mg
- Vitamin A: 3.45 mcg
- Vitamin C: 0.75 mg

'My family needs a hot breakfast every day—no cornflakes, no sandwich, no khakra will do. I tried making this porridge on three occasions and I am happy to say they loved it every time. While the lockdown was on, I used dates to sweeten'

—Malika Sharma, Pune

# OATS (JAEE)

*Avena sativa*, commonly known as oats, is a great breakfast cereal and one of the healthiest foods you can eat. Its beta glucan fibres, resistant starch, avenanthramide antioxidants, avenalin proteins, zinc, manganese, selenium, iron, copper and thiamine content not only protect against heart disease but also help lower post-meal blood sugar and insulin levels, lower LDL cholesterol levels, build immunity, reduce inflammation, suppress appetite, slow the rate of digestion, increase satiety, prevent constipation, aid in weight loss and, when included in the weaning foods of babies, it can also lower the risk of the child developing asthma. It is no wonder, then, that oats are highly recommended by nutritionists the world over. If oats are processed in factories that do not process wheat, they can be safely classified as gluten-free.

*Pro-tip:* If you want to soothe your skin after being out in the sun all day, or treat skin that is itchy or inflamed from eczema, acne or rashes, use oatmeal to bring relief. Finely grind 2 tablespoons of jumbo, steel-cut or even unflavoured instant oats and form an oatmeal paste with 1 teaspoon of pure gulab jal and some cold water. The consistency should neither be too thick nor too runny. Apply this paste on inflamed skin and sit back and relax for 10 minutes. Wash off with cold water. Aveeno, the skin cosmetic brand, derives inspiration for its brand name form 'avena', the botanical name for oats.

## HEALTHY OATMEAL BARS

Avoid undermining all your hard work at the gym by not paying attention to your post-workout meal or snack. These oatmeal bars have a combination of proteins and carbohydrates. They help repair worn-out and sore muscle tissue, and refill depleted energy levels. Our healthy oatmeal bars are ideal to refuel the body for optimal recovery and maximum results, right after you have completed a strenuous workout.—*Savlyene*

*Preparation time* 15 minutes, plus 8 hours to set in the refrigerator
*Cooking time* 0 minutes
*Serves* 16

*Ingredients*

* 200 gm oats (not the instant variety)
* 50 gm almonds, chopped
* 50 gm walnuts, chopped
* 50 gm chia seeds (or flax seeds)
* 50 gm coconut, toasted
* 50 gm pumpkin seeds (or sunflower seeds)
* 150 gm peanut butter
* 150 gm honey, jaggery or date syrup
* 1 tbs cinnamon powder
* 1 tsp vanilla extract
* 1/2 tsp salt

*Method*

* Line a 10-inch square baking pan with 2 long strips of criss-crossed parchment or butter paper. Press the paper

down so that it snugly fits the base and sides of the baking pan.

- Mix the oats with the chopped nuts, toasted coconut and seeds in a large mixing bowl.
- Add the cinnamon and salt, and combine well.
- Mix the peanut butter with the sweetener and vanilla extract, and pour it into the mixing bowl containing the dry ingredients.
- Mix well until the liquid ingredients completely coat the dry ingredients.
- Transfer into the lined baking pan, spread evenly and firmly pat down using the palms of your hands or the base of a drinking glass. The mixture should be tightly packed into the baking pan.
- Cover and let it set in the refrigerator overnight.
- After 8 hours, check if the bars have set. Then remove them from the pan by lifting out the opposite corners of the butter paper.
- Place on a chopping board and slice into 16 equal-sized bars using a sharp knife.
- Wrap each bar in parchment or butter paper and store in the refrigerator.
- Do not forget to carry one in your gym bag!

*Nutritive value per serving*

- Energy: 226.6 kcal
- CHO: 19.2 gm
- Protein: 6.70 gm
- Fat: 13.67 gm
- Sodium: 35.42 mg
- Potassium: 71.93 mg
- Calcium: 37.90 mg

- Iron: 1.17 mg
- Vitamin A: 0.04 mcg
- Vitamin C: 0.10 mg

'This crunchy, sweet, salty bar is addictive and yet good for you. I would love to add some dried cranberries the next time I make it. I used a baking tray with individual rectangular moulds. So I did not need to line the tray with butter paper. I just packed the oat mix tightly into each mould, and a few hours later, they easily slipped out'

—Deanne Pinto, Toronto

## OATMEAL UTTAPAM

Your snack right after a sweat session need not be sweet. It is important to consume good carbs and a minimum of 20 gm protein to replenish all those depleted stores of energy and amino acids. You can hit that nutritional mark by adding 1 scoop of whey protein powder to this recipe. This added protein will make these uttapams a perfect post-workout meal on the go. Omit the whey protein if you haven't worked out.—*Savlyene*

*Preparation time* 15 minutes
*Cooking time* 10 minutes
*Serves* 4

*Ingredients*

- 150 gm oatmeal (not instant oats)
- 100 gm rice flour

- 1 onion, finely chopped
- 2 green chillies, finely chopped
- 4 tbs veggies (corn, tomatoes with the peel and seeds, carrots with the peel, capsicum with the seeds, mushrooms with the stalks, etc.), all finely chopped
- 2 tbs coriander with the stalks, freshly chopped
- 1 tsp ginger, grated with the peel
- 150 gm yoghurt, whisked
- Salt to taste
- 1 tbs vegetable oil
- 1 scoop whey protein powder (optional)

*Method*

- Put the whisked yoghurt into a large mixing bowl.
- Add the oatmeal, rice flour and salt. Mix well and add water to make a batter with a consistency similar to pancake, crepe or dosa batter.
- Let this batter rest for 5 minutes.
- You may now add the whey protein powder (to make it a post-workout snack).
- At this stage, you may choose to add the chopped veggies, onions, green chillies, coriander and grated ginger to the batter. Or add them while the uttapams are being made.
- Heat a griddle, a tawa or a pan, and lightly grease with vegetable oil.
- Stir the batter well and pour a ladle of batter on the pan.
- If you haven't added the veggies previously, you can sprinkle some of them now.
- Cover and cook until the base is done.
- Flip and cook well on the other side as well.

- Repeat until you finish the batter. You should be able to make 8 uttapams.
- Serve warm or cold.

*Nutritive value per serving*

- Energy: 244.47 kcal
- CHO: 36.53 gm
- Protein: 13.04 gm
- Fat: 5.11 gm
- Sodium: 50.34 mg
- Potassium: 327.75 mg
- Calcium: 110.29 mg
- Iron: 3.60 mg
- Vitamin A: 41.72 mcg
- Vitamin C: 9.71 mg

'My mom tried this recipe. The uttapams tasted like pizza!'

—Aarav Phull, Mumbai

# PEARL MILLET (BAJRA)

Pearl millet is a gluten-free grain that finds wide use in the cuisines of people living in Rajasthan, Gujarat, Maharashtra and Uttar Pradesh. Among cereals, pearl millet has the highest folic acid, iron, calcium and potassium content. This makes it an ideal grain choice for pregnant women and for lactating mothers. It is a good weaning food for babies. It makes for a nutritionally complete protein meal when consumed with lysine-rich foods such as soya beans, eggs, sardines, codfish, red meat, tofu and cheese. It offers protection against cancer, diabetes, cardiovascular disease, Alzheimer's disease, anaemia, arthritis and gastrointestinal disturbances, and can even help lower the risk of gallstone formation and prevent insomnia.

*Pro-tip:* Eat this grain in moderation because of its goitrogen content. Goitrogens suppress the normal functioning of the thyroid gland and may cause goitre or enlargement of the gland. Fermentation of this grain further increases goitrogenic activity. So if you have an abnormally functioning thyroid gland, please avoid eating fermented bajra.

## BAJRE KI KHEER/PEARL MILLET PUDDING

Kheer, a one-pot traditional dessert, is made from milk, jaggery or sugar, some cardamom powder and a variety of bases, ranging from rice to grated pumpkin, sago, carrots, broken wheat, vermicelli, ragi, corn and even garlic. Bajra kheer is popular in Rajasthan, and this particular recipe is from one of our staff from Fatehpur who takes great pride in his Shekhawati heritage. I have modified the recipe a bit, because the original made it extremely sweet.—*Charlyene*

*Preparation time* 10 minutes
*Cooking time* 15 minutes
*Serves* 4

*Ingredients*

- 6 tbs pearl millet, boiled or pressure-cooked (preferable to soak for an hour and then cook)
- 1 tbs ghee
- 3 cups milk
- 3 tbs jaggery
- 10 strands of saffron
- 1/4 tsp cardamom powder
- 1/4 tsp nutmeg powder

*Method*

- Soak the strands of saffron in 4 tablespoons of water and keep aside.
- Heat ghee in a pan and fry the cooked pearl millet for 4 to 5 minutes until it browns a bit.
- Add the milk and cook until the milk thickens, for about 10 minutes.
- Add the spice powders.
- Adjust the consistency with more milk or water. It should neither be too thick nor too thin.
- Remove from the stovetop and add the jaggery and the saffron water, along with the strands of saffron.

- Pour into earthen pots (optional) and serve warm or cold, garnished with a few nuts (optional).

*Nutritive value per serving*

- Energy: 280.62 kcal
- CHO: 32.58 gm
- Protein: 8.46 gm
- Fat: 12.94 gm
- Sodium: 48.97 mg
- Potassium: 341.15 mg
- Calcium: 227.64 mg
- Iron: 2.23 mg
- Vitamin A: 8.85 mcg
- Vitamin C: 3.56 mg

'I have regularly eaten this porridge kheer at Charmaine Ma'am's place as a mid-evening snack. When I tried making it at home, it was too thick the first time. But I have aced the consistency since then and my parents now think I am a great cook'

—Namrata Rahul, Mumbai

## BAKEDBAJRAKOTHIMBIRVADI/SPICYMILLETSQUARES

The Maharashtrian staple kothimbir vadi is a spicy snack made with chickpea flour. It is first steamed, then cut into squares and deep-fried. I used bajra flour instead of chickpea flour once to make the vadis and it tasted so good that I just had to make them again. This time around, I baked the vadis. Every step you take to make food healthier counts!—*Charmaine*

*Preparation time* 15 minutes
*Cooking time* 20 minutes
*Serves* 4

*Ingredients*

- 200 gm bajra flour, roasted
- 6 tbs fresh coriander with the stalks, finely chopped
- 2 tbs peanuts, roasted and coarsely ground
- 1 tbs home-made ginger-garlic-green-chilli paste
- 4 tbs yoghurt
- 1/2 tsp turmeric powder
- A pinch of pepper powder
- 1/2 tsp red chilli powder
- 1/2 tsp cumin powder
- 1 tbs white sesame seeds
- Salt to taste
- 1 tsp jaggery powder

*For tempering*

- 1/2 tbs vegetable oil
- 1/2 tsp mustard seeds
- A pinch of asafoetida

*Method*

- Preheat the oven to 180 degrees.
- In a large bowl, mix all the ingredients, with the exception of the sesame seeds and the oil.

- Add some water to make a very thick batter.
- Leave aside for 15 minutes.
- Pour this batter into a greased baking pan and sprinkle the sesame seeds on top.
- Bake on the centre rack of the oven, preferably in a water bath, until an inserted toothpick comes out clean.
- Once it cools, cut into squares.
- Heat the oil in a pan, temper the mustard seeds until they splutter, add the asafoetida and pour this over the baked vadis.
- Serve hot with green chutney or tomato sauce.

*Nutritive value per serving*

- Energy: 253.56 kcal
- CHO: 35.73 gm
- Protein: 7.95 gm
- Fat: 8.76 gm
- Sodium: 9.15 mg
- Potassium: 273.17 mg
- Calcium: 46.93 mg
- Iron: 3.75 mg
- Vitamin A: 3.121 mcg
- Vitamin C: 0.15mg

'Both measurement-wise and taste-wise, this recipe is perfect. Baking time in my oven is around 25–30 minutes. I feel that curry leaves can also be added while tempering these vadis. This is a good, healthy snack'

—Tejal Malani, Hyderabad

# RICE (CHAWAL)

There are over 40,000 varieties of rice—the seed of the grass species *Oryza sativa*, grown worldwide on every continent, except in Antarctica. Our Indian long-grain basmati rice is one of the three most famous varieties, the other two being the fragrant Thai jasmine rice and the Italian Arborio rice, which is used for making risotto. Uncooked white rice will stay on the shelf for more than ten years, but uncooked brown rice will last for not more than six months because of the oxidation of the bran coat. The texture of cooked rice is largely affected by its amylose and amylopectin starch content. Sticky rice has more amylopectin and lesser amylose, and cooks into a glutinous mass ideal for making sticky rice pudding. Basmati rice, on the other hand, has more amylose and lesser amylopectin, and hence cooked rice grains stay separate and do not clump together. The higher the amylose content of the rice variety, the more difficult it is to digest. So sticky rice is easily digested, but the downside is that this quick digestion leads to an unhealthy spike in blood sugar levels, which is more pronounced if one is diabetic. Brown rice, which has both bran as well as germ, has a lower glycaemic index (GI, a measure of how foods affect post-meal blood sugar levels) and can help control blood sugar levels.

*Pro-tip:* Food Protein-Induced Enterocolitis Syndrome (FPIES), a condition affecting babies and younger children, is commonly triggered by rice consumption. It is not a typical allergic reaction but more of an immune response. The gastrointestinal symptoms include vomiting, bloody diarrhoea, dehydration, inflammation of the small and large intestines, low blood pressure and lethargy. FPIES triggers could also include milk and soya-based infant formulas, potatoes, sweet potatoes, fish and certain shellfish. Avoid the food triggers if a baby or a child exhibits these symptoms.

## ARANCINI DI RISO

These Sicilian rice balls are a delicious way of using up leftover rice or risotto. *Arancini* means 'little oranges' in Italian. The original recipe shared by my uncle makes use of leftover risotto, is stuffed with mozzarella, tomato sauce or a meat sauce, dipped in flour, beaten eggs and breadcrumbs, and deep-fried. He loves to surprise his guests by changing the filling and leaving them guessing as they pop each ball of yumminess in their mouths. Well, we at GHA have your good health to think of, right? So I've used lesser cheese, added paneer, stuffed them with a previously made mango chipotle jam (p. 264), omitted the eggs and air-fried them.—*Charlyene*

*Preparation time* 1 hour 25 minutes
*Cooking time* 35–40 minutes
*Serves* 8

*Ingredients*

- 2 cups leftover cooked rice (Arborio or any short-grain rice)
- 2 tbs pumpkin seeds, roasted and coarsely ground
- 50 gm Parmesan cheese, grated
- 100 gm paneer, crumbled
- 2 tbs fresh parsley or coriander with the stalks, finely chopped

- 5 fresh basil leaves, finely chopped
- 2 tbs of any filling, such as finely chopped sauteed mushrooms or tomato concasse (p. 225). I've used some of our mango chipotle jam (p. 264)
- 1 cup breadcrumbs
- Salt to taste
- 1–2 tbs vegetable oil

## Method

- Heat the leftover rice in a pan with 4 tablespoons of water until it gets soft (you can add a small amount of butter too).
- In a large bowl, combine the cooked rice, pumpkin seeds, Parmesan cheese, paneer, basil and parsley, and set aside.
- Add salt to taste.
- Shape the mixture into table tennis-size balls.
- Stuff the centre of each ball with a small amount of the filling and reshape into balls.
- Roll the balls in a bowl of the breadcrumbs and cool overnight or for a minimum of 1 hour.
- After bringing them out from the fridge, you may have to roll them in breadcrumbs again.
- Heat the air fryer on high and fry in batches after greasing the base with vegetable oil.
- You can use a paniyaram or appe pan instead of an air fryer.
- Serve hot with a dipping sauce of your choice.

## Nutritive value per serving

- Energy: 216.12 kcal
- CHO: 25.14 gm

- Protein: 7.83 gm
- Fat: 9.36 gm
- Sodium: 109.28 mg
- Potassium: 35.15 mg
- Calcium: 185.11 mg
- Iron: 0.54 mg
- Vitamin A: 30.18 mcg
- Vitamin C: 4.98 mg

'We all love the idea that the leftover rice gets used up to make a great dish, and also that we can use any filling we want. I tried mushrooms once and spicy carrot pickle another time. I do not have an air fryer, so I lightly fried them. It's a great recipe. Thank you'

—Sudha V. Trivedi, Ranchi

## VAGHARLELO BHAAT

This Gujarati tempered-rice preparation is a quick, easy, tasty and healthy way to use up the leftover rice just lying in your refrigerator. Throwing food into the garbage bin is something I abhor. When I was younger, I would even get someone else to discard my plate waste, probably because an old house help had scared me into believing that God would not forgive me if I ever did this! So now, when I find leftover rice, depending on the time I have to spare, I use it to make dishes that range from croquettes, dosas, Arancini balls and sticky rice puddings to this quick and deeply satisfying meal in a bowl. Do try it.—*Charlyene*

*Preparation time* 5 minutes
*Cooking time* 7–8 minutes
*Serves* 4

## Ingredients

+ 2 large cups leftover cooked rice
+ 1 tsp tamarind paste
+ 1 tsp red chilli powder
+ 1 tsp cumin powder
+ 1 tsp coriander powder
+ 1/2 tsp turmeric powder
+ 1/4 tsp pepper powder
+ 1 tbs peanuts, roasted
+ 2 tbs lime juice (reserve the lime for chutneys, pickles, etc., or infuse it in a bottle of water to drink through the day)
+ Salt to taste

## For tempering

+ 1 tbs vegetable oil
+ 1/2 tsp mustard seeds
+ 3/4 tsp cumin seeds
+ 10 curry leaves

## Method

+ To the leftover cooked rice, add all the spice powders and tamarind paste, and mix well.
+ Heat oil in a pan and temper the mustard seeds.
+ Once they pop, add the cumin seeds and the curry leaves.
+ Add the previously spiced cooked rice and salt to taste.

- Allow the rice to heat well and then remove from the stovetop.
- Add the roasted peanuts and a squeeze of lemon juice, and give it a quick stir.
- Serve warm with some chilled dahi or raita.

*Nutritive value per serving*

- Energy: 294.91 kcal
- CHO: 59.56 gm
- Protein: 6.18 gm
- Fat: 3.55 gm
- Sodium: 1.23 mg
- Potassium: 143.7 mg
- Calcium: 6.56 mg
- Iron: 0.36 mg
- Vitamin A: 3.21 mcg
- Vitamin C: 0.04 mg

'My husband and son love spicy food, so I added more red chilli powder to the dish. We eat the rice with dahi and I am happy that I do not need to make more dishes. It is a complete dinner in itself'

—Meena Pereira, Bengaluru

# SORGHUM (JOWAR)

This gluten-free grain has evolved from being a crop grown specifically to feed livestock to a multifaceted grain that is a boon to people with irritable bowel syndrome (IBS), celiac disease and gluten sensitivity. Until a few years ago, molasses made from sorghum were widely used in place of expensive sweeteners. The grain and flour are nutritious staples, with many essential health benefits. It promotes gut health, enhances heart health, boosts energy levels, strengthens bones, improves blood haemoglobin levels, aids in weight loss and helps improve the health of the largest organ of your body—the skin. The antioxidants and phytochemicals present in sorghum, such as anthocyanins, phenolic acids, phytosterols and tannins, are anti-inflammatory in nature. Sorghum has a low GI and is a good cereal choice for diabetic patients and those with insulin resistance. It is a healthy alternative to all-purpose flour, maida or refined flour.

*Pro-tip:* Use sorghum flour to make a face pack by mixing it with equal parts whisked yoghurt. Add a few drops of honey and the white of an egg (optional), and leave the pack on your face for about 20 minutes. Rinse off with cold water, pat dry and apply an ice cube in circular motions. Radiantly glowing and well-hydrated skin will be your reward.

## SORGHUM BHELPURI

Bhelpuri is a popular street food thought to have originated in Mumbai, India's maximum city. No trip to Mumbai is complete without a visit to Chowpatty, or the Juhu beach, to tuck into this snack. It has a medley of tastes and textures—sweet, salty, spicy, tangy and very crunchy. You will find a bhel vendor on practically every street corner in Mumbai, each with his own set of clients. The recipe for this bhel was given to us by a Jain client, so it does not have any onions in it. You can add chopped onions and also serve this with a garlic chutney if you like. It has a great mix of carb-rich sorghum and protein-rich paneer.—*Savlyene*

*Preparation time* 10 minutes
*Cooking time* 20 minutes
*Serves* 8

*Ingredients*

- 250 gm wholegrain jowar (soaked overnight in water, rinsed well and pressure-cooked over 4 whistles)
- 200 gm paneer, crumbled (preferably made at home from 1 litre of cow's milk). Save the whey for soups, gravies, etc., or to add to roti dough
- 2 tomatoes, chopped, with the peel and seeds
- 1 cucumber, chopped, with the peel
- 1 capsicum, chopped, with the seeds
- 2 green chillies, finely chopped
- 1/2 cup mint, chopped, with the stalk
- 1/2 cup coriander, chopped, with the stalk
- 1 tsp oregano, dried
- 1 tsp red chilli flakes
- 1/2 tsp thyme, dried
- 1 lime juice
- 1 tsp chaat masala (optional)

- 1 tbs pumpkin and melon seeds
- Salt to taste

## Method

- In a big bowl, mix the cooked jowar and crumbled paneer.
- Add the remaining ingredients and mix well.
- Set aside for 5 minutes.
- Serve with a green chutney (optional).

## Nutritive value per serving

- Energy: 181.55 kcal
- CHO: 26.09 gm
- Protein: 7.71 gm
- Fat: 5.15 gm
- Sodium: 10.8 mg
- Potassium: 226.67 mg
- Calcium: 138.59 mg
- Iron: 1.87 mg
- Vitamin A: 50.28 mcg
- Vitamin C: 36.29 mg

'Simple, easy and nutritious is what I expect in a recipe from Savlyene. I have tried the bhel once and enjoyed it, and so did my eighty-two-year-old mum. Next time I will be trying it without the chaat masala to see the difference'

—Benaifer N. Iranee, Kolkata

## SORGHUM BHAKRIS

These healthy flatbreads made with sorghum flour are a staple in most parts of India, especially in Maharashtra and Karnataka, where they are called 'jolada roti'. Every year, in the second week of February, we drive down to the Shrine of the Infant Jesus in Nashik for the annual feast mass. Most of the time, our pilgrimage is a single-day trip. However, there have been times when we have driven down a few days earlier to not only pray more but to eat more! Nashik can be extremely cold in February, and dinner at a local restaurant famous for its Malvani delicacies is compulsory. What do we enjoy the most? No, no, not the Malvani chicken masala or spicy fried fish, but the piping hot bhakris served with generous amounts of desi ghee and organic jaggery! I've used jowar flour here.—*Savlyene*

*Preparation time* 10 minutes
*Cooking time* 15 minutes
*Serves* 4

*Ingredients*

- 200 gm sorghum flour
- 1 tbs wheat flour (optional; it makes binding easier)
- 1/2 tsp salt
- Hot water for kneading the dough

*Method*

- Sift the sorghum flour with the wheat flour (optional) and the salt.
- Place the flour in a large mixing bowl.
- Make a well at the centre and pour about 1/2 cup of hot water into it.

- Gradually incorporate the flour with the hot water to make a firm dough.
- You may need some more hot water to form the dough.
- If the dough feels sticky, do not worry—just add some more sorghum flour.
- Cover with a damp muslin cloth and keep aside for 30 minutes.
- Divide the dough into equal-sized balls.
- Flatten out into rotis/bhakris on a board liberally dusted with flour or between the palms of your hands.
- Cook on both sides on a heated griddle and finish off the roasting process directly on a flame.
- Serve hot with white butter or ghee, a sabji of your choice or jaggery.

*Nutritive value* per serving

- Energy: 174.76 kcal
- CHO: 36.24 gm
- Protein: 5.38 gm
- Fat: 0.92 gm
- Sodium: 196.28 mg
- Potassium: 175.66 mg
- Calcium: 14.96 mg
- Iron: 2.13 mg
- Vitamin A: 0.70 mcg
- Vitamin C: 0.03 mg

'These bhakris go best with a simple tuvar dal and buttermilk. Simply delicious GHA recipe'

—Ira Jain, Hyderabad

# WHEAT (GEHU)

Over the past few years, this basic grain has received so much flak—and the debate continues. The health benefits of wheat depend on the form in which you consume it. If your wheat consumption is limited to food items such as bread, pasta and biscuits, which use refined, bleached white flour or maida, you need to know more about the refining process. About 40 per cent of the original wheat grain gets removed during the refining process, which means that you are losing out on the most nutritious parts of the grain—the bran and the germ. Apart from this, refined, bleached white flour has reduced amounts of B-complex vitamins, important minerals and fibre, as they are lost in the refining process. So if you want to weigh less, reduce your risk of developing metabolic syndrome (obesity, diabetes, dyslipidemia and hypertension), check conditions associated with chronic inflammation, prevent gallstone formation, improve gut health, clear your bowels well every morning and get protection against breast cancer (irrespective of whether you are male or female), choosing wholegrains over refined ones is the only way to go.

*Pro-tip:* A wheat poultice—a thick paste made of wholewheat flour, Epsom salts, herbs such as ginger juice, turmeric powder, onion juice and garlic juice, and mixed in some warm water—can be applied on the body to treat abscesses and insect bites, relieve inflammation and promote healing. The warmth of the poultice increases blood flow to the affected area—an important part of the healing process. Please avoid using this poultice on any wound that appears to be seriously infected, in which case, visit a doctor immediately.

## BAKED MASALA PURIS

What time is your snack o'clock? You know the time I am talking about. The time it feels like lunch was eaten hours ago and dinner will not be served for another few hours. I get the munchies between 5 p.m. and 6 p.m. I've realized that ignoring my hunger pangs at that time is not only hard to sustain but, like any form of deprivation, sets you up for a debacle at the dinner table. Over the years, I've wisened up and now make sure that I have healthy home-made snacks on hand for these times. Baked masala puris is just one of these snacks. You must make a big batch, because it doesn't last long.—*Charlyene*

*Preparation time* 25 minutes
*Cooking time* 20 minutes
*Serves* 10

*Ingredients*

- 150 gm wholewheat flour
- 50 gm rice flour
- 50 gm oat flour
- 1 tsp cumin seeds
- 1 tsp kalonji (Nigella Seeds)
- 1 tsp red chilli flakes
- 3 tbs vegetable oil
- Salt to taste

*Method*

+ Preheat the oven to 180 degrees.
+ Make a stiff dough using the flours, 1 tablespoon oil and some hot water.
+ Add the salt, chilli flakes, cumin seeds and kalonji.
+ Cover with a damp cloth and keep aside for 20 minutes.
+ Roll out into thin chapatis.
+ Cut into small discs.
+ Pierce with a fork or a toothpick.
+ Place on a greased baking tray after brushing the top of each disc with some oil.
+ Bake until golden brown.
+ Turn the puris around, brush some more oil and bake that side too until golden brown.
+ Cook and store in an airtight container.

*Nutritive value per serving*

+ Energy: 126.27 kcal
+ CHO: 16.42 gm
+ Protein: 3.38 gm
+ Fat: 5.23 gm
+ Sodium: 193.80 mg
+ Potassium: 46.65 mg
+ Calcium: 10.56 mg
+ Iron: 1.07 mg
+ Vitamin A: 0.06 mcg
+ Vitamin C: 0.021 mg

'We fry puris regularly, and I am always asking my cook to use less oil. When we got this GHA recipe to try out, I insisted that Maharaj bake the puris. I am happy with the healthy puris and Maharaj cannot make excuses any more'

—Tripti Javeri, Brussels

## WHOLEWHEAT GARLIC BUNS

Whether you are a beginner at baking or love baking cakes and muffins but find baking bread a bit daunting, you must try your hand at making wholewheat garlic buns. You can omit the garlic in the butter if you are not a fan, and use dried herbs or plain butter. You will come up with a winner every time. The same recipe can be used to make bread rolls, dinner rolls/knots, chutney rolls, cheese buns, mushroom-stuffed buns, masala buns—the options are endless once you get the basics right. Have a go at it—there will be no turning back.—*Savlyene*

*Preparation time* 1 hour
*Cooking time* 20 minutes
*Serves* 8

*Ingredients*

- 2.5 cups wholewheat atta (flour)
- 4 tbs maida
- 4 tbs warm milk
- 1 tbs jaggery sugar
- 2 tbs instant dry yeast

- 2 tbs oil
- 1/2 tbs garlic butter (1 tsp finely minced garlic for every 100 gm butter)
- 1 tsp baking powder
- 1 tsp salt
- Some cold milk and some melted butter for brushing

*Method*

- Combine the milk, the jaggery sugar and the dry yeast in a deep mixing bowl and keep aside for 20 minutes.
- Sift both flours with the baking powder and salt.
- Once the yeast has risen, add the sifted flours and knead into a soft dough, along with 3/4 cup warm water, oil and garlic butter.
- The dough is ready when it forms a smooth ball and readily springs back when you lightly press it down with the tip of a finger.
- Grease another mixing bowl and transfer the dough into it.
- Cover the dough with a slightly damp muslin cloth and leave aside to prove.
- After about 1 hour, the dough will have doubled in size. If you repeat the process of lightly pressing it with the tip of one finger, it will not spring back.
- Knock it down and knead again, pulling and stretching it to make it more elastic.
- Divide into 12 equal-sized smooth, round balls and place them a bit apart on a greased baking tray.
- Cover with the damp muslin cloth and let it prove for another 25–30 minutes.
- Brush with cold milk.

- Preheat your oven to 200 degrees in the meantime.
- Bake the garlic buns on the centre rack for 20 minutes, until it gets a golden crust.
- Remove and quickly brush with some melted butter.
- Serve warm.

*Nutritive value per serving*

- Energy: 233.44 kcal
- CHO: 38.44 gm
- Protein: 7.32 gm
- Fat: 5.60 gm
- Sodium: 256.29 mg
- Potassium: 174.65 mg
- Calcium: 32.89 mg
- Iron: 2.15 mg
- Vitamin A: 0.49 mcg
- Vitamin C: 0.15 mg

'My son loves to bake but had never baked bread before. So he readily accepted the GHA recipe-try-out challenge. The resulting soft, spongy wholewheat garlic rolls were a good accompaniment to soup'

—Thelma K., Mumbai

# AMARANTH (RAJGIRA)

This native Peruvian crop has nutritionally rich leaves and seeds. Ancient Aztecs baked amaranth cakes in the shape of images of their deities. Amaranth greens have nutritional properties similar to those of spinach and other dark-green leafy vegetables. The beige, small and round amaranth grains are the only ones that provide vitamin C and contain the amino acid lysine, not commonly found in other vegetable sources. These gluten-free grains have three times the amount of calcium and are also good sources of potassium, iron, folate, phosphorus, manganese and magnesium. Their beneficial peptides, such as lunasin, and phytochemicals, such as rutin and nicotiflorin, help lower high blood pressure levels and the incidence of cancer. Include these wonder grains in your diet for improved cardiovascular health, better blood sugar levels, reduced cholesterol levels, a better immune system, stronger bones, sharper vision, lower blood pressure levels and possibly even reduced tumour-marker activity. Like buckwheat and quinoa, these 'pseudocereals', which grow from flowering plants, are classified as grains, which grow from grasses, because of their similar properties.

*Pro-tip:* Amaranth oil is a natural bactericide. Use a tablespoon of it to practise oil pulling or oil swishing every morning. This should be done as soon as you wake up, even before you brush your teeth. Start with swishing for 3–5 minutes and gradually move to 10 minutes. Spit out the oil once done. This will not only help remove dental plaque and clean your teeth and tongue, but also help with swollen gums and oral ulcers.

## AMARANTH CREPES

Shrove Tuesday or Pancake Tuesday is also called Mardi Gras or Fat Tuesday. It is the last day of indulging before the start of the Lenten season. Since 'mindful eating' is key to good health, here is our GHA take on the traditional Christian coconut-stuffed crepes made on this day. We made the crepes using a variety of flour combinations, including rice and oat flours, but found that the amaranth-flour variety looked and tasted the best. They were also the least cumbersome to make. We then stacked them with fresh seasonal fruits such as grapes, apples, dragon fruit and orange segments. A star-anise-and-cinnamon-infused orange sauce provided another element altogether. You can stuff these amaranth crepes with a wide variety of fillings both sweet and savoury. You needn't limit to just stacking them—you can also form a wrap or a roll.—*Savlyene and Charlyene*

*Preparation time* 15 minutes
*Cooking time* 25 minutes
*Serves* 4

*Ingredients*

- 200 gm amaranth flour
- 50 gm wheat flour
- 2 eggs, large, or 2 tbs ground flax and 6 tbs water (flax eggs), or 1/2 tsp baking powder
- 1 cup milk

+ 1 tbs butter
+ A pinch of salt

*Method*

+ Sift the amaranth flour with the wheat flour and salt (and the baking powder, if you are using that option).
+ Beat the eggs well (else beat the ground flax with the water and let it swell for 10 minutes).
+ Gradually incorporate the flour and the milk in the beaten eggs or flax eggs and continue whisking to form a smooth batter. You may need to adjust the consistency with water. It should neither be too thick nor too runny.
+ Keep aside for 10 minutes.
+ Heat a small pan and add a little butter to grease the pan.
+ Pour out small amounts of the batter into the pan and swirl it around to get a thin, even layer.
+ Cook for a minute or two and then flip it to cook the other side for another minute.
+ Repeat the process with the remaining crepe batter.
+ Serve warm with a topping of your choice.

*Nutritive value per serving*

+ Energy: 288.34 kcal
+ CHO: 40.60 gm
+ Protein: 11.19 gm
+ Fat: 9.02 gm
+ Sodium: 544.75 mg
+ Potassium: 309.2 mg
+ Calcium: 136.53 mg
+ Iron: 4.85 mg

- Vitamin A: 31.34 mcg
- Vitamin C: 0.75 mg

'I had followed the GHA recipe for these crepes twice. Once with fruits, and once with Nutella. Both were excellent. Will try again and have it with a healthy walnut butter I just made'

—Arun Shah, Delhi

## AMARANTH SALAD WITH MANGO CHIPOTLE COCONUT OIL DRESSING

We made this salad for two French friends from our yoga class who were pining for a healthy meal in a bowl. They had never tasted amaranth before and, looking at the bowl, one of them, Renne, even thought that we were offering them caviar! If you look at the picture closely, you will see that the glossy, cooked red amaranth grains do look a bit like sturgeon roe, so Renne could not be faulted for her assumption.—*Savlyene and Charlyene*

*Preparation time* 20 minutes
*Cooking time* 25 minutes (for amaranth)
*Serves* 6

*Ingredients*

*For the salad*

- 200 gm red amaranth grains, soaked overnight
- 1 bunch arugula leaves with the stalks

- ◆ 2 onions, diced
- ◆ 4 tomatoes, chopped, with the peels and the seeds
- ◆ 4 tbs pomegranate seeds
- ◆ Salt to taste
- ◆ Lime juice, as required

*For the dressing*

- ◆ 4 tbs mango chipotle jam (p. 264)
- ◆ 2 tbs extra-virgin coconut oil

*Method*

*For the dressing*

- ◆ Mix the mango chipotle jam well with the extra-virgin coconut oil.
- ◆ Add 4 tablespoons hot water and blend in a small mixer/ grinder/blender to get a mayonnaise-like consistency.
- ◆ Transfer this dressing to a clean glass container and refrigerate.

*For the salad*

- ◆ Steam-cook the soaked red amaranth grain for about 25 minutes. Set aside to cool.
- ◆ In the meantime, put the arugula leaves in a bowl of ice-cold water for 10 minutes and roughly tear the leaves with your hands. Do not chop them with a knife, else the leaves will wilt faster.
- ◆ Mix the cooled, cooked red amaranth with the arugula, pomegranate, tomatoes and onions.
- ◆ Add salt to taste and a squeeze or two of lemon juice, and toss well.

* Serve cold with a dollop of the mango chipotle dressing.

*Nutritive value per serving*

* Energy: 208.71 kcal
* CHO: 30.42 gm
* Protein: 5.67 gm
* Fat: 7.15 gm
* Sodium: 335.07 mg
* Potassium: 329.55 mg
* Calcium: 100.62 mg
* Iron: 3.22 mg
* Vitamin A: 109.65 mcg
* Vitamin C: 15.01 mg

'I had only eaten amaranth chikki before this—never anything else made from amaranth. So trying this exotic recipe was a bit scary. I am glad my husband encouraged me to do so. It turned out great. Next time I will be doubling the recipe'

—Geeta N. Garg, Pune

# BUCKWHEAT (KUTTU)

This pseudocereal is gluten-free and not related to wheat, despite its name. Fagopyritol and D-chiro-inositol, the soluble carbs in buckwheat, help to prevent unhealthy spikes in post-meal blood sugar levels. Buckwheat husk contains resistant starch, which is excellent for gut health. When you eat dark buckwheat flour, not only is it more satiating, but it also has a good probiotic effect. Its resistant starch gets fermented by the good bacteria in the large intestine. These good bacteria then produce butyrate, which serves as a food source for colon cells, improves gut health and reduces risk of colon cancer. The antioxidants quercetin, rutin, vitexin and D-chiro-inositol are responsible for many of the health benefits of this pseudocereal. Buckwheat flour is a good source of protein for vegetarians. Although rare, allergies to buckwheat may cause skin rashes and welts, hives, swelling of the lips, abdominal bloating and diarrhoea. This mainly holds true for those who are already allergic to latex products and to rice.

*Pro-tip:* Like all other grains, buckwheat groats should be thoroughly washed a couple of times in cold running water. To cook the groats for a porridge or kasha, the thumb rule is 2 parts water for 1 part buckwheat groats. Pressure-cook over 4 whistles. Do not discard the liquid used for cooking. Save it and add it to soups and gravies, or even to knead roti dough.

## BUCKWHEAT MOLTEN CAKE

The lockdown has ensured that we stay indoors, but video-conferencing applications such as Zoom have allowed us to continue our interactions with relatives, friends, clients and co-workers from the safety of our homes. So we spend part of our Sunday evenings online with our cousins, participating in a bakery challenge. One cousin sends out a recipe a few days in advance, we collect the ingredients and get set to bake at a designated time. This molten cake recipe is courtesy of our youngest cousin, who is all of twelve. The original recipe had all-purpose flour, butter, semi-sweet chocolate and refined sugar, and tasted heavenly. We recreated the cake using buckwheat flour, coconut oil, carob chips and jaggery. Looked nearly the same, tasted just as good but was so much healthier.—*Charlyene and Savlyene*

*Preparation time* 10 minutes
*Cooking time* 12 minutes
*Serves* 4

*Ingredients*

- 40 gm buckwheat flour
- 20 gm wheat flour
- 1/4 tsp salt
- 3 eggs or 3 tbs ground flax with 6 tbs water (flax egg)
- 130 gm jaggery sugar
- 120 gm carob or chocolate chips
- 130 ml coconut oil
- 1/2 tsp vanilla extract
- 1/2 tsp instant coffee powder (optional)

*Method*

- Preheat the oven to 175 degrees.
- Lightly grease 4 medium-sized ramekins and set aside.
- Sift the flours with the salt and instant coffee powder, and set aside.
- In a large mixing bowl, gently warm the coconut oil and add the carob chips and jaggery sugar.
- Remove from the stovetop and whisk well until it cools.
- Add the eggs or flax eggs and continue to whisk.
- Add the vanilla extract.
- Gently fold in the sifted flour until it just combines. Do not overmix.
- Divide the batter between the 4 greased ramekins.
- Bake for 10–12 minutes. The edges should be firm, but the centre should be slightly soft.
- Remove and let it stand for a minute.
- Carefully invert each ramekin on to a serving plate and serve warm.

*Nutritive value per serving*

- Energy: 481.34 kcal
- CHO: 37.30 gm
- Protein: 5.14 gm
- Fat: 34.62 gm
- Sodium: 3.76 mg
- Potassium: 241.4 mg
- Calcium: 54.17 mg
- Iron: 3.68 mg
- Vitamin A: 45.08 mcg
- Vitamin C: 1.06 mg

'I used flax eggs for the first time, and I was so happy with the result. I will be trying out this egg substitute for other cakes too. Since I did not have carob chips, I replaced them with regular chocolate chips and added 1 teaspoon coffee powder instead of 1/2. My tip would be to bake these just before you want to serve then. Amazing result'

—Mona Sanghvi, Jaipur

## BUCKWHEAT ROTIS

A perfect alternative to wheat rotis, these delicious buckwheat rotis are gluten-free and vegan too. Yes, they do have an acquired taste and texture, but their health benefits are plenty. It can get difficult to make a smooth, non-sticky buckwheat flour dough because of the lack of gluten. The trick here is to make the dough in advance and use some mashed potato and warm water to bind the dough together. This will also ensure that the rotis do not crack when you are rolling them out. The edges of the rotis will not be perfectly round and will have cracks. I've often been teased about serving cracked-edge rotis but I just insist that 'rustic' is the way to go!—*Savlyene*

*Preparation time* 20 minutes
*Cooking time* 30 minutes
*Serves* 4

*Ingredients*

♦   250 gm buckwheat flour

- 1 potato, large, with the peel (wash the potato well and then boil and finely mash with the peel)
- 2 tbs fresh coriander, finely chopped, with the stalks
- Salt to taste
- 1 tbs vegetable oil

## Method

- Sift the buckwheat flour with the salt.
- In a large bowl, mix the sifted flour with the mashed potato and chopped coriander.
- Add a little warm water to facilitate better binding.
- Cover with a damp cloth and keep aside for 15 minutes.
- Divide the dough into 8 balls and roll out medium-thick rotis on a board well dusted with buckwheat flour.
- Cook the rotis well on both sides on a hot griddle or a tawa.
- Smear with a little oil.
- Serve hot.

## Nutritive value per serving

- Energy: 246.29 kcal
- CHO: 42.69 gm
- Protein: 6.89 gm
- Fat: 5.33 gm
- Sodium: 497.04 mg
- Potassium: 334.82 mg
- Calcium: 52.14 mg
- Iron: 10.15 mg
- Vitamin A: 48.1 mcg
- Vitamin C: 4.68 mg

'Adding potatoes to buckwheat rotis makes them soft and easier to roll out. I set the dough aside for 30 minutes, and it becomes even more pliable. No one at home complained about the potato-peel addition—they didn't even notice'

—Juhi Anurag, Singapore

# QUINOA

This miracle grain from the Andes is a pseudocereal. In its wholegrain form, quinoa may be effective in preventing and treating atherosclerosis, breast cancer, diabetes and insulin resistance. It is close to one of the most complete foods in nature, because it contains amino acids, enzymes, vitamins and minerals, fibre, antioxidants such as quercetin, and phytonutrients. The quercetin content in quinoa is even higher than in cranberries. Quinoa is the superfood of today. It is popular with vegetarians, vegans, diabetics, cardiac patients, athletes, people who are lactose- or gluten-intolerant or those who have celiac disease. Since it is gluten-free, it is easy to digest. It acts as a prebiotic, which feeds the microflora (good bacteria) in our intestines.

*Pro-tip:* To enhance its nutritional value, sprout quinoa by soaking it in water for some time. The grains have an outer coat that contain bitter-tasting saponins. These saponins make them inedible. Be sure to rinse the sprouted quinoa in water a couple of times to get rid of these saponins. You will now be able to taste the nutty flavour of the grain. If you skip this step, your quinoa dish will be bitter and unpalatable. Quinoa is available in three colours—red, white and black. I find the tricolour quinoa the tastiest. The white quinoa can easily replace semolina in most recipes.

## SPROUTED QUINOA CROQUETTES

These little snack/party-time finger foods are a delicious take on the French classic—potato croquettes. Quinoa is such a versatile grain to cook with, and these croquettes are crispy on the outside, tender on the inside and flavourful in a subtle yet soul-satisfying way. I love to serve these croquettes with a small dollop of dip made from hung curd, garlic and sun-dried tomatoes.—*Charlyene*

*Preparation time* 30 minutes
*Cooking time* 30 minutes
*Serves* 8

*Ingredients*

*For the croquette mixture*

- 200 gm sprouted quinoa (sprout by soaking in water for 2–3 hours. The bitter saponin-containing seed coat will loosen and float on top, indicating that the grain has sprouted. Rinse well a couple of times, drain and keep aside or refrigerate if using later)
- 3 tbs flax seeds, ground
- 1 tbs pepper, freshly ground
- 2 tbs celery stalks, chopped, with the leaves
- 4 tbs red bell pepper, finely diced, with the seeds
- 1 tbs mint leaves, finely chopped, with the stalks
- 1 tbs coriander leaves, finely chopped, with the stalks
- Salt to taste
- 2 tbs vegetable oil

*For the seed crumb mixture*

- Mix together equal parts of breadcrumbs, coarsely ground pumpkin seeds and coarsely ground sunflower seeds with a small amount of cornflour. Store in an airtight container in the refrigerator.

*For the hung curd dip*

- 2 cups dahi, hung for a few hours in a muslin cloth potli
- 1 tbs garlic, finely minced
- 2 tbs sun-dried tomato paste
- Salt to taste

*Method*

*For the hung curd dip*

- Mix the hung curd with the minced garlic and the sun-dried tomato paste.
- Add salt to taste.
- Store in an airtight container in the refrigerator.

*For the croquettes*

- In a large bowl, combine all the ingredients, except the vegetable oil.
- Set aside for 10 minutes.
- Shape into croquettes about 2 inches long.
- Coat the croquettes in the seed-crumb mixture and refrigerate for 10 minutes.
- Set the air fryer on high heat.
- Lightly grease the base and air-fry the croquettes in small batches, until they are golden brown. Alternatively, you can bake or fry them.
- Serve with the hung curd dip.

*Nutritive value per serving*

- Energy: 96.98 kcal
- CHO: 6.98 gm
- Protein: 2.82 gm
- Fat: 6.42 gm
- Sodium: 4.66 mg
- Potassium: 160.57 mg
- Calcium: 49.96 mg
- Iron: 1.56 mg
- Vitamin A: 32.27 mcg
- Vitamin C: 9.75 mg

'The use of seeds instead of breadcrumbs makes these croquettes so much more nutritious and tasty. I plan to replace breadcrumbs with seed crumbs for all other recipes too. The second time I made these croquettes, I froze a batch for later use. They tasted as good as the first lot'

—Adrian Silveira, Goa

## SPROUTED QUINOA UPMA

I like the nutty taste of this upma even better than that of the regular semolina upma. I first made it when I was longing to eat some home-cooked upma and couldn't find the box of semolina in our pantry. I'm quite bad when it comes to finding stuff—especially when it is lying inches from my flared nostrils! Instead, I checked the refrigerator and found sprouted quinoa that Mum had saved for some new kitchen experiment.

I decided to use it to make upma and Mum was more than happy when she tasted it. If you have sprouted quinoa kept in your refrigerator, this dish will be ready in a jiffy. Don't just take my word for it. Try it someday and your family will thank you for it. Hey, but then you must thank me!—*Savlyene*

*Preparation time* 20 minutes (longer if you have to sprout the quinoa from scratch)
*Cooking time* 20 minutes
*Serves* 4

*Ingredients*

- 200 gm sprouted quinoa (white or tricolour)
- 3 large onions, finely chopped
- 150 gm red, yellow and green bell peppers, chopped, with the seeds
- 1 tsp ghee
- 1/4 tsp mustard seeds
- 1/2 tsp red chilli flakes
- Himalayan pink sea salt to taste
- 1 tsp pine nuts or cashews (optional)

*Method*

- Heat the ghee in a pan and temper the mustard seeds and red chilli flakes.
- Add the chopped onions and allow them to sweat for 3 minutes.
- Add the sprouted quinoa and mix well.
- Add a mug of warm water and allow it to cook for 10 minutes.
- Add the bell peppers and sea salt to taste.

* Allow it cook for 5 more minutes.
* Serve warm with some toasted nuts (optional).

*Nutritive value per serving*

* Energy: 197.41 kcal
* CHO: 30.81 gm
* Protein: 7.79 gm
* Fat: 4.81 gm
* Sodium: 529.65 mg
* Potassium: 380.23 mg
* Calcium: 111.645 mg
* Iron: 4.1 mg
* Vitamin A: 17.10 mcg
* Vitamin C: 44.00 mg

'The GHA tip of sprouting the quinoa before using it was very helpful. I did not know that it was simple but so essential. It improved the digestibility of quinoa. This recipe was a hit. Now my family doesn't want sooji upma—only quinoa upma'

—Rita Silveira, Goa

# PULSES

More and more diets the world over are looking at pulses as a source of protein. This macronutrient comprises of twenty amino acids as its building blocks. Nine of these amino acids cannot be produced by the human body and are called essential amino acids. Most of the proteins present in plants lack one or more of these essential amino acids. So should you not eat plant sources of protein? No, you just need to know which plant sources to combine and eat protein from a variety of sources, so that you can avail of all the proteins you need from your meal.

Pulses and lentils are low-fat sources of two important nutrients—protein and fibre. Scientific studies show that people who consume a minimum of half a cup of pulses and lentils every day get more protein, fibre, calcium, magnesium, potassium, iron, zinc and folate as compared to people who do not consume the same amount of pulses and lentils every day. Pulses are also a more affordable and sustainable source of protein when compared to other plant-based and animal sources.

Just 1 cup of cooked pulses provides more than half the amount of dietary fibre needed for the day. This fibre is of both soluble and insoluble types. Soluble fibre is needed to keep body weight down, maintain blood sugar levels and lower blood cholesterol levels. Insoluble fibre maintains the health of the gastrointestinal tract by aiding in digestion and preventing constipation. The starch component of pulses is of the resistant type, which is good for patients with dyslipidemia, diabetes and gut issues.

# BENGAL GRAM

Belonging to the legume family, the Bengal gram is also known as chickpeas or garbanzo beans. Middle Eastern cookery has made use of this pulse in a variety of dishes, ranging from hummus to falafel and tabouleh. Owing to their nutty taste and grainy yet creamy texture, chickpeas can be added to soups, smoothies, stir-fries, gravies and even cakes, cookies and other baked products. Their protein and fibre content provides satiety for a longer period. Thus, they may reduce appetite and are great for those on a weight-loss diet. Apart from this, the proteins in chickpeas help with muscle-building and strength development, provided they are combined with the right foods. This is because they lack the essential amino acid methionine. The magnesium and potassium content of chickpeas can boost heart health and prevent hypertension. The soluble fibre in chickpeas helps lower triglycerides and LDL cholesterol. They have a low GI and help release glucose slowly, rather than causing a spike in post-meal blood sugar levels. Their soluble fibre content is good for improving gut health because they help increase the number of healthy gut bacteria and prevent the increase in the number of unhealthy gut bacteria. This positively impacts conditions such as IBS and colon cancer.

*Pro-tip:* Aqua faba is the water left from cooking chickpeas and other legumes in a pressure cooker, a slow cooker or the stovetop. Do not discard this. Not only can you add it to gravies and soups, but it is also a great vegan egg replacer or substitute. Whisk this slightly viscous liquid and it will be the same consistency as egg whites. Continue whisking and you will be able to use it for vegan desserts such as meringues, pavlovas, mousses, nougats, marshmallows, macarons, brownies and even for vegan mayonnaise.

## CHICKPEA PATE/PATE DE FAUX GRAS

Yes, you read that right—this isn't a goose-liver pate/pate de foie gras, but a yummy vegan version. Pate de foie gras is a French delicacy made from goose or duck liver. The birds are force-fed corn to fatten them and their livers up. Foie gras literally translates to 'fat liver', and the dish is a must on Christmas and New Year's Eve parties. If you are vegetarian, can't tolerate the cruelty of force-feeding or just want to take a break from non-vegetarian food, do try this faux gras for your year-end party.—*Savlyene*

*Preparation time* 20 minutes
*Cooking time* 10 minutes
*Serves* 8

*Ingredients*

- 150 gm mushrooms, chopped, with the stalks
- 2 large onions, sliced
- 20 cloves of garlic, chopped
- 300 gm boiled chickpeas (reserve the cooking liquid for soups and gravies)
- 2 large beetroots, boiled with the skin
- 100 gm walnuts, pine nuts or almonds, coarsely ground

- 2 tbs Italian seasoning
- 2 tbs olive oil
- 2 tbs white wine (optional)
- Salt to taste

## Method

- Heat the oil in a pan and sauté the onions until translucent.
- Add the garlic and cook for 2 minutes.
- Add the mushrooms, salt and Italian seasoning.
- Cook for 2 minutes.
- Remove from the stovetop and cool completely.
- Purée in a blender, along with the chickpeas, beets and ground walnuts, pine nuts or almonds.
- Add the white wine (optional).
- Adjust the salt to taste.
- Transfer to a clean airtight glass container and refrigerate.
- You can top with olive oil if you wish.
- Serve with garlic toast or baked chips.

## Nutritive value per serving

- Energy: 299.18 kcal
- CHO: 31.34 gm
- Protein: 12 gm
- Fat: 13.98 gm
- Sodium: 46.83 mg
- Potassium: 421.69 mg
- Calcium: 50.60 mg
- Iron: 2.61 mg
- Vitamin A: 1.06 mcg
- Vitamin C: 6.09 mg

'I had tasted this for our staff Christmas party last year. So Charmaine Ma'am was pretty sure I would be able to do justice to this recipe. She didn't know that I had never tried cooking anything—I could just heat water. So I had to take my mother's help. But this was easy to make. I also used it as a sandwich spread'

—Sonal Jagdish, Mumbai

## SCOTCH EGGS

A soft-boiled egg wrapped in minced sausage meat, coated in breadcrumbs and baked or fried, the original British version is very much like our Nargisi kofta!

We've made a meatless version using a falafel mixture. What can you use for an eggless version? Boiled and puréed chana dal to look like the egg yolk, boiled and pureed rice to look like the egg white—shaped to resemble a boiled egg! The cereal-pulse combo is a good source of protein, just like an egg.—*Charlyene*

*Preparation time* 15 minutes
*Cooking time* 10 minutes
*Serves* 4

*Ingredients*

- 4 eggs, boiled and shelled
- 150 gm chickpeas, boiled
- 1 onion, finely chopped
- 6 cloves of garlic, minced

- 1 tbs white sesame seeds
- 1 tbs mint, finely chopped
- 2 tsp coriander, finely chopped, with the stalks
- 1/2 tsp cumin powder
- 1/2 tsp red chilli powder or paprika
- 1/2 tsp dill, dried
- 1/2 tsp pepper powder
- 1 tbs vegetable oil
- Salt to taste

*For the crumbling*

- A mix of seeds such as pumpkin, sunflower and melon, coarsely ground

*Method*

- Pulse the chickpeas in a blender and add the onion, garlic, sesame and the remaining herbs and spices.
- Remove from the blender and add salt to taste.
- Mix well and portion out into 4 balls.
- Take each ball and flatten it in the palm of your hand. You may need to grease your palms with a little oil.
- Place a boiled and shelled egg in the centre and cover completely with the falafel mixture of about 1/4-inch thickness.
- Repeat with the rest of the eggs.
- Crumb each egg by rolling it in the seed-crumb mixture.
- Set the air fryer on high; grease it lightly.
- Air-fry the Scotch eggs for 8–10 minutes or until golden brown.
- Serve hot with a side of dill pickles and salad, sauce or chutney.

*Nutritive value per serving*

- Energy: 239.22 kcal
- CHO: 28.68 gm
- Protein: 15.69 gm
- Fat: 6.86 gm
- Sodium: 88.44 mg
- Potassium: 275.12 mg
- Calcium: 64.52 mg
- Iron: 2.3 mg
- Vitamin A: 5.65 mcg
- Vitamin C: 4.87 mg

'We make Nargisi kofta very often. So making Scotch eggs was easy. The difficult part was when I had to make it the second time, replacing the boiled egg with rice and dal. Initially I forgot to season the dal. Charlyene had said that I could make the vegetarian eggs (of yellow dal round balls covered with white rice to look like boiled eggs) earlier, and let them cool. It was a great tip that my pure vegetarian friends love'

—Shagufta M., Mumbai

# BLACK-EYED PEAS/COWPEAS (CHAWLI)

This pulse, with its eye-like black spot, is a bean, not a pea. Well loved for their flavour, these beans are a staple in Indian cooking. High in polyphenol antioxidants, they are also good sources of copper, iron and folate. Their protein content may reduce the hunger hormone ghrelin, thereby keeping you feeling full for longer. The fibre content not only helps reduce hyperacidity and digestive problems, but acts as a prebiotic, stimulating the growth of good bacteria in the gut. These beneficial bacteria improve immunity and reduce inflammation in the body. Like other pulses, the regular consumption of black-eyed peas also helps keep levels of blood sugar and blood cholesterol in check.

*Pro-tip:* As with other pulses, the speed of cooking and the digestibility quotient are improved by soaking for 6–8 hours in water. Another benefit of soaking the black-eyed peas and then cooking them is the reduction in the raffinose and physic acid content of the peas. Raffinose is a fibre that may cause digestive problems such as gas, bloating, stomach ache and cramps.

Phytic acid is an antinutrient that binds to minerals such as iron, magnesium, calcium and zinc.

## ALSANYACHE TONAK

A mouth-watering Goan vegetarian speciality, the tonak masala used here is like a garam masala that can be made ahead in a larger batch and refrigerated. You can also use store-bought tonak masala, but the home-made version always tastes better. I'm half Goan and half east Indian, so I sometimes use the east Indian bottle masala instead!—*Charmaine*

*Preparation time* 15 minutes
*Cooking time* 40 minutes
*Serves* 4

*Ingredients*

*For the tonak masala*

- 100 gm coriander seeds
- 50 gm cumin seeds
- 25 gm cinnamon sticks
- 6 Kashmiri red chillies
- 8 star anise
- 10 green cardamom
- 10 cloves
- 1 tbs black peppercorns

*For the alsanyache tonak*

- 150 gm black-eyed peas, soaked overnight
- 2 onions, sliced
- 4 cloves of garlic
- 1 large potato, cubed, with peel
- 1 tomato, chopped, with peel and seeds
- 50 gm coconut, freshly grated
- 2 tbs tamarind paste
- 2 tbs tonak masala
- 1 tbs vegetable oil
- Salt to taste

*Method*

*For the tonak masala*

- Dry-roast all the ingredients, stirring regularly until they change colour slightly.
- Cool and transfer to a blender.
- Grind to form a fine masala powder.
- Store in an airtight container in the refrigerator

*For the alsanyache tonak*

- Wash the black-eyed peas and pressure-cook over 4 whistles in 4 cups of water with some salt to taste.
- Once the pressure cooker has cooled and let off steam, open it and drain the peas, reserving the cooking liquid.
- In a pan, heat the oil and fry the onion until translucent.
- Add the garlic, grated coconut and tonak masala, and cook until the coconut browns.
- Add the potato and cook for 2 minutes before adding the tomato.
- Add 2 cups of the black-eyed peas cooking liquid and cook well.
- When the gravy thickens, add the peas and salt to taste.
- Finally add the tamarind paste and stir well.
- Serve hot with steamed rice or bread/pao.

*Nutritive value per serving*

- Energy: 264.29 kcal
- CHO: 34.57 gm
- Protein: 10.24 gm
- Fat: 9.45 gm
- Sodium: 15.56 mg

- Potassium: 878.6 mg
- Calcium: 54.77 mg
- Iron: 3.02 mg
- Vitamin A: 57.19 mcg
- Vitamin C: 25.01 mg

'I am Marwari and my husband is Mangalorean. This chawli tonak is similar to what his mother makes back home. I sent this recipe to my mother-in-law. She, too, said it was very good'

—Gunjan Pinto, Mumbai

## ATOLA

All Souls Day is a solemn feast to commemorate the deceased members of a family and society. East Indians generally make atola on this day to appease the souls of their ancestors. It is a porridge made from newly harvested rice, black-eyed peas, coconut milk and jaggery. As with other kinds of porridge, it tastes great either hot or cold. In our home, atola is made quite regularly and polished off really quick, so I really cannot comment on how it tastes nine days old—as per the famous nursery rhyme!—*Charlyene*

*Preparation time* 20 minutes
*Cooking time* 1 hour
*Serves* 4

*Ingredients*

- 50 gm black-eyed peas, soaked overnight

- 100 brown rice, soaked overnight
- 25 gm sprouted ragi
- 25 gm steel-cut oats
- 150 ml coconut milk (not coconut cream)
- 100 gm palm jaggery
- 2 tbs mixed seeds
- 1 tbs black dates or raisins, chopped
- 1/4 tsp nutmeg, freshly grated
- 1/4 tsp cardamom powder
- Salt to taste

## Method

- Wash the rice and black-eyed peas well and pressure-cook over 4 whistles in 3 cups of water, along with the sprouted ragi, oats and some salt to taste.
- Once the cooker has cooled and let off steam, open it and add the coconut milk and jaggery.
- Bring to one quick boil, then add the spice powders, mixed seeds and black dates or raisins.
- Adjust consistency with more coconut milk, if needed.
- Serve hot or cold.

## Nutritive value per serving

- Energy: 368.64 kcal
- CHO: 58.62 gm
- Protein: 8.70 gm
- Fat: 11.04 gm
- Sodium: 14.61 mg
- Potassium: 232.55 mg
- Calcium: 449.82 mg
- Iron: 2.005 mg

- Vitamin A: 0.16 mcg
- Vitamin C: 0.045 mg

'When we lived in Mumbai, we had east Indian neighbours. So atola was a dish I was familiar with. I didn't know it was so easy to make, though. My daughters love it and so does the rest of the family'

—Pallavi Das, Raipur

# GREEN CHICKPEAS (HARA CHANNA)

The perfect superfood from the Fabaceae family, these beans are high in protein and fibre, have a lower sodium content, are low in saturated fat and have a low GI. They are a good source of vitamin B9 or folate, and vitamins A and C. They have a unique and flavourful taste, and are nutrition-packed. Their high fibre content contributes to longer periods of satiety, better bowel movement, an improved lipid profile, better blood sugar readings and better weight management. The potassium in green chickpeas helps maintain normal blood pressure readings. When you consume these beans regularly, there is an improvement in the metabolism of carbohydrates, proteins and fats. This is because of their vitamin B1 thiamine and B6 pyridoxine content. These vitamins act as enzyme co-factors for the metabolism of macronutrients.

*Pro-tip:* Although pulses are good sources of protein, they lack one or more essential amino acid. If you want to stick to a plant-based diet and yet ensure that you are getting all the essential amino acids your body requires, you must ensure that you consume cereals such as rice or wheat along with pulses. They provide the methionine that pulses lack, thereby making your meal a balanced one.

## HARA CHANNA CHAAT

Here is a good evening snack for times when your lunch has been light and dinner might be late. After having this chaat, you will not have to worry about hunger pangs for the next few hours. Rest assured, you will be satiated right up to dinner time and might even eat lesser.—*Charlyene*

*Preparation time* 10 minutes
*Cooking time* 0 minutes
*Serves* 4

## Ingredients

- 150 gm green chickpeas, boiled
- 100 gm amaranth, roasted
- 4 tbs onion, chopped
- 1 tsp ginger, chopped, with the peel
- 2 green chillies, chopped
- 2 tsp chaat masala
- 50 gm pumpkin seeds
- 2 tsp black sesame seeds, toasted
- 1 tsp white sesame seeds, toasted
- 4 tbs lemon juice
- Salt to taste

## Method

- Combine all but the last two ingredients in a large bowl.
- Add salt to taste.
- At the time of serving, add lime juice.
- Serve immediately.

*Nutritive value per serving*

- Energy: 282.44 kcal

- CHO: 36.18 gm
- Protein: 13.55 gm
- Fat: 9.28 gm
- Sodium: 12.74 mg
- Potassium: 222.09 mg
- Calcium: 102.09 mg
- Iron: 4.60 mg
- Vitamin A: 0.39 mcg
- Vitamin C: 3.44 mg

'I had never tasted amaranth in a chaat before. So I found this a great way to up the nutrition value and make it a complete meal in itself. Thank you, Team GHA. I love to add lots of lemon juice to my lentils and greens, so I added 6 tablespoons instead of the recommended 4 tablespoons'

—Munna Shaikh, Hyderabad

## GREEN CHICKPEA CURRY

Lentils and whole pulses occupy pride of place in our pantry. This is probably the only section that has neatly lined glass jars with tightly fitted maroon lids containing our plant-based proteins. There is always a stock of creamy soya beans, orange masoor dal, golden yellow lentils, green vatana, maroon rajma, black-eyed peas, whitish broad beans and mixed chowli. As kids, we were fascinated by how green chickpeas changed to brown in the pressure cooker. This recipe brings back so many fond memories.—*Savlyene*

*Preparation time* 15 minutes
*Cooking time* 20 minutes
*Serves* 4

*Ingredients*

- 150 gm green chickpeas, soaked overnight
- 2 large onions, finely chopped
- 2 large tomatoes, finely chopped, with peel and seeds
- 2 green chillies, finely chopped
- 1 tbs ginger-garlic paste, home-made
- 1 tsp mustard seeds
- 1 tsp cumin seeds
- 1/2 tsp turmeric powder
- 1/4 tsp pepper powder
- 1 tsp red chilli powder
- 1/2 tsp garam masala powder
- 1/8 tsp asafoetida
- 1 tbs vegetable oil
- Salt to taste

*To garnish*

- Coriander, chopped, with the stalks

*Method*

- Heat the oil in a pressure cooker and temper the mustard seeds in it.
- When they start sputtering, add cumin seeds and fry for a few seconds.
- Add a pinch of asafoetida.
- Add the finely chopped onions, along with ginger-garlic paste and the chopped green chillies.

- Fry until the onions become soft and light brown in colour.
- Add puréed or finely chopped tomatoes.
- Fry the gravy until the tomatoes are cooked.
- Add the turmeric powder, pepper powder, red chilli powder, garam masala powder and salt to the gravy.
- After this, add the soaked green chickpeas and 2 cups of warm water.
- Pressure-cook over 3 whistles.
- Open the pressure cooker once it has cooled completely and after all the steam has released.
- Garnish with chopped coriander leaves.
- Serve it hot, with rice or roti.

*Nutritive value per serving*

- Energy: 216.33 kcal
- CHO: 29.26 gm
- Protein: 9.05 gm
- Fat: 7.01 gm
- Sodium: 14.92 mg
- Potassium: 253.005 mg
- Calcium: 52.29 mg
- Iron: 2.7 mg
- Vitamin A: 35.46 mcg
- Vitamin C: 12.14 mg

'I am a dal lover. I can eat it for breakfast, lunch and dinner, without rice or roti. I tried this recipe yesterday and it turned out great. I love a smoky flavour, so later I gave this dish a charcoal smoking—divine'

—Sheetal Shetty, Bengaluru

# BLACK GRAM (URAD DAL)

These unique legumes have soluble fibre in the form of mucilaginous polysaccharides. This bulks up the colonic wastes and protects mucosal cells of the colon by binding toxins and carcinogenic substances. It also decreases the reabsorption of the cholesterol-binding bile acids in the colon. The beans are iron, calcium, copper, potassium, phosphorus, magnesium and zinc. They help improve cognitive ability, memory and haemoglobin levels. Black gram is an excellent source of folate from the B-complex group of vitamins. Folic acid is essential during the pre-conception phase and during pregnancy, to prevent any neural tube defects in newborns. The isoflavones in these beans, namely daidzein, formononetin, glycitein and genistein, are being studied for the role they play in reducing osteoporosis and cancers that occur in post-menopausal women.

*Pro-tip:* Black gram-infused sesame oil is a good remedy for joint pains and also used to nourish the scalp. Boil 2 tablespoons of black gram in 150 ml sesame oil. Once it comes to a boil, switch off the flame and cover it. Let it steep overnight. Then strain and store in a dark-coloured glass bottle. When gently massaged on the scalp, it prevents dry-flake formation. To use for joint pains, warm the oil first and then apply on the affected joints, using as little pressure as possible.

## LANGARWALI DAL

Our trip to Amritsar would not have been complete without partaking of the langar feast at the Golden Temple. The coldest day in December that year, the sanctity of the temple, the sacred way in which the free langar meal was prepared and served with love to every visitor, irrespective of religion, caste, creed or ethnicity—all of this added to the amazing taste of this simple preparation. It won our hearts, and the lingering flavour cannot be erased from my memory.—*Charlyene*

*Preparation time* 20 minutes
*Cooking time* 30 minutes
*Serves* 6

*Ingredients*

- 100 gm whole black gram, soaked for 2 hours
- 100 gm split Bengal gram, soaked for 2 hours
- 4 tbs onion, finely chopped
- 1 large tomato, chopped, with the peel and seeds
- 1/2 tsp turmeric powder
- 1/4 tsp pepper powder
- 1/2 tsp red chilli powder
- 2 tsp ghee
- Salt to taste

*For the tempering*

- 1 tsp cumin seeds
- 1 small red chilli, dried

- 2 green chillies
- 1 tsp ginger with the peel, julienned
- 1/2 tsp garam masala powder
- A pinch of asafoetida
- 1 tbs ghee

## Method

- Wash the soaked lentils thoroughly.
- Heat the ghee and sauté the onions and tomatoes in a pressure cooker.
- Add the washed lentils, turmeric, pepper and red chilli powder, along with salt to taste and 3–4 cups of warm water.
- Pressure-cook over 6 whistles.
- Once the pressure cooker has cooled and let off steam, open it and mash the pulses.
- Heat ghee for the tempering and add the ingredients to be tempered.
- Pour the tempering over the langarwali dal.
- Serve hot with parathas.

## Nutritive value per serving

- Energy: 153.77 kcal
- CHO: 17.71 gm
- Protein: 7.93 gm
- Fat: 5.69 gm
- Sodium: 333.37 mg
- Potassium: 445.71 mg
- Calcium: 37.86 mg
- Iron: 2.7 mg

- Vitamin A: 24.18 mcg
- Vitamin C: 2.65 mg

'We relish this preparation each time we visit gurdwaras, and making it at home with a taste that reminded us of the temple was like a blessing. Thank you, Charmaine, for inviting us to be part of your recipe trials'

—Pradeep and Deepti Agarwal, Raipur

## NO-BAKE BLACK GRAM COOKIES

These are easy, fun to prepare and make for an extremely nutritious snack. There is no baking involved. If you are trying to inculcate good eating habits in children, you could probably start with these cookies. After all, everyone loves cookies. Just place the ingredients in individual bowls in front of the young ones and get them to mix and mould these. Just great for enhancing their fine motor skills. Plus, a great way to incorporate pulses into their diet.—*Savlyene*

*Preparation time* 20 minutes
*Cooking time* 0 minutes
*Serves* 10

*Ingredients*

- 150 gm black gram, boiled, cooled and mashed
- 75 gm roasted oats
- 75 gm desiccated coconut
- 100 gm cocoa powder

+ 100 gm date paste
+ 50 gm raisins or berries

## Method

+ Mix the oats and desiccated coconut, and place on a tray.
+ Add the date paste and cocoa powder to the mashed black gram.
+ Mix well.
+ Add the raisins or berries.
+ Form into 1-inch balls.
+ If the mixture is too dry, add some milk or the liquid in which the black gram was cooked.
+ Add some more date paste to increase the sweetness (if needed).
+ The consistency of the mixture should be soft and pliable, just sufficiently so for the cookies to hold their shape.
+ Roll the cookies in the oat-and-coconut mixture.
+ Flatten a bit.
+ Place on a butter-paper-lined tray and set in the refrigerator.
+ Once set, transfer to an airtight container and store in the refrigerator.

## Nutritive value per serving

+ Energy: 179.95 kcal
+ CHO: 25.11 gm
+ Protein: 5.68 gm
+ Fat: 6.31 gm
+ Sodium: 11.61 mg
+ Potassium: 187.85 mg
+ Calcium: 12.91 mg

- Iron: 1.02 mg
- Vitamin A: 0.14 mcg
- Vitamin C: 0.09 mg

'Our boys aged six and eight are experts at making these no-bake cookies. We just finished making a third round! They love the taste, but love making them for their grandparents even more than they love eating them. This recipe is a winner, Savlyene. Thank you'

—Sheela and Tony Sanghi, Chandigarh

# MUNG BEANS

Counted among the best plant-based sources of protein, these legumes are a good source of the essential amino acids phenylalanine, leucine, isoleucine, lysine, saline and arginine. Their antioxidants include phenolic acid and cinnamic acid. These neutralize the free radical damage linked to the growth of cancer cells in the lungs and the stomach. Mung bean soup may be an excellent hydration solution to heat stroke. Apart from this, the beans have a positive effect on the heart, the pancreas and the lungs. They help lower blood pressure, improve digestion and provide resistant starch that boosts immunity and lowers the risk of colon cancer. Pregnant women need more iron, folate and protein, all of which are present in mung beans. However, it is not advisable for them to eat raw mung beans.

*Pro-tip:* Mung beans can be sprouted and eaten raw, or lightly steamed once sprouted. Sprouting increases their vitamin C content, and frees up more amino acids and nearly six times the original amount of antioxidants. It also decreases their phytic acid content. Phytic acids are antinutrients that reduce the absorption of important minerals such as magnesium, calcium and zinc. Simply soak the beans in water for 8 hours and then place them in a sprouter or a muslin cloth bag for three days, making sure to aerate and hydrate them regularly. Wash them a couple of times in cold water before adding them to salads or dosa batters.

## SPROUTED MUNG BEAN MUFFINS

The sprouting of mung beans ups its nutrition quotient and increases its digestibility. Crunchy mung sprouts taste amazing in a salad or a stir-fry. Our GHA mung-bean muffins incorporate the health benefits of sprouts and are a visually appealing treat, especially for those who like their muffins savoury, not sweet!—*Savlyene*

*Preparation time* 10 minutes, plus 1 hour to rest the batter
*Cooking time* 25 minutes
*Serves* 8

*Ingredients*

- 200 gm mung sprouts
- 150 gm yoghurt, whisked
- 100 gm rice flour
- 50 gm besan
- 50 gm oat flour
- 10 spinach leaves, chopped, with the stalks
- 2 tbs carrots, diced, with the peel
- 2 tbs green peas
- 1/2 tsp turmeric powder
- 1/4 tsp pepper powder
- 1/2 tsp red chilli powder
- 1/2 tsp coriander seeds, coarsely crushed
- 1/2 tsp cumin seeds
- 2 tbs vegetable oil
- Salt to taste

*Method*

- Put the sprouts in a blender along with the whisked yoghurt, and blend well.
- Pour into a large bowl and set aside for an hour.
- After an hour, add the rest of the ingredients to the fermented batter.
- Stir well and fill cupcake moulds up to 3/4th the depth with the batter.
- Steam or bake until an inserted toothpick comes out clean.
- Serve with green chutney.

*Nutritive value per serving*

- Energy: 199.52 kcal
- CHO: 26.51 gm
- Protein: 9.96 gm
- Fat: 5.96 gm
- Sodium: 257.69 mg
- Potassium: 332.91 mg
- Calcium: 64.41 mg
- Iron: 2.29 mg
- Vitamin A: 34.03 mcg
- Vitamin C: 2.63 mg

'Baking has never been my forte, but these muffins looked so interesting and super healthy. I just had to try this GHA recipe. What I liked about it were the easy pantry ingredients needed to make these amazing muffins. I will be using this recipe to also make pancakes and delicious dosas. This is definitely going to be a breakfast staple in my house'

—Aparna Dharira, Mumbai

## SPROUTED MUNG BEAN ROTLAS

High-protein snacks are always in demand post workout or between main meals. Make a stack of these and keep them handy. They go well with a glass of buttermilk, coconut water or nimbu pani. The sprouting of the beans increases their vitamin C value threefold and is just what is needed for muscle recovery.—*Charlyene*

*Preparation time* 20 minutes
*Cooking time* 20 minutes
*Serves* 8

*Ingredients*

- 150 gm mung sprouts
- 150 gm yoghurt, whisked
- 100 gm wholewheat flour
- 100 gm coconut sugar or jaggery sugar
- 1/2 tsp elaichi powder
- 1/2 tsp dried ginger powder
- 2 tbs vegetable oil or ghee

*Method*

- Blend the sprouts with the whisked yoghurt in a blender.
- Pour the batter into a bowl and add the rest of the ingredients, except the oil.
- Continue mixing to get a soft, smooth dough. You may need to add a little water if the dough is too stiff or more wheat flour if it is too slack.
- Roll out small, thick rotlas on a floured board.
- Grease a griddle and roast the rotlas well on both sides.

* Add a drop of oil or ghee just before turning them around.
* Serve warm.

*Nutritive value per serving*

* Energy: 171.16 kcal
* CHO: 26.26 gm
* Protein: 4.83 gm
* Fat: 5.2 gm
* Sodium: 30.4 mg
* Potassium: 258.59 mg
* Calcium: 95.22 mg
* Iron: 1.01 mg
* Vitamin A: 2.19 mcg
* Vitamin C: 0.02 mg

'I am waiting for schools to reopen. These rotlas will make for a satiating school snack for my children. I teach in the same school, so I am sure I will be visiting them at break time to eat from their dabbas. Thank you, Charlyene'

—Rachna Joshi, Mumbai

# RED KIDNEY BEANS

Kidney beans are available in a variety of colours—black, white, cream, purple and deep red. They are the richest plant-based sources of protein. Even though they may not have all the essential amino acids that meat does, they are nearly comparable and might even be referred to as 'the poor man's meat'. They contain proteins such as lectins, protease inhibitors and phaseolin. Their starchy, slow-release carbohydrates are amylose- and amylopectin-based. This makes them a good choice for type 2 diabetics. They have a good content of resistant starch, which improves the health of the colon and protects against colon cancer, but their galactoside content may cause flatulence, bloating and diarrhoea in some consumers. These beans are a rich source of vitamins and minerals such as folate, iron, copper, manganese, molybdenum, potassium and vitamin K. They are also a good source of antioxidants such as isoflavones and anthocyanins.

*Pro-tip:* Although kidney beans are beneficial for human health, the raw form of red kidney beans contains a toxic protein called phytohaemagglutinin. It may cause bloating, flatulence and diarrhoea when the beans are consumed in raw form. To avoid this, soak the beans overnight, wash them well and then pressure-cook them. This eliminates the toxins and makes red kidney beans safe to eat. Soaking and pressure-cooking the beans also inactivates the antinutrient content that includes phytic acid, protease inhibitors and starch blockers, which would otherwise have impaired the absorption of nutrients in the digestive tract.

## ANTIOXIDANT SOUP

Anthocyanins are plant pigments that give grains, fruits and vegetables their red, blue, purple and black colours. These flavonoids offer antiviral, anti-cancer and anti-inflammatory health benefits. Our soup incorporates two sources of this plant pigment—red kidney beans and black carrots—which combine to give this soup a beautiful purplish hue.—*Charlyene*

*Preparation time* 10 minutes
*Cooking time* 30 minutes, or 8 hours in a Crockpot or slow cooker
*Serves* 4

*Ingredients*

- 200 gm red kidney beans, soaked overnight
- 200 gm black carrots, chopped, with the peel
- 1 bay leaf
- 2 onions, chopped
- 6 cloves of garlic, minced
- 1 tsp dried tarragon
- 1 tbs vegetable oil or butter
- Salt and pepper to taste

*Method*

- If you are using a Crockpot or a slow cooker, switch it on high, else use a regular pressure cooker.
- Heat the oil or butter and temper the bay leaf.

- Add the onions and cook until translucent.
- Add the garlic, the beans and the carrots, and sauté for 5 minutes.
- Add the tarragon, salt to taste and 4 cups of water.
- Pressure-cook over 5 whistles or set the Crockpot on low for 8 hours.
- Once cooked, you can puree and add water to adjust the consistency to get a smooth, thick soup. Or you can have it as is, if you want a chunky soup.
- Portion out in bowls and add pepper and salt to taste.
- Serve warm.

*Nutritive value per serving*

- Energy: 179.34 kcal
- CHO: 25.41 gm
- Protein: 8.76 gm
- Fat: 4.74 gm
- Sodium: 32.5 mg
- Potassium: 713.25 mg
- Calcium: 73.43 mg
- Iron: 2.8 mg
- Vitamin A: 452.08 mcg
- Vitamin C: 6.09 mg

'I made the soup in the pressure cooker and used orange carrots, so I got an orangish-coloured soup. Taste-wise it was fantastic. I will be making it more often in the coming weeks'

—Meena Sakpal, Dubai

## CRINKLE COOKIES

You are super-stressed, completing a work assignment that just does not seem to end. You suddenly crave a heavenly morsel of goodness to pair well with the mug of hot beverage you are also craving for. You stop work. You go into the kitchen. You bake. Baking is a major stressbuster. A few hours later, you emerge from your haven, energized, refreshed and ready to take on another assignment—or two, or three! Bring it on, Mom!—*Savlyene*

*Preparation time* 45 minutes
*Cooking time* 15
*Serves* 8

*Ingredients*

- 100 gm red rajma puree (blend the pressure-cooked rajma in some of the cooking liquid until you get a fine paste). Reserve the rest of the cooking liquid to add to soups, gravies, etc.
- 100 gm wheat flour
- 1 tsp baking powder
- 1 tsp baking soda
- 1/2 tsp salt
- 1 tsp coffee powder
- 75 gm cocoa powder
- 180 gm jaggery sugar or coconut sugar
- 100 ml vegetable oil
- 1 tsp vanilla extract
- 50 gm sugar, powdered (to dust on the cookies after they have been baked)

*Method*

- Sift the wheat flour with the baking powder, baking soda, salt, cocoa powder and coffee powder, and set aside.
- In a large bowl, beat the oil and jaggery sugar until well combined.
- Add the rajma puree and continue whisking until soft and smooth.
- Gently fold in the sifted flour mixture.
- Add the vanilla extract and stir well.
- Using an ice-cream scooper to portion out spoonfuls on to a lined baking tray.
- Freeze for 10 minutes.
- Preheat the oven to 180 degrees.
- Bring out the cookie tray from the freezer and dust with the powdered sugar.
- Bake for 12 minutes, until the edges are done and the inside appears soft and gooey.
- Allow to cool on a wire rack.
- Store in an airtight container.

*Nutritive value per serving*

- Energy: 184.03 kcal
- CHO: 38.14 gm
- Protein: 5.19 gm
- Fat: 1.19 gm
- Sodium: 351.1 mg
- Potassium: 253.60 mg
- Calcium: 33.69 mg
- Iron: 1.96 mg

- Vitamin A: 0.072 mcg
- Vitamin C: 0.003 mg

'I was very happy with the final product. The cookies are crispy on the outer edges and chewy-soft at the centre. The best part is that my grandchildren do not know they are eating rajma cookies—they think it is chocolate'

—Meena Sakpal, Dubai

# RED LENTILS (MÀSOOR)

Lentils are edible legumes. They are of different types. The brown lentils have an earthy flavour and hold their shape well during cooking. Puy lentils have a peppery taste and greenish colour. Green lentils taste great in soups and stews. Yellow and red lentils have a sweet, nutty flavour and are available in the split form as dals. The tiny black beluga lentils look almost like caviar, hence the name. They are generally used as a base in warm salads. Irrespective of the type of lentil, they are all a great source of disease-protecting phytochemicals, B-complex vitamins, zinc, iron, potassium and magnesium. They help in managing diabetes, cancer, hypertension, cardiovascular disease, obesity and gut health. However, their antinutrient content of trypsin inhibitors, tannins, lectins and phytic acid may impact the absorption of other nutrients. So it is best to soak them for a minimum of 2 hours prior to cooking.

*Pro-tip:* Use a masoor-dal pack to remove or lighten a tan, exfoliate your skin and refresh it. Soak 3 tablespoons of masoor dal in water overnight. Grind it to form a thick paste with some milk. Then add a teaspoon of lemon juice and 2 teaspoons of mint juice. Apply on your face, arms and back. Leave it on for 20–30 minutes. Rinse off with cold water. Pat dry and apply an ice cube in circular motion. Pat dry again.

## GREEN TEA MASOOR

Boost your metabolic rate and your antioxidant quotient with this curry. The green tea not only impacts the taste of this curry but also the aftertaste. Each spoonful is rich, tasty and releases all those feel-good endorphins your body needs. Make sure to make this at least once a week, if not more.—*Charmaine*

*Preparation time* 15 minutes
*Cooking time* 25 minutes
*Serves* 8

*Ingredients*

- 250 gm red masoor dal, soaked for 2 hours
- 2 sachets of green tea
- 2 medium onions, finely chopped
- 4 cloves of garlic, minced
- 2 tsp ginger, grated, with the peel
- 2 small tomatoes, chopped, with the peel and seeds
- 1 tsp cumin seeds
- 1 tsp garam masala powder
- 1/2 tsp red chilli powder
- 1/2 tsp nigella seeds
- 1 tbs vegetable oil
- Salt to taste
- Lime juice

*To garnish*

- Coriander, freshly chopped, with the stalks

*Method*

- Place the green tea sachets in a bowl and infuse them in 400 ml boiling-hot water. Cover and set aside.
- Heat the oil in a pressure cooker and sauté the cumin and nigella seeds.
- Add the onions, ginger and garlic, and sauté for 2 minutes.
- Add the chopped tomatoes and, when they have softened, add the garam masala and red chilli powders.
- Cook for 5 minutes, then add the soaked red masoor dal.
- Add the green tea decoction 2 minutes later, after squeezing out the tea bags.
- Add another 2–3 cups water.
- Add salt to taste.
- Pressure-cook over 3 whistles.
- Serve hot with a squeeze of lime juice and some chopped coriander.

*Nutritive value per serving*

- Energy: 132.28 kcal
- CHO: 19.84 gm
- Protein: 7.38 gm
- Fat: 2.6 gm
- Sodium: 8.75 mg
- Potassium: 502.65 mg
- Calcium: 34.53 mg
- Iron: 1.57 mg
- Vitamin A: 21.99 mcg
- Vitamin C: 4.01 mg

'Green tea in dal? Was this for lunch or a 5 p.m. snack? That's what my kids kept asking me, knowing my penchant for green tea every evening. To our surprise, the subtle flavour of the green tea made our masoor dal even more tasty and energizing. My hubby feels it will help with his BP too'

—J.S. Sabherwal, Mumbai

## MOROCCAN LENTIL HARIRA

This traditional Moroccan soup had lots of lamb in it when we tasted it for the first time in Marrakech. There are so many variations to harira, and we have made the vegetarian option many times. It is a chunky, hearty, flavoursome soup that can also be served as a one-pot meal if you add some rice or vermicelli to it. If you have a Moroccan earthen tagine, try making the harira in it.—*Charmaine*

*Preparation time* 20 minutes
*Cooking time* 45 minutes
*Serves* 8

*Ingredients*

- 200 gm whole masoor, soaked for 2 hours
- 1 large onion, finely chopped
- 1 cup fresh coriander, finely chopped, with the stalks
- 4 tomatoes, chopped, with the peel and seeds
- 4 stalks celery stalks, chopped, with the leaves
- 1 tbs ginger, finely grated, with the peel

- 1 tsp cumin powder
- 1 tsp cinnamon powder
- 1 tsp pepper powder
- 1/2 tsp turmeric powder
- 2 tbs vegetable oil
- 4 cups vegetable stock or plain water
- 1 cup rice or vermicelli bits (optional)
- Salt to taste

*Method*

- Heat the oil in a pressure cooker and sauté the onions until translucent.
- Add the ginger and tomatoes, and cook for 2 minutes.
- Add the rest of the ingredients.
- If adding rice or vermicelli, make sure you add more cooking liquid.
- Pressure cook over 3 whistles.
- Serve hot.

*Nutritive value per serving*

- Energy: 126.75 kcal
- CHO: 15.82 gm
- Protein: 6.62 gm
- Fat: 4.11 gm
- Sodium: 5.40 mg
- Potassium: 277.34 mg
- Calcium: 26.02 mg
- Iron: 2.09 mg
- Vitamin A: 25.17 mcg
- Vitamin C: 4.99 mg

'A delicious, filling soup that brought back memories of a Berber restaurant in Fez. I did add lots of lemon at the end'

—Kumud Hirawat, Mumbai

# DRIED GREEN PEAS (VATANA)

Apart from being a very good source of cholesterol and blood sugar-lowering soluble fibre, these legumes provide sufficient insoluble fibre. This helps sweep digestive waste through the gastrointestinal tract, increases stool bulk, promotes bowel regularity and prevents constipation, IBS and diverticulosis. They also provide proteins, B-complex vitamins such as folate and B1, and minerals such as copper, manganese, phosphorus, potassium (which helps stabilize blood pressure) and molybdenum. If your diet is high in preserved foods, you will benefit from adding these legumes to your meal. This is because many preserved foods have sulphites added as preservatives. People who are sulphite-sensitive experience headaches, disorientation and an increase in heart rate because of this. Molybdenum, a trace mineral present in dried green peas, helps detoxify these sulphites. Apart from this, dried green peas contain cancer-fighting antioxidant compounds such as sterols and flavonoids.

*Pro-tip:* The iron content in dried green peas is not as easily absorbed as the iron in animal tissues. To boost iron absorption from all pulses, you should eat your dals, vatana, channa, etc., with a good food source of vitamin C such as lime juice, tamarind juice or green chillies. So go ahead and squeeze lime juice on your dal or add tamarind or chilli paste to your channa chaats.

## PESTO VATANA MOUSSE

The humble dried green pea, normally used in the making of a simple but tasty curry in our home, just got fancy! We've used it to make this beautiful savoury mousse. It is velvety-soft and yet has a grainy texture because of the pesto. When we serve this to guests, they cannot believe its main component is vatana and not avocado!—*Savlyene*

*Preparation time* 30 minutes
*Cooking time* 0 minutes
*Serves* 4

*Ingredients*

*For the seed-crumb base*

- 4 tbs pumpkin seeds
- 4 tbs melon seeds
- 1 tbs east Indian bottle masala or garam masala powder
- Salt to taste
- 2 tsp vegetable oil

*For the pesto vatana mousse*

- 30 basil leaves
- 5 tbs pumpkin seeds
- 2 tsp white sesame seeds
- 4 cloves of garlic
- 2 tbs olive oil
- 150 gm green vatana, soaked overnight, pressure-cooked and drained. Reserve the cooking liquid to add to soups, gravies, etc.
- Salt to taste

*Method*

*For the seed-crumb base*

+ Dry-roast the seeds.
+ Add the oil, the masala powder and salt to taste.
+ Roast until it changes colour.
+ Cool completely and coarsely grind.
+ Refrigerate.

*For the pesto vatana mousse*

+ Take 1 cup of aqua faba (the cooking liquid of the vatana) and whisk until it resembles beaten egg whites. Set aside.
+ Place the pumpkin seeds, sesame seeds and garlic in a blender and grind them.
+ Add the basil leaves and continue blending while slowly adding the olive oil.
+ Add salt to taste.
+ Your seed pesto is ready.
+ Add the cooked vatana and blend until smooth. Add salt if needed.
+ Transfer to a bowl and gradually incorporate the whipped aqua faba.

*To assemble*

+ Using a greased cookie cutter as a guide, place 2 tablespoons of the seed-crumb base per mousse.
+ Press down firmly.
+ Top with the pesto vatana mousse.
+ Repeat for the other three.
+ Let it set for an hour in the refrigerator.

- Bring out the mousse and gently remove the cookie cutter.
- Garnish with basil leaves.
- Serve cold.

*Nutritive value per serving*

- Energy: 462.21 kcal
- CHO: 12.84 gm
- Protein: 18 gm
- Fat: 37.65 gm
- Sodium: 305.54 mg
- Potassium: 203.27 mg
- Calcium: 66.52 mg
- Iron: 4.05 mg
- Vitamin A: 15.33 mcg
- Vitamin C: 0.45 mg

'I took this recipe up as a challenge, because who uses vatana to make a mousse? Tried it and it turned out great. Everyone thought I had used avocado despite the lockdown, when getting simple vegetables was difficult. I am happy to share the recipe (if Savlyene agrees) but not sure if my friends will believe that I used dried green vatana'

—Mukta Sen, Chennai

## VATANA CHITAPS

Chitaps, or rice flour crepes, are an east Indian delicacy. Traditionally they are made from rice flour, eggs and coconut milk, and are fermented overnight with toddy. No east Indian wedding buffet table is complete without these soft, porous, coconut-flavoured, spongy crepes, which are just ideal to mop up the yummy curries that the community is famous for. We've used a puree of cooked dried green peas, coconut milk and rice flour—no eggs or toddy. The signs of a perfect chitap are the million little holes that give them a lacy look, the golden-brown colour and the crispy edges. You would be forgiven if you thought these delicate crepes were a lacy handkerchief to use at the end of your meal!—*Charlyene*

*Preparation time* 30 minutes
*Cooking time* 10 minutes
*Serves* 4

*Ingredients*

- 120 gm cooked green vatana, soaked overnight, pressure-cooked and drained
- 300 ml coconut milk (not coconut cream)
- 80 gm rice flour
- 2 level tsp baking powder (if you do not want to use baking powder, use 2 eggs, else omit and leave the batter in the refrigerator overnight to ferment)
- 1/2 tsp salt
- 1/2 tsp coconut sugar
- 2 tsp vegetable oil

*Method*

- Sift the rice flour with the baking powder and salt. Keep aside.

- In a blender, puree the cooked green vatana and add the coconut milk to form a smooth batter.
- Add the coconut sugar and gradually add the sifted flour.
- Blend until there are no lumps and leave aside for 15–20 minutes.
- Adjust the consistency with warm water. It should be neither too thin nor too thick.
- Heat a small skillet over high heat and lightly grease the base with a few drops of oil.
- Pour just enough batter to get a thin crepe, while moving the skillet around to spread the batter out evenly, just as you would for a dosa or an uttapam.
- When the edges start to brown slightly, run a wooden spatula around to loosen the crepe and flip it around.
- Cook for another 30 seconds.
- Repeat for the rest of the batter, making sure the skillet is always very hot.
- Serve hot.

*Nutritive value per serving*

- Energy: 299.06 kcal
- CHO: 26.96 gm
- Protein: 8.52 gm
- Fat: 17.46 gm
- Sodium: 800.95 mg
- Potassium: 179.43 mg
- Calcium: 30.58 mg
- Iron: 2.24 mg
- Vitamin A: 2.05 mcg
- Vitamin C: 0.7 mg

'My staunch east Indian mother would never have let me change her original chitap recipe. I am glad I tried the GHA variation out when she was asleep, because when she woke up and tasted these dried green pea chitaps, she said, "It is different, but nice. Now go make more." I know my mother well and know she loves these green chitaps but will not admit it—so I'm just going to make lots more'

—Serena Dias, Mumbai

# SOYA BEANS

When it comes to sources of plant-based protein, soya beans are counted among the best. They have a good amount of glycinin and conglycinin protein. Unfortunately, some people show allergic reactions to these two protein types. Regular consumption of soya protein may decrease blood cholesterol levels marginally. Soya bean oil has linoleic acid. They are also a good source of vitamins such as B1, B9 (folate) and K1, and minerals such as molybdenum, copper, phosphorus and manganese. They are a good source of isoflavone phytonutrients genistein and daidzein, which are plant-based oestrogenic compounds, or phytoestrogens, which mimic the role of oestrogen, the female sex hormone. Having said this, it is important to add that phytoestrogens in soya may alleviate menopausal symptoms only in women (especially Japanese) who have a particular type of gut bacteria that converts soya isoflavones to equol. Equol is responsible for soya's female-health benefits, such as prevention of osteoporosis and alleviation of menopausal symptoms. Studies show that the isoflavones and lunasin in soya beans may be responsible for certain cancer-preventing actions but are not conclusive on whether they can also cause cancer. So it is always better to eat a wide variety of foods from different food groups to ensure a healthy, balanced diet.

*Pro-tip:* The incidence of hypothyroidism because of a decrease in thyroid-hormone production may be attributed to high intake of soya foods. The soya isoflavones can suppress thyroid function, especially in those individuals with an underactive thyroid gland. Soya goitrogens block iodine absorption and thyroid-hormone production. So avoid eating these beans for three months if you have been diagnosed with hypothyroidism and check if this impacts your TSH levels positively.

## SOYA KHEEMA BUNS

Textured vegetable protein is a popular, cheaper and healthier substitute for meat. It is available in the form of soya chunks and soya granules. Since it is impossible to discern a meat dish from a well-prepared soya dish, we have had the pleasure of treating the most hard-core non-vegetarians to many 'mock meat' preparations, and they have always come back for more! These soya-mince-stuffed buns are a great example. So round up the ingredients and get started. Your family and friends will thank you for it.—*Savlyene*

*Preparation time* 10 minutes
*Cooking time* 30 minutes
*Serves* 4

*Ingredients*

- 100 gm soya granules
- 2 large onions, cut lengthwise
- 1 tbs ginger-garlic paste
- 2 tbs tomatoes, chopped, with the peel and seeds
- 1 tbs east Indian bottle masala or garam masala
- 1 tsp cumin seeds
- 2 tbs coriander, chopped, with the stalks

- 1 tbs vegetable oil
- Salt to taste
- 2 tbs lime juice
- 4 large or 8 small wholewheat garlic buns (p. 39)

*Method*

- Soak the soya granules in warm water for 10 minutes. Drain and set aside.
- Heat oil in a pan and sauté the cumin seeds.
- Add the onions and cook until brown.
- Once the onions have browned, add the east Indian bottle masala or the garam masala powder, and ginger-garlic paste. Cook for 2 minutes.
- Add the chopped tomatoes and cook until they soften.
- Add the soaked and drained soya granules next.
- Keep stirring until the masala coats the granules and add a cup of warm water.
- Cover and cook for 10 minutes.
- Add salt to taste.
- Keep stirring until the water dries out and add the lime juice and chopped coriander.
- Cool.
- Slit each bun and fill with the soya kheema. Alternatively, if you are using our recipe for wholewheat garlic buns, you may choose to stuff the soya kheema filling into each ball of dough and then bake them.

*Nutritive value per serving*

- Energy: 373.15 kcal
- CHO: 50.45 gm

- Protein: 21.08 gm
- Fat: 9.67 gm
- Sodium: 260.23 mg
- Potassium: 264.82 mg
- Calcium: 138.43 mg
- Iron: 7.56 mg
- Vitamin A: 12.04 mcg
- Vitamin C: 4.21 mg

> 'Heart disease runs in my family, because no one runs in the family! Ha! So using soya mince is my way of ensuring a healthy quotient in their diet. I feel the stuffed buns looked better and were easier to eat. Looks like a great party/picnic snack too, post lockdown'
>
> —Greta L. Ferro, Mumbai

## CROCKPOT SOYA UNDHIYU

Surat is well known for its textiles, saris, diamonds and, most importantly, its undhiyu. This winter speciality uses many fresh winter veggies and is traditionally cooked in an earthen pot sealed and placed upside down in a fire pit specially dug out for this delicacy. It is slow-cooked for many hours, ending up in a preparation that is rustically delicious. We use our Crockpot, but you can make this in a pressure cooker, slow cooker or on the stovetop. Another twist is the incorporation of soya beans to up the protein value of the dish.—*Charlyene*

*Preparation time* 30 minutes
*Cooking time* 4 hours in a Crockpot
*Serves* 8

*Ingredients*

- 150 gm soya beans, soaked overnight
- 100 gm surti papdi (flat beans), chopped
- 100 gm lilva papdi (small flat beans), chopped
- 2 medium potatoes, chopped, with the peels
- 4 medium eggplants (2 cross slits at one end going halfway down to hold the masala)
- 1 medium yam, chopped, with the peel
- 1 medium sweet potato, chopped, with the peel
- 2 raw bananas, chopped, with the peel

*For the masala*

- 100 gm coconut, freshly grated
- 8 tbs coriander, finely chopped, with the stalks
- 2 tbs peanuts, roasted and coarsely ground
- 2 tbs ginger-garlic paste
- 1 tbs green chilli paste
- 2 tsp garam masala powder
- 1 tsp red chilli powder
- 1 tsp turmeric powder
- 1/4 tsp pepper powder
- 2 tsp coriander powder
- 2 tsp cumin powder
- 1 tbs white sesame seeds
- Salt to taste
- 2 tsp jaggery sugar
- 4 tbs vegetable oil

*To serve*

♦   10 methi muthia (this can be store-bought)

*Method*

♦   Mix all the ingredients for the masala in a large bowl and set aside.
♦   When prepping the vegetables, please ensure they are all chopped to equal size.
♦   Stuff the eggplants with some of the masala and place them at the bottom of the lightly greased Crockpot.
♦   Place the soaked soya beans and the other veggies in the masala bowl, and toss well to ensure the masala is distributed evenly.
♦   Place this in the Crockpot above the stuffed eggplants.
♦   Add some water to the masala bowl and draw out all the remaining masala.
♦   Add this to the Crockpot.
♦   Taste for salt and add more if needed.
♦   Set the Crockpot on high for 1 hour and then on low for another 3 hours. Alternatively, you may choose to make the undhiyu in the pressure cooker for 3–4 whistles.
♦   Serve warm after adding the methi muthias.

*Nutritive value per serving*

♦   Energy: 311.54 kcal
♦   CHO: 22.61 gm
♦   Protein: 9.06 gm
♦   Fat: 20.54 gm
♦   Sodium: 15.28 mg

- Potassium: 737.76 mg
- Calcium: 89.86 mg
- Iron: 3.13 mg
- Vitamin A: 13.12 mcg
- Vitamin C: 19.99 mg

'We all love this Gujarati special winter meal, but we have never made it before because of the long process. This recipe is a quick one—ideal for inaugurating my new slow cooker, a gift from hubby on our anniversary six months ago. Loved the fact that I didn't have to fry the methi muthia at home. I used the baked ones from a store in Mumbai'

—Armin D., Mumbai

# YELLOW PIGEON PEAS (TUVAR DAL)

One of the most important and widely used food legume crops, yellow pigeon peas are legumes that grow abundantly. Like other legumes, they are an excellent source of minerals such as magnesium, calcium, phosphorus and potassium, besides copper, manganese and zinc. Potassium acts as a vasodilator and lowers blood pressure. Pigeon peas are good sources of vitamins B2, B3, B6 and B9, needed for the metabolism of carbohydrates and fats, and also to boost energy levels. Their protein content helps bone, tissue, muscle and cell formation. The folate in yellow pigeon peas helps prevent folic acid deficiency anaemia. The soluble dietary fibre content in these peas helps lower cholesterol and prevent heart disease, while the insoluble fibre content prevents bloating, abdominal pain, cramping, diarrhoea and constipation. The sprouting of pigeon peas enhances their digestibility. It is always best to soak the peas for a few hours, wash them well and pressure-cook them.

*Pro-tip:* Sometimes tuvar dal is oiled to increase its shelf life. The oil acts as a natural preservative and prevents infestation. If you have purchased this type of oiled dal, it is best to wash it thoroughly in hot water to remove all the oil. As with regular dal, always continue soaking and washing until the water is no longer foaming and appears clearer.

## DAL TADKA

A bowl of lentils tempered with spices and pure ghee, served on a bed of soft-cooked rice, with a side of vegetables and an accompaniment of fresh home-made pickle or chutney—that is the description of our go-to meal, a meal bursting with flavour, soothing and satiating, a meal that has so much nostalgic value. Dal tadka is a staple in most Indian homes, and there are so many different versions of it. This is our basic version.—*Charmaine*

*Preparation time* 15 minutes
*Cooking time* 30 minutes
*Serves* 4

*Ingredients*

- 150 gm yellow pigeon peas, soaked for an hour
- 2 onions, finely chopped
- 1/2 tsp turmeric powder
- 1 tsp cumin seeds
- 1/2 tsp gingelly seeds
- 6 cloves of garlic, finely chopped
- 1 tsp ginger, finely chopped, with the peel
- 2 tomatoes, pureed, with the peels and seeds
- 1 tsp garam masala powder
- 1/2 tsp cumin powder
- 1/2 tsp saunf powder
- 1 tsp coriander powder
- 1 bay leaf
- 1 tbs ghee

*   Salt to taste
*   A piece of charcoal

*Method*

*   Pressure-cook the soaked dal along with the chopped onions, turmeric powder and salt over 4 whistles.
*   Once cool, puree the dal and set aside.
*   In the meantime, heat the ghee in a large pan and temper the bay leaf, cumin and gingelly seeds.
*   Cook the ginger and garlic for 2 minutes.
*   Add the tomato puree and the rest of the masala powders.
*   Once the mix is well roasted, add the dal puree.
*   Adjust for salt and cook for 5 minutes. The dal should be thick in consistency.
*   When ready to serve the dal, heat the charcoal piece until red-hot and immerse it in a small bowl with a tablespoon of ghee.
*   Place the charcoal bowl in the dal pan and cover immediately.
*   This will give the dal a smoky flavour.
*   Remove the charcoal bowl after 5 minutes.
*   Serve hot with steamed rice or rotis.

*Nutritive value per serving*

*   Energy: 179.36 kcal
*   CHO: 25.90 gm
*   Protein: 7.96 gm
*   Fat: 4.88 gm
*   Sodium: 14.12 mg

- Potassium: 555.8 mg
- Calcium: 77.48 mg
- Iron: 15.38 mg
- Vitamin A: 13.12 mcg
- Vitamin C: 4.72 mg

'I loved this different way of making dal tadka. I had never used charcoal smoking for lentils before. This was definitely good, because it got my son Zane's approval. He gave up his regular favourite curd rice to have this smoked dal tadka'

—Lisette-Ann D'Silva, Mumbai

## RED CURRANT BAKED SOUFFLÉ

The first time I baked a soufflé with lentil puree, I did not let the family know that I had surreptitiously added some healthy ingredients. When they asked me to make it again, I had to share the secret. Why? The ramekins were lined up, the fruit puree was ready and just as I was adding the pureed tuvar dal, my two detectives walked in! Over the years I have used many seasonal fruits and dried fruits, but this red currant variety is a family favourite.—*Charmaine*

*Preparation time* 10 minutes
*Cooking time* 20 minutes
*Serves* 4

## Ingredients

- 150 gm yellow pigeon peas, soaked, pressure-cooked and pureed
- 100 gm red currant puree (soak the dried red currants in some warm water and puree)
- 150 gm hung curd (save the whey for soups, gravies, roti dough, etc.)
- 100 gm castor sugar
- 100 ml milk

## For garnishing

- 12 red currants and a few mint leaves

## Method

- Preheat the oven to 180 degrees.
- Place all the ingredients in a food processor or blender and blend on high speed until smooth.
- You may need to add a little more milk to adjust the consistency.
- Pour this mixture into 4 ramekins and cover each with butter paper. Since it is eggless, it will not rise like a classic French soufflé but will taste just as delicious.
- Place the ramekins in a baking tray with 1 glass water to form a water bath.
- Bake for 18–20 minutes.
- Garnish with the remaining red currants and the mint leaves.
- Serve warm or cold.

*Nutritive value per serving*

- Energy: 308.92 kcal
- CHO: 61.17 gm
- Protein: 8.86 gm
- Fat: 3.2 gm
- Sodium: 23.82 mg
- Potassium: 565.85 mg
- Calcium: 134.45 mg
- Iron: 2.02 mg
- Vitamin A: 13.51 mcg
- Vitamin C: 46.37 mg

'I called Charlyene at GHA twice to check if there was an error in the recipe. Tuvar dal in a French dessert? I learnt something new that day and my husband also benefited from the health point of view. I did not have red currants, so I used mango instead. It worked very well. I will use red currants whenever I am able to get them after this lockdown period'

—Fatima D'Mello, Hong Kong

# VEGETABLES

A balanced diet that includes ample nutrient-dense vegetables and fruits can have positive effects on your life, and your physical and mental health. It can lower your blood pressure and blood sugar levels, prevent some types of cancer, reduce your risk of heart disease, strokes, eye disease and digestive disorders. It can provide satiety, keep your appetite under control and may even promote healthy weight loss. The important thing to remember is that no single vegetable or fruit will provide all the nutrients your body needs to stay fit and active. So you need to choose from a wide variety of vegetable and fruit types and colours. This will ensure that you are getting all the vital nutrients from the different plant compounds.

The fresh, edible portions of herbaceous plants, such as roots, stems, leaves, flowers, fruits and seeds, are broadly known as vegetable matter. There are root vegetables such as beets, yams, carrots, radishes, sweet potatoes and turnips. Asparagus is a stem vegetable while potatoes are edible tubers. Leafy vegetables include cabbage, spinach, kale, mint, celery and lettuce. Onions and garlic are bulb vegetables, while cauliflower and broccoli are flower or head vegetables. Tomatoes, cucumbers, eggplant, peppers, okra, etc., are actually fruits. Seed vegetables include peas and beans.

Vegetables are a source of important nutrients such as dietary fibre, essential vitamins, minerals and trace elements, all of which are important for human nutrition. However, they may contain antinutrients such as solanine, enzyme inhibitors, oxalic acid, tannins, etc., which come in the way of the absorption of essential nutrients. The good news is that most of these antinutrients can be deactivated by cooking vegetables adequately.

# BITTER GOURD (KARELA)

Let me introduce you to a close relative of the veggies we all love, such as cucumber, pumpkin and zucchini—bitter gourd/ bitter melon/karela. You may be wondering if this is the proverbial black sheep of the family. After all, very few people love bitter gourds, right? Its bitter taste, which may not be very delectable, is attributed to its alkaloids and glucosides. So why is karela clubbed with other veggies? Well, they are all fruits belonging to the same family of gourds and pack in several important nutrients. If you need to increase your immunity, improve bone health, heal wounds quickly, get quick relief from indigestion, piles and hyperacidity, disintegrate kidney stones, reduce split ends and premature greying of hair, prevent cell damage, see better, enhance skin glow, get rid of belly fat, avoid a hangover after a night of binge-drinking, cleanse your liver, prevent cancer-cell formation, maintain cholesterol levels, lower blood pressure and control blood sugar levels, look no further than a bowlful of 'bitter is better' karela!

*Pro-tip:* Small green bitter gourds are more palatable. The bitterness increases as the fruit grows and orangish bitter gourds are extremely bitter. When prepping bitter melons, slice them without removing the peels and then discard the white pith. Parboil the slices in boiling hot water to reduce some of the bitterness. Remove the slices and save the water. This water, or 'bitter melon tea', can be consumed throughout the day for its health benefits.

## KARELA PEEL KADHI

Kadhi is a velvety-smooth, subtly spiced buttermilk curry that acts as comfort food in most north Indian homes. You may have tasted various versions from different parts of India. The Punjabi kadhi is thick and creamy, with onion pakodis dunked in it. Sindhi kadhi has an assortment of vegetables and uses tomatoes as a base instead of yoghurt. The spicy Rajasthani kadhi is a thin golden-yellow gravy that is accompanied by steamed rice and a large amount of desi ghee. The affable Gujaratis make their kadhi distinctly sweet. Down south, Tamilians love their paruppu urrundai mor kuzhambu, or buttermilk curry, with lentil dumplings. I've even tasted a version with mango bits and grilled prawns! Gently cooking buttermilk will lessen its vata-inducing properties and help boost digestion. Taking advantage of kadhi's ability to adapt and adopt to a variety of add-ons, I've used bitter melon peels—and the taste is amazing.—*Charmaine*

*Preparation time* 10 minutes
*Cooking time* 10 minutes
*Serves* 4

*Ingredients*

- 100 gm bitter gourd peel, chopped, boiled in water and drained
- 200 gm yoghurt
- 50 gm Bengal gram flour
- 4 cloves of garlic, finely chopped
- 1 large onion, finely chopped
- 1 tsp cumin seeds
- 1 tsp cumin and coriander powder

- 1 tsp chilli powder
- 1/2 tsp turmeric powder
- 1/8 tsp pepper powder
- 1/4 tsp asafoetida
- 1 tsp jaggery sugar
- 2 tsp vegetable oil
- Salt to taste

## Method

- Whisk the yoghurt with 4 cups of water.
- Add the Bengal gram flour and mix well to prevent the formation of lumps.
- Heat oil in a pan and temper the cumin seeds and asafoetida.
- Add garlic and onions, and lightly cook.
- Add the rest of the ingredients, except the yoghurt mixture, salt and jaggery sugar.
- A minute later, add the yoghurt mixture, along with the salt and the jaggery sugar. Bring to a gentle boil.
- Adjust the consistency with more water, if needed.
- Serve hot with steamed rice.

## Nutritive value per serving

- Energy: 200.82 kcal
- CHO: 21.91 gm
- Protein: 10.61 gm
- Fat: 7.86 gm
- Sodium: 57.87 mg
- Potassium: 380.04 mg
- Calcium: 386.97 mg
- Iron: 2.62 mg

- Vitamin A: 7.04 international units (IU)
- Vitamin C: 12.78 mg

> 'I made a thicker kadhi, but I am sure it will taste better with a thinner consistency. My boys needed that extra bit of jaggery to cut down the bitterness of the karela peels. Will make it again'
>
> —Devika Goel, Mumbai

## BITTER GOURD PICKLE

This accompaniment to a simple meal hits all the right spots—it is slightly spicy, mildly sweet, perfectly salty, subtly sour and pleasantly bitter. This balance ensures good health. Served with steamed rice and a basic dal or kadhi, this pickle will have your family asking for second helpings. So be sure to make lots of it and keep a bottle handy in the refrigerator for times when you are hard-pressed for time or low on energy and unable to whip up a multicourse meal. It can stay well in the refrigerator for a month. When my girls were in school, I would make banana theplas or sweet potato rotis and stuff them with this pickle. Their lunch boxes were always wiped clean!—*Charmaine*

*Preparation time* 15 minutes
*Cooking time* 25 minutes
*Serves* 15

*Ingredients*

- 250 gm bitter gourd, deseeded and cubed, with the peel

- 4 tbs cumin seeds
- 4 tbs coriander seeds
- 2 tbs mustard seeds
- 4 tbs fennel seeds
- 1 tbs fenugreek seeds
- 1/2 tbs asafoetida
- 4 tbs tamarind paste
- 150 gm jaggery
- Salt to taste

*For tempering*

- 35 curry leaves
- 2 tbs coconut oil
- 1 tbs mustard seeds
- 1 tbs urad dal

*Method*

- Roast the cumin seeds, coriander seeds, mustard seeds, fennel seeds and fenugreek seeds in a heated pan.
- Just before you turn off the heat, add the asafoetida and mix well.
- Cool and grind it in a blender.
- Cook the bitter gourd cubes in hot water for 8–10 minutes, or until well cooked but not soft. Strain and reserve the water to drink as bitter gourd cleansing tea throughout the day.
- Blend the tamarind paste with the jaggery, add 4 tablespoons of hot water and bring to a gentle boil.
- Add the roasted spice powder and the cooked bitter gourd cubes.
- Add salt to taste.

- You may need to adjust the flavour by adding more salt, jaggery or tamarind paste to bring about a balance.
- Temper the curry leaves, mustard seeds and urad dal in coconut oil.
- Add to the bitter gourd pickle.
- Store in a clean glass jar.

*Nutritive value per tablespoon serving*

- Energy: 83.73 kcal
- CHO: 13.57 gm
- Protein: 2.21 gm
- Fat: 2.29 gm
- Sodium: 12.28 mg
- Potassium: 299.21 mg
- Calcium: 93.35 mg
- Iron: 2.95 mg
- Vitamin A: 5.39 mcg
- Vitamin C: 9.19 mg

'We are extremely fond of pickles and chutneys, but stay away as per our nutritionist's advice. Then when she herself sends a pickle recipe, who can resist? So different from salty, oily, regular store-purchased pickles. A very good tip of saving the karela water to drink during the day. My family loved the karela pickle with chapati. I am going to make a big jar of this pickle soon'

—Rita Salunkhe, Nashik

## STUFFED BITTER GOURD

The quintessential Indian thali is a complete meal, with an assortment of delicious dishes, recipes of which are procured from different regions of India. Sometimes, when Mum needs an able assistant (ha ha) for one of her talks/workshops, she takes me along. When the said talk/workshop is in another part of the country, partaking of a regional feast is one of the many perks of my job—shopping and sightseeing are other benefits! Ahmedabad is well known for its delicious food, and we once had a memorable dinner in an old palace that had been converted into a dining place. Not only were the courses numerous and sumptuous, but they were also served in different areas—the snacks were served in a dining hall, the main course on the terrace, and desserts and post-meal mukhwas and paan in the well-lit lawns. The bharwan karela was served piping hot, filled with nuts, dried fruit and coconut, and oozing in fat. This is my healthier, air-fried version. You can also bake it.—*Charlyene*

*Preparation time* 35 minutes
*Cooking time* 15 minutes
*Serves* 4

*Ingredients*

- 4 green bitter gourds, with the peels
- 2 tbs pumpkin seeds, roasted
- 2 tbs chironji seeds, roasted
- 2 tbs melon seeds, roasted
- 4 tbs peanuts, roasted
- 2 tsp mustard seeds

* 1 tbs red chilli powder
* 1 tbs cumin powder
* 1 tbs coriander powder
* 4 tbs coriander, freshly chopped, with the stalks
* 1 tbs pomegranate seeds or anardana, dried
* 1 tbs dried raw mango powder or amchur
* 2 tbs jaggery powder
* 2 tbs vegetable oil
* Salt to taste

## Method

* Carefully trim the edges of the bitter gourds, leaving the peel intact.
* Slit off one end to allow a scoop to fit in, so you can gently remove the pith and the seeds.
* Parboil, remove the gourds and set aside to cool.
* Coarsely grind the roasted peanuts and seeds.
* Heat oil in a pan and temper the mustard seeds.
* Add the red chilli powder, cumin powder and coriander powder.
* Once it changes colour slightly, add the coarsely ground peanuts and seeds, and cook until coated with the masalas.
* Add the chopped coriander, anardana, amchur, jaggery powder and salt.
* Fill the bitter gourds with this mixture.
* You can seal the open end with some besan paste or mashed potato (optional) and also apply some oil to the bitter gourd peel (again, optional).
* Air-fry for 8–10 minutes on high heat or bake on a lightly greased baking tray.
* Serve hot with a tangy mint chutney or tomato sauce.

*Nutritive value per serving*

- Energy: 362.43 kcal
- CHO: 16.02 gm
- Protein: 12.06 gm
- Fat: 27.79 gm
- Sodium: 18.94 mg
- Potassium: 556.12 mg
- Calcium: 85.07 mg
- Iron: 5.87 mg
- Vitamin A: 21.83 mcg
- Vitamin C: 55.15 mg

'What a great idea of stuffing the karela with so many nutritious seeds! The bitter gourd tea was a great cleanser too. A very good recipe. I strongly recommend it to everyone'

—Madhu Agarwal, Agra

## BITTER GOURD CHIPS

Along with beetroot, jackfruit, yam, tapioca, kale, potato and sweet potato chips, bitter gourd chips are readily available at every grocery store and namkeen/farsaan mart. However, more often than not, these so-called 'healthy munchies' are loaded with salt and hidden fats, defeating the very purpose of the label 'health'. If you want to have control on what is going into your body, try making these simple chips at home. Your body will thank you for it.—*Savlyene*

*Preparation time* 30 minutes
*Cooking time* 20 minutes
*Serves* 6

## Ingredients

- 6 medium bitter gourds, with the peel
- 2 tbs Bengal gram flour
- 3 tbs rice flour
- 1 tbs corn flour
- 1 tsp red chilli powder
- 1 tsp dried oregano
- 1 tbs chaat masala or amchur powder
- 2 tbs tamarind paste
- 2 tbs vegetable oil
- Salt to taste

## Method

- Trim the edges off the bitter gourd and slice them into thin circles.
- Remove the pith and the seeds.
- Mix the tamarind pulp with enough water to soak the bitter gourd slices with some salt for 30 minutes.
- While the slices are soaking, mix the Bengal gram flour, rice flour, corn flour, red chilli powder, oregano and chaat masala. Stir well and set aside.
- After 30 minutes, squeeze the tamarind water out of the bitter gourd slices and place them on a paper towel to soak off as much liquid as possible.
- Sprinkle the prepared mix over the bitter gourd slices and mix thoroughly.

- Preheat the air fryer at 175 degrees for about 5 minutes.
- Brush the tray of the air fryer with oil and evenly spread out a small batch of the coated bitter gourd slices.
- Air-fry for about 15 minutes, tossing them around intermittently to ensure even cooking.
- You may need to brush on some more oil. Alternatively, you can also bake them.

*Nutritive value per serving*

- Energy: 133.64 kcal
- CHO: 16.08 gm
- Protein: 4.28 gm
- Fat: 5.80 gm
- Sodium: 16.25 mg
- Potassium: 440.1 mg
- Calcium: 32.45 mg
- Iron: 2.33 mg
- Vitamin A: 21.88 mcg
- Vitamin C: 54.48 mg

'I will never buy karela chips from a store again. The label may say 'oil-free' but they are always so salty. The GHA recipe for bitter gourd chips was super. Melt-in-the-mouth crunchiness, flavoursome, awesome'

—Anita Ravi, Jaipur

# CABBAGE (PATTA GOBI)

This simple crucifer is a powerhouse of phytonutrients. It contains glucosinolates and sulforaphane, which help eliminate free-radical build-up in the body. Patients with aggressive cancers of the bowel, colon and the prostate gland benefit immensely from increasing their cabbage intake. Apart from being a very good source of fibre, cabbage also contains vitamin K and vitamin C. These vitamins help in expediting wound healing and bruising. If you mistakenly eat poisonous mushrooms, please drink half a cup of cabbage juice with a pinch of cumin-seed powder. The juice acts as an antidote. The excessive consumption of raw cabbage may cause gastrointestinal disturbances, bloating, flatulence and hyperacidity. Thiocyanates in raw cabbage can impact iodine nutrition and interfere with thyroid health. So decrease your consumption if you have hypothyroidism. The white inner core of a cabbage, called the heart, is crunchy and can be eaten in different ways. Simply slice it and serve it with a dip or add it to a salad or slaw to create another textural dimension; pickle it; or add it to a soup or a gravy.

*Pro-tip:* You can make a great body scrub by mixing together 2 tablespoons of grated cabbage heart, 4 teaspoons of rice flour, a tablespoon of lemon juice and 1 egg (optional). It reduces wrinkles, makes the skin taut and gives it a refreshing glow.

## CABBAGE BOWLS

The outer leaves of cabbage make appealing bowls that are perfect for a host of nutritious fillings. The first time I had this bowl was at our favourite Chinese restaurant in south Mumbai. The owner had curated a special meal for us, and the dishes were from different provinces in China. The bowls were filled with exotic veggies, some minced pork, Sichuan peppers and a very tangy sauce. I tried a variety of vegetarian options at home and everyone who tried them felt that the rajma–paneer combination was the best.—*Charmaine*

*Preparation time* 10 mins
*Cooking time* 0 mins
*Serves* 4

*Ingredients*

- 4 outer leaves of a large Chinese or regular cabbage
- 150 gm red kidney beans, cooked
- 80 gm paneer, crumbled
- 1 onion, diced
- 2 tomatoes, diced, with the peels and seeds
- 1 green capsicum, diced, with the seeds
- 1 yellow or red bell pepper, diced, with the seeds
- 1 tsp red chilli flakes
- 1 tbs lemon juice
- 4 tbs orange juice (reserve the zest for jams, marmalades, tea infusions, etc.)
- 1 tbs olive oil
- Salt to taste

*Method*

* Place the outer leaves of the cabbage (as close to a bowl shape as possible) in a basin of cold water and leave aside.
* Combine the cooked red kidney beans with the crumbled paneer and the rest of the vegetables.
* Mix the lemon juice, orange juice and olive oil well.
* Add the red chilli flakes and salt to taste.
* Pour this dressing over the other ingredients and mix until the beans are well coated.
* Remove the cabbage bowls from the basin of cold water and pat dry.
* Divide the mixture into four parts and place them carefully in the cabbage bowls.

*Nutritive value per bowl*

* Energy: 210.42 kcal
* CHO: 24.34 gm
* Protein: 11.84 gm
* Fat: 7.3 gm
* Sodium: 10.59 mg
* Potassium: 605.78 mg
* Calcium: 151.03 mg
* Iron: 2.65 mg
* Vitamin A: 30.09 mcg
* Vitamin C: 25.11 mg

'We got our staff at the restaurant to make these healthy bowls and everyone enjoyed the fresh taste'

—Michelle Seo, Delhi

## FERMENTED SPICY SAUERKRAUT

This lactobacillus-fermented, spicy cabbage pickle is very easy to make. Just remember to use fresh cabbage. Just like Korean kimchi, Japanese miso and natto, and kefir from eastern Europe, this German/Russian/Polish sauerkraut is full of natural probiotics that help your gut stay healthy. It also gives a boost to your immune, upper respiratory and cardiovascular systems. Sour cabbage has vitamin K in the form of menaquinone, which is good for bone health. Just a small amount will be a great accompaniment to any meal, and it goes especially well with burgers, Russian pierogi, roasted potatoes and Thanksgiving turkey. Please avoid eating large bowlfuls, as it will result in bloating and flatulence due to trisaccharide raffinose, which the human small intestine is unable to break down.—*Charlyene*

*Preparation time* 20 minutes
*Pickling time* 4 days
*Serves* 12

*Ingredients*

- 1 kg cabbage with the outer leaves
- 1 carrot, grated, with the peel
- 1 large onion, chopped
- 8 cloves of garlic, minced
- 4 tbs red chilli flakes
- 1 tsp caraway seeds
- 3 tbs sea salt

*Method*

- Keeping 1 outer leaf aside and cut the cabbage into quarters.

- Shred thinly, along with the core.
- Place all the ingredients in a large bowl.
- Gently massage the cabbage mixture for a few minutes with clean hands until it starts to release its liquids.
- Ensure that the spices and condiments are evenly and completely mixed.
- The shredded cabbage will release water and shrink.
- Place a plate over the cabbage to cover it completely.
- Weight the plate down with something heavy, such as a mortar and pestle.
- Or put something heavy, such as a jar filled with water, over the cabbage mixture.
- This will ensure that the cabbage continues releasing its juices and is submerged in the brine.
- Keep aside for about 3 hours.
- Pack the cabbage mixture into a sterilized glass jar.
- Pour any leftover brine into the jar.
- Place the outer cabbage leaf, which you had set aside, on top of the kraut in the jar. You may have to cut it.
- Once again weight down the top of the cabbage leaf to keep pressure on the kraut and keep it submerged in the brine.
- Cover with a muslin cloth and tightly secure with a band to allow air to flow but keep dust out.
- Check the brine level after 24 hours, and add some saltwater if there isn't enough brine.
- Allow the cabbage to ferment for 3–4 days at room temperature on your kitchen counter.
- Taste for sourness and continue to ferment for a few more days until it gets as sour as you would prefer.
- Remove the muslin cloth and the weight, close the jar with its clean lid and keep refrigerated to stop further fermentation.

- If you see any mould, skim that part out immediately, the rest of the sauerkraut is fine.
- If you keep the sauerkraut refrigerated, it should last for two months.

*Nutritive value per serving*

- Energy: 39.77 kcal
- CHO: 6.1 gm
- Protein: 1.95 gm
- Fat: 0.88 gm
- Sodium: 1555.29 mg
- Potassium: 311.9 mg
- Calcium: 48.07 mg
- Iron: 0.39 mg
- Vitamin A: 18.1 mcg
- Vitamin C: 28.32 mg

'Not only has this GHA version of sauerkraut helped with my digestion, but it has also reduced my bone pain. I have been using it every day for twelve days now. Thank you, Charlyene, for inviting me for the recipe trial. Loved it'

—Kanika Loomba, New York

## GADO GADO

This traditional Indonesian salad has it all—crunchy vegetables, a chilli peanut sauce that owes its flavour to galangal, the freshness of coriander and the goodness of tofu. As long as the sauce remains the same, the vegetables can be altered, according to what is readily available in your pantry. They just have to be fresh and crunchy. I sometimes add some steamed brown rice and one or two boiled eggs to make it a basic, simple but hearty meal bowl.—*Savlyene*

*Preparation time* 10 minutes
*Cooking time* 10 minutes
*Serves* 4

## Ingredients

- 150 gm cabbage, shredded, with the outer leaves and the inner core
- 100 gm tofu cubes, fried
- 100 gm tempeh, fried
- 100 gm French beans, chopped
- 100 gm cucumber, diced, with the peel
- 1 bunch spinach leaves, blanched, with the stalks
- 200 gm bean sprouts

## For the peanut sauce

- 4 tbs peanut butter, crunchy
- 4 cloves of garlic, crushed
- 1 small onion, finely chopped
- 1-inch piece of galangal or ginger, grated, with the peel
- 1 tsp cumin powder
- 1/2 tsp chilli powder
- 1 tsp lime juice
- 1 tsp tamarind paste
- 1 tsp jaggery sugar
- 1 tbs sesame oil
- Salt to taste

*For the garnish*

* 1 tbs onion slices, fried
* 1 tsp green chilli, finely chopped
* 1 tbs peanuts, roasted and salted

*Method*

* Lightly steam the cabbage and the French beans.
* Steam the bean sprouts for 2 minutes.
* Cool completely and place them in a serving bowl, bean sprouts first.
* Add the blanched spinach, tofu, tempeh and cucumber.

*For the peanut sauce*

* Heat oil in a pan and cook the onion and garlic.
* Add the galangal, cumin and chilli, and cook for another minute.
* Finely add the lime juice, tamarind paste, jaggery and crunchy peanut butter, and mix well.
* Add salt to taste.
* You may need to add some hot water to adjust the consistency, so that it becomes a coating sauce.
* Spoon some of the sauce over the veggies.
* Garnish with the onions, peanuts and chilli.
* Serve the remaining sauce separately.
* You may also choose to serve the veggies and tofu separately on a platter, with the dipping sauce at the centre.

*Nutritive value per serving*

* Energy: 265.01 kcal
* CHO: 14.73 gm

- Protein: 14.49 gm
- Fat: 16.48 gm
- Sodium: 130.04 mg
- Potassium: 782.87 mg
- Calcium: 124.89 mg
- Iron: 3.23 mg
- Vitamin A: 182.16 mcg
- Vitamin C: 50.65 mg

'Took me back to Bali with this recipe, Team GHA! Great!'

—Jason Ling, Delhi

## CABBAGE FOOGATH

An east Indian speciality, this is one dish that is cooked on days when staunch non-vegetarians have eaten too much meat and are looking to give their systems a break! The Goans call it 'fugad de repolho'. This dish is also a favourite in south India. Dad is an expert at making this foogath, because it requires finely sliced cabbage and he just loves chopping veggies. So whenever I have to make it, which is a couple of times a week, I wait till Dad is around and available to do mise en place! My family loves adding peanuts to everything. I'm not particularly fond of monkey food, so when I cook foogath, I give peanuts a miss. A simple, wholesome dish—just stuff a few tablespoonfuls into a chapati, crepe or a roti wrap, and you will have a great lunch-box snack.—*Savlyene*

*Preparation time* 10 minutes
*Cooking time* 20 minutes
*Serves* 4

*Ingredients*

+ 500 gm cabbage, finely sliced, with the outer leaves and inner core
+ 2 large onions, finely chopped
+ 4 tbs coconut, freshly grated
+ 4 green chillies, slit finely
+ 1 tsp mustard seeds
+ 15 curry leaves
+ 1 tsp grated ginger
+ 5 cloves of garlic, crushed
+ 1 tsp turmeric powder
+ 1/2 tsp pepper powder
+ 2 tbs vegetable oil
+ Salt to taste

*Method*

+ Heat the oil in a pan and temper the mustards seeds and curry leaves.
+ Add the onions and cook until soft.
+ Add the green chillies, turmeric powder, pepper powder, ginger and garlic.
+ Add the cabbage and cover.
+ Add a cup of hot water and cook for a short while. The cabbage should be crunchy, not overcooked.
+ Add salt to taste.

- Lastly add the grated coconut.
- Serve hot with chapatis and yoghurt.

*Nutritive value per serving*

- Energy: 220.37 kcal
- CHO: 10.54 gm
- Protein: 4.31 gm
- Fat: 17.91 gm
- Sodium: 24.52 mg
- Potassium: 574.08 mg
- Calcium: 110.21 mg
- Iron: 2.45 mg
- Vitamin A: 35.14 mcg
- Vitamin C: 45.55 mg

'In our home, everyone detests cabbage. Boiled quarters, lightly seasoned with salt and pepper. But now that we have tried the foogath, our love for cabbage and Indian food is at an all-time high'

—Grace Meyers, Stockholm, Sweden

# CARROT (GAJAR)

Beta carotene, the orange-red flavonoid pigment, gives red and orange carrots their colour. Regular consumption of carrots in a balanced meal helps treat rheumatoid arthritis, helps in digestion and bowel movement, lowers cholesterol levels, regulates the release of insulin and glucose in the body, prevents brain-cell degeneration by reducing the beta-amyloid plaque deposition in the brain, improves vision, lowers your risk of macular degeneration and slows down the development of cataracts.

Kanji (the fermented probiotic winter drink loaded with antioxidants) is what comes to mind when one sees black carrots in sabji *mandi*s in northern India. These carrots get their purplish-black colour from anthocyanins, pigments that help lower bad cholesterol (LDL) and protect arteries against oxidation. They also protect from various cancers and neurological disorders such as Alzheimer's. Black carrots additionally provide phenols, beta carotene, vitamins C and K, calcium, iron and zinc. Their antioxidant activity is four times that of red and orange carrots. They are anti-inflammatory as well.

*Pro-tip:* The GI is a measure of how quickly foods raise your blood sugar levels after a meal. Raw carrots have a comparatively lower GI, as compared to cooked carrots. Pureeing carrots further increases their GI value. So if you want to keep a tight control on your blood sugar and enjoy

147

the health benefits of this root vegetable, go ahead and choose the correct option.

## BLACK CARROT CAKE

A sudden urge to eat carrot cake got me marching into the kitchen to take stock of the ingredients, armed with our prized black diary, the one that has most of our tried-and-tested recipes. I found all the healthy flours, organic jaggery sugar, the spices and the eggs. What did I miss? Carrots, of course! Not a single orange carrot in sight, but a sackful of black carrots had just arrived from a farm in Delhi. So was I going to change my mind and make another cake? No, I would put the black carrots to good use. Try this cake for its outstanding spice flavour and super moist crumb.—*Savlyene*

*Preparation time* 25 minutes
*Cooking time* 45 minutes
*Serves* 12

*Ingredients*

- 400 gm black carrots, grated, with the peel
- 160 gm refined flour
- 110 gm oat flour
- 90 gm ragi flour
- 2 tsp baking powder
- 1/2 tsp salt
- 2 tsp cinnamon powder
- 1 tsp nutmeg powder
- 400 gm jaggery sugar
- 6 eggs

Lemon Barley

Bajre Ki Kheer/Pearl Millet Pudding

Vagharlelo Bhaat

Sorghum Bhakris

Baked Masala Puris

Wholewheat Garlic Buns

Amaranth Salad

Buckwheat Molten Cake

Buckwheat Rotis with
Tomato Concasse

Sprouted Quinoa Croquettes

Chickpea Pate

Scotch Eggs with
Bengal Gram

Alsanyache Tonak

Atola

Hara Channa Chaat

Langarwali Dal

No-Bake Black
Gram Cookies

Sprouted Mung
Bean Muffins

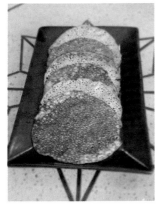

Vatana Chitaps

Soya Kheema Buns

Dal Tadka

Bitter Gourd Pickle

Stuffed Bitter Gourd

Fermented Spicy Sauerkraut

Pesto Vatana Mousse

Cabbage Foogath

Black Carrot Cake

Rajasthani Carrot Sabji

Moringa Pancakes

Drumstick Soup

Crockpot Avial

Eggplant and Tofu Stacks

Ravaiya

Roasted Red Pumpkin Soup

Red Pumpkin Bhaji

Red Pumpkin Seed and Peel Munchies

Ridge Gourd Chutney

Ridge Gourd Dry Chutney

Ridge Gourd Curry

Ridge Gourd Theplas

Sweet Potato Bebinca

Sweet Potato Chips

Sweet Potato Cutlets

Tomato Concasse

Tomato Rogan Josh

Banana Cucumber Bread

Banana Peel Thoran

Vegan Jackfruit 'Pulled Pork' Burgers

Mango Chia Pudding

Mango Chipotle Jam

Pear Frangipane Tart

Poached Pear

Strawberry Grape
and Chia Spread

Watermelon and Feta Salad

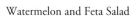

Chocolate Soil Pots

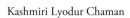

Kashmiri Lyodur Chaman

Khoya Amba Haldi Ladoos

Khoya Dry-Fruit Ladoos

Date and Cinnamon Smoothie

Soya-Milk Chocolate Pudding

* 300 ml vegetable oil
* 1 tbs vanilla extract

*Method*

* Preheat the oven to 180 degrees.
* Sift the three flours with the baking powder, salt, cinnamon powder and nutmeg powder.
* In a large bowl, whisk the vegetable oil and jaggery sugar until light and fluffy.
* Add the eggs and whisk until smooth.
* Fold in the sifted flour and the grated carrots.
* Add the vanilla extract and combine well.
* Pour the batter into a greased 8-inch springform pan.
* Bake for 45 minutes.
* Tastes delicious plain, but you can jazz it up with some cream cheese frosting and garnish with candied walnuts, like I did.

*Nutritive value per serving*

* Energy: 483. 41 kcal
* CHO: 52.43 gm
* Protein: 6.54 gm
* Fat: 27.53 gm
* Sodium: 242.24 mg
* Potassium: 328.91 mg
* Calcium: 99.93 mg
* Iron: 3.12 mg
* Vitamin A: 180.59 mcg
* Vitamin C: 2.28 mg

'My family loves the traditional carrot cake with walnuts. I decided to try this black carrot cake after Charmaine sent the recipe to me along with a few black carrots. Glad to report that this cake was well appreciated by my children. We are awaiting winter to make this once again.'

—Sabina Shaikh, Mumbai

## BLACK CARROT OATMEAL

Most of the times when we go grocery shopping, if there is one food item we buy in jumbo-sized packs, it's oats. We grind some of the oats either finely or coarsely to use as a replacement for wheat flour in rotis, pancakes, crepes, etc., to make uttapams and dosas. The rest we use in porridges, granola bars, smoothies and to extract oat milk. Here is the recipe of a black carrot oatmeal that is quick and very easy to make. It energizes you until lunchtime, is healthy and very pretty. Serve it in a plain white bowl, and you will see what I am talking about—the purplish hue is stunning.
—*Charmaine*

*Preparation time* 10 minutes
*Cooking time* 30 minutes
*Serves* 4

*Ingredients*

- 1 cup black carrots, grated, with the peel
- 2 cups oats

* 3 cups water
* 1 cup milk
* 1 tsp cardamom powder
* Salt to taste (optional)
* Jaggery to sweeten (optional)

*Method*

* Boil the oats and grated carrots in the water for about 20 minutes.
* Add the milk and allow the oats to cook until they thicken and absorb most of the liquid, for 7–8 minutes.
* Add the cardamom powder and switch off the heat.
* Add salt and jaggery to taste (optional).
* Serve warm.

*Nutritive value per serving*

* Energy: 315.94 kcal
* CHO: 51.46 gm
* Protein: 11.46 gm
* Fat: 7.14 gm
* Sodium: 32.5 mg
* Potassium: 159.02 mg
* Calcium: 101.87 mg
* Iron: 2.67 mg
* Vitamin A: 170.02 mcg
* Vitamin C: 3.29 mg

'Being diabetic, I like to choose food carefully so as to not increase my sugar levels. Glad I received this recipe to try out. A satisfying breakfast keeps me full for at least 3 hours. Sugar levels stay in range too. Also taking the Good Health Always spice mix. Will follow this regularly'

—Ravi Berari, Ranchi

## CARROT AND SOYA KOFTA CURRY

Every Catholic home has a tried-and-tested recipe for meatball curry. Finely minced lamb or chicken with lots of spices are shaped into balls and cooked in a thick, spicy coconut gravy. Soya granules are a good meat substitute and I've enhanced the nutritive value of this vegan dish by using carrots. You can use cashew, oat or almond milk instead of coconut milk.
—*Charmaine*

*Preparation time* 30 minutes
*Cooking time* 40 minutes
*Serves* 4

*Ingredients*

*For the koftas*

+ 150 gm red/orange carrot, grated and steamed, with the peel
+ 120 gm potato, boiled and mashed, with the peel
+ 120 gm soya granules, boiled
+ 4 tbs onions, finely chopped
+ 4 small green chillies, finely chopped

* 1 tbs ginger-garlic paste
* 1 tsp garam masala powder
* Salt to taste

*For the gravy*

* 1 cup tomato puree
* 1/2 cup onion paste
* 2 tbs ginger-garlic paste
* 1 tsp tamarind paste
* 1 tbs garam masala powder
* 1 tsp cardamom powder
* 1 tsp star anise powder
* 1 cup coconut milk (or almond/cashew/oat milk). Reserve the coconut or nut meal for chutneys, cookies or to thicken gravies
* 2 tbs vegetable oil
* Jaggery sugar to taste
* Salt the taste

## Method

*For the koftas*

* Mix the grated and steamed carrots, boiled and mashed potato, and the boiled soya granules well in a large bowl.
* Add the remaining ingredients and combine until smooth.
* Adjust the salt.
* Check if you can form small kofta-sized balls without them falling apart; else add some cornflour.
* Keep aside.

*For the gravy*

* Heat oil in a pan and sauté the onion paste until light brown.

- ◆ Add the ginger-garlic paste and tamarind paste, and continue cooking.
- ◆ Add the tomato puree and the spice powders.
- ◆ Cook further with 1 cup warm water.
- ◆ Once the gravy has come to a boil, gently add the koftas one at a time and cook for another 5 minutes or until the gravy has thickened.
- ◆ Just before turning off the heat, add the coconut milk, give it one boil and add salt and the jaggery sugar to taste.
- ◆ Serve hot.

*Nutritive value per serving*

- ◆ Energy: 326.43 kcal
- ◆ CHO: 28.69 gm
- ◆ Protein: 18.65 gm
- ◆ Fat: 15.23 gm
- ◆ Sodium: 89.29 mg
- ◆ Potassium: 391.15 mg
- ◆ Calcium: 150.07 mg
- ◆ Iron: 8.14 mg
- ◆ Vitamin A: 171.88 mcg
- ◆ Vitamin C: 21.31 mg

'Carrot kofta curry instead of our meatball curry would be difficult for my boys to accept. Or so I thought. Surprisingly, they loved it. The gravy was great to eat with rice. Carrot koftas held their shape in the gravy, even one day later. Happy to have been part of the recipe trial'

—Shelley Gomes, Mumbai

## RAJASTHANI CARROT SABJI

Rajasthan is famous for its maharajas, its historical temples, its forts, palaces and havelis, its warm people, its handicrafts, its music and its varied cuisine. Marwaris are known for their hospitality and feed their guests a plethora of dishes, from tangy welcome drinks to crunchy starters, spicy sabjis, piping-hot rotis, chutneys and achaars, cooling chaas and mouth-watering desserts. This recipe comes to you straight from the Marwari heart. I do hope you enjoy it.—*Charlyene*

*Preparation time* 15 minutes
*Cooking time* 35 minutes
*Serves* 4

*Ingredients*

* 250 gm carrots, chopped into medium-sized bits, with the peel. Wash well, trim the ends and chop
* 150 gm cluster beans, chopped into medium-sized bits
* 1 onion, finely chopped
* 1 tbs Rajasthani garam masala
* 1 tsp red chilli powder
* 1 tsp turmeric powder
* 1/2 tsp pepper powder
* 2 tbs roasted Bengal gram flour
* 2 tbs vegetable oil
* Salt to taste

*For the Rajasthani garam masala*

* 3 tbs cumin seeds
* 1 tbs coriander seeds

- 1 tbs fennel seeds (saunf)
- 1 tbs carom seeds (ajwain)
- 2 black cardamom (badi elaichi)

## Method

### For the Rajasthani garam masala

- Heat a pan (preferably iron) on high heat and dry-roast the spices until they change colour.
- Cool and grind to a fine powder.
- Store in an airtight container.

### For the Rajasthani carrot sabji

- Heat oil in a pan and sauté the onions until soft.
- Add the carrots and cluster beans, cover and allow to steam-cook for 2 minutes.
- Add the Rajasthani garam masala powder, red chilli powder, turmeric powder and pepper powder, and mix well.
- Add a glass of warm water and allow to cook for 10 minutes.
- Once the vegetables are cooked, thicken the gravy with the roasted Bengal gram flour.
- Season with salt and serve warm with rotis.

### Nutritive value per serving

- Energy: 224.92 kcal
- CHO: 20.17 gm
- Protein: 7.62 gm
- Fat: 12.64 gm

- Sodium: 65.9 mg
- Potassium: 884.91 mg
- Calcium: 300.7 mg
- Iron: 7.51 mg
- Vitamin A: 312.34 mcg
- Vitamin C: 11.63 mg

'The gravy got too thick the first time, so I made it again and made sure to not overcook. Result was a very nice sabji, which we ate with sorghum rotis'

—Dipti A. Mehta, Coimbatore

# DRUMSTICK

The roots, bark, leaves, flowers, fruits and seeds of the drumstick tree (*Moringa oleifera*) are all edible and make for an amazing medicinal and nutritive 'meal in a tree'. The roots taste like horseradish. The seeds, along with their long, immature pods, are called drumsticks and are an essential ingredient in south Indian sambars. The roots and seeds inhibit the growth of disease-producing micro-organisms or pathogens because of their antimicrobial properties.

Moringa leaves can be eaten like any other leafy vegetable. They provide the most nutrition, and if you do not have access to the tree, you might never even see the leaves—let alone eat them and benefit from their health properties. They are a rich source of iron, which prevents anaemia. Moringa provides large amounts of chlorogenic acid, quercetin, kaempferol, zeatin, beta sitosterol, caffeoylquinic acid, rutin and vitamin C, all of which are powerful antioxidants that reduce inflammation in the body and up your immunity. Chlorogenic acid also helps manage blood sugar levels. The leaves are rich in calcium, the mineral associated with bone health. The leaves provide the fibre necessary to impact heart health in a positive way. When used in diets for cancer patients, it makes tumour cells more sensitive and responsive to chemotherapy. Moringa powder is now available in most health stores.

*Pro-tip:* Pregnant women will benefit from eating moringa leaves and drumsticks, especially because of their high iron and vitamin C content. A low haemoglobin level leads to anaemia and may be caused by iron and folic acid deficiency. This has a negative impact on foetal development. However, they should avoid consuming the bark or bark extracts. The bark has chemicals that can induce uterine contractions and cause a miscarriage.

## MORINGA AND BELL PEPPER HUMMUS

We were blessed to have grown up in a lovely tiled-roof cottage surrounded by coconut palms, drumstick trees, and mango and other fruit trees. All this in the heart of Mumbai! The upside was having access to lots of fresh produce; the downside was lots of stones falling on the tiles during mango season! Preparing dishes that required moringa leaves was never a problem. The real problem was how to prevent the tonnes of leaves from going to waste. So here are some delicious ways to use the leaves.—*Savlyene*

*Preparation time* 15 minutes
*Cooking time* 15 minutes
*Serves* 8

*Ingredients*

- 1 cup fresh moringa leaves, steamed (save the cooking liquid to drink as a cleansing tea)
- 300 gm chickpeas (soak overnight, rinse well and pressure-cook over 3 whistles)
- 2 red bell peppers, roasted (in the oven or on a direct flame until the outer skin splits)
- 4 garlic cloves, crushed

- ◆ 4 tbs tahini or white sesame paste (preferably home-made, using toasted white sesame seeds with olive oil and salt)
- ◆ 1 tbs cumin powder
- ◆ 100 ml olive oil (preferably extra-virgin)
- ◆ 4 tbs lemon juice
- ◆ Salt to taste

*Method*

- ◆ Blend all the ingredients, except the chickpeas, until smooth and creamy.
- ◆ Add the chickpeas and continue blending until well incorporated.
- ◆ Store in an airtight glass jar in the refrigerator.
- ◆ Serve with salad veggie sticks or crudites, vegetable chips (think healthy karela chips here), pita, lavash, crackers or even baked matris and puris.
- ◆ We served them with some interesting pistachio and pumpkin-seed thins.

*Nutritive value per serving*

- ◆ Energy: 273.48 kcal
- ◆ CHO: 17 gm
- ◆ Protein: 7.78 gm
- ◆ Fat: 19.43 gm
- ◆ Sodium: 30.36 mg
- ◆ Potassium: 216.75 mg
- ◆ Calcium: 92.72 mg
- ◆ Iron: 2.8 mg
- ◆ Vitamin A: 554.64 mcg
- ◆ Vitamin C: 41.79 mg

'A healthy twist to a regular dip. It is a great party snack—so tasty, easy to make and nutritious. Plus, I got to know about aqua faba, the water from cooking chickpeas. So now I am waiting to use that in macaroons'

—Radha G.K., Hyderabad

## MORINGA PANCAKES

As long as we had access to fresh moringa leaves, quickly making this breakfast snack was never a problem. The fresh leaves were washed, sun-dried and roasted in an iron pan. Once cooled, the leaves were ground to a fine powder and stored in an airtight glass container in the refrigerator. These moringa pancakes are a breakfast staple and can be made sweet or savoury. Either way they will always be tasty.—*Charlyene*

*Preparation time* 10 minutes
*Cooking time* 20 minutes
*Serves* 8

*Ingredients*

- 2 tbs moringa powder
- 1 cup oat flour
- 1 cup wheat flour
- 2 tsp baking powder
- 1/2 tsp salt
- 4 bananas, mashed
- 1 cup milk

- 1 tbs coconut or sesame oil
- 1 tsp vanilla extract

## Method

- Sift the oat and wheat flours with the baking powder and salt.
- In a large bowl, mix the mashed bananas with the moringa powder.
- Add the milk and stir well.
- Add the sifted flours.
- Whisk until smooth.
- Add the vanilla extract.
- Heat oil in a frying pan and fry scoopfuls of the batter until lightly golden on both sides.
- Serve the pancakes warm with honey or butter, and fresh fruit.
- For savoury pancakes, omit the bananas and use vegetable puree and some herbs and spices.

## Nutritive value per serving

- Energy: 239.73 kcal
- CHO: 42.37 gm
- Protein: 7.01 gm
- Fat: 4.69 gm
- Sodium: 149.41 mg
- Potassium: 308.96 mg
- Calcium: 57.51 mg
- Iron: 2 mg
- Vitamin A: 116.77 mcg
- Vitamin C: 7.75 mg

'With the health benefits of moringa being made so popular, we were waiting for a good recipe. I made sweet moringa pancakes as per the recipe, and spicy ones with grated beet and green chillies. Both were very tasty, light and healthy. Thank you'

—Ratna Jaisinh, Jaipur

## DRUMSTICK SOUP

This soup is for anyone who needs better immunity, stronger bones, better hair, skin and nails, improved haemoglobin, blood sugar and cholesterol levels, improved digestive and bowel health, better eyesight and stronger gums. Well, just about everyone will benefit from this soup.—*Charlyene*

*Preparation time* 15 minutes
*Cooking time* 20 minutes
*Serves* 4

*Ingredients*

- 8 drumsticks, cut into 3-inch pieces
- 2 large onions, finely chopped
- 2 tomatoes, chopped, with the peel and seeds
- 6 cloves of garlic
- 1 tsp ginger, grated, with the peel
- 1/2 tsp turmeric powder
- 1 tsp pepper powder
- 1 tbs vegetable oil
- Salt to taste
- A few spoons of freshly squeezed lime juice

*Method*

- Heat the oil in a pressure cooker and sauté the onions over medium heat.
- Add the ginger and garlic, and cook for 2 minutes.
- Add the tomato concasse or the chopped tomatoes, along with the turmeric and pepper powders.
- Add the drumstick pieces.
- Cover with 4 cups of hot water, add salt to taste and pressure-cook over 5 whistles.
- Cool completely and remove the pressure-cooker lid.
- Put the cooked drumstick pieces in a bowl and transfer the soupy liquid into a blender.
- Carefully press out the drumstick flesh/sap with a spoon and discard the fibrous pod.
- Add this to the soupy liquid in the blender and blend well.
- Transfer to a pan, bring to a gentle boil and adjust the taste with salt and pepper, along with the consistency with water or milk.
- Just before serving add a squeeze of lime.
- Serve hot.

*Nutritive value per serving*

- Energy: 82.73 kcal
- CHO: 7.91 gm
- Protein: 3.48 gm
- Fat: 4.13 gm
- Sodium: 25.96 mg
- Potassium: 535.19 mg

- Calcium: 49.07 mg
- Iron: 1.31 mg
- Vitamin A: 31.23 mcg
- Vitamin C: 80.75 mg

> 'My in-laws are above eighty years old, and this is such a nourishing soup for both of them, as well as the rest of our family. I am told that the lime juice helps with mineral absorption. This is a good soup'
>
> —Mariola D'Cunha, Mumbai

## CROCKPOT AVIAL

A couple of years ago, I was in Pune for one of our Good Health Always workshops—the ones where Mum needs an able assistant ha ha!!! With assisting comes benefits of shopping, sightseeing, tasting local delicacies, etc. The mall next to our hotel held a pleasant surprise—a store filled with stuff that I had only previously seen in Toronto. Bread makers, roesti pans, fondue pots, mandolines, Crockpots, instant pots and even mini snow-cone machines! This was much before they became common household items in India. Mum grudgingly agreed to buy the Crockpot, and I did not mind that I would have to forgo my stipend for that month. We've used the Crockpot to steam our traditional Christmas pudding, roast chickens, make biryani, undhiyu and chole, and I will now share a recipe of the Keralite avial, generally made during Onam.—*Charlyene*

*Preparation time* 30 minutes
*Cooking time* 3 hours in a Crockpot (else 30 minutes in a pressure cooker)
*Serves* 4

*Ingredients*

- 3 drumsticks, cut into 2-inch pieces
- 2 large potatoes with the peel, cut into 2-inch pieces
- 2 carrots with the peel, cut into 2-inch pieces
- 12 French beans, stringed and cut into 2-inch pieces
- 1 green banana with the peel, cut into 2-inch pieces
- 8–10 pieces of yam with the peel, cut into 2-inch pieces
- 1 tsp mustard seeds
- 1 tsp cumin seeds
- 25 curry leaves
- 2 green chillies, slit in half
- 3/4 tsp turmeric powder
- 1/2 tsp pepper powder
- 4 tbs grated coconut
- 2 tbs coconut oil
- 4 tbs yoghurt, whisked
- Salt to taste

*Method*

- Set the Crockpot on high heat.
- Add the coconut oil and temper the mustard seeds and cumin, followed by the curry leaves.
- Add the green chillies, turmeric and pepper powders, and stir well.
- Once fried well, add the chopped vegetables, followed by the grated coconut. Mix well.

- Add the whisked yoghurt and 4 cups of hot water, along with salt.
- Cover the Crockpot and set on medium to low heat for 3 hours.
- I prefer to make this at night, so it cooks overnight and set off to 'warm' mode post that. If you do this, you will wake up to piping-hot avial that is ready to pack into lunch boxes in the morning before you set out to work.
- Alternatively, you can make this in a pressure cooker or a regular vessel on a stovetop.

*Nutritive value per serving*

- Energy: 239.21 kcal
- CHO: 31.96 gm
- Protein: 5.89 gm
- Fat: 9.77 gm
- Sodium: 61.64 mg
- Potassium: 1046.08 mg
- Calcium: 116.7 mg
- Iron: 2.52 mg
- Vitamin A: 283.94 mcg
- Vitamin C: 57.58 mg

'I use my Crockpot for a number for dishes but I had never made this delicacy. Glad to say that it tasted awesome and was so easy to prepare'

—Vibha V. Kamath, Sacramento, the US

# EGGPLANT (BRINJAL)

This king of Indian vegetables is actually a fruit belonging to the nightshade family of plants, Solanaceae, along with tomatoes, bell peppers and potatoes. Botanically, eggplants are berries, just like blueberries and tomatoes, while in culinary terms, eggplants are vegetables. They are a staple in Mediterranean cuisine, in classic dishes ranging from the Greek moussaka, Italian aubergine parmigiana and French ratatouille to the Turkish imam bayeldi and Middle Eastern baba ganoush. Eggplants provide dietary fibre, folate, magnesium, manganese, copper, sodium, potassium, B-complex vitamins and vitamin C. They are also a good source of phytophenols, the antioxidants that prevent heart disease and cancer. Nasunin, the anthocyanin found in the peel of eggplants, prevents damage to cell membranes of the brain—another reason to eat the peels. However, you may need to limit your intake if you have renal and bone issues, because of their oxalic acid content. Eggplants contain very minuscule amounts of nicotinic acid—about 0.01 per cent. In terms of the nicotine in one cigarette, that amounts to about 8–9 kg of eggplant!

*Pro-tip:* Please remember that eggplants are capable of absorbing large amounts of fat, as they are being cooked. This makes dishes with eggplant very rich and calorie-dense. The rich sauces that they are cooked in can do further damage if you are on a calorie-restricted diet plan. Even simple masala-marinated eggplant thick rounds will pack in a lot of oil and no amount of absorbent tissue paper will help reduce the oil content. In our kitchen experiments, we have found that if you salt the eggplant slices, along with a little lemon juice and rice flour or cornflour, about 15 minutes before applying the masala marinade or continuing with your recipe, not only will the eggplant slices not turn brown due to oxidation but will also absorb much lesser oil.

## RATATOUILLE

This classic French stew perfectly pairs eggplant with red bell peppers, tomatoes, zucchini, onion and lots of fresh herbs. 'Rata' comes from the French word for a warm, chunky stew and 'touiller' means to stir up. This was the first 'French' dish I learnt to cook, and I like to serve it with basic pasta. You can also eat it with pulao, quinoa or couscous. I've even made a cauliflower pizza base and used the veggies from the ratatouille as a topping, along with some grated cheese.—*Charlyene*

*Preparation time* 15 minutes
*Cooking time* 1 hour
*Serves* 4

*Ingredients*

- 700 gm eggplant, cubed, with the peel
- 1 cup of tomato concasse (p. 225)
- 1 zucchini, cubed, with the peel
- 2 red and yellow bell peppers, cubed, with the seeds
- 4 tbs onion, finely chopped
- 2 tbs garlic, minced

- 1 tsp red chilli flakes
- 1 tbs oregano, dried
- 1 tsp pepper, freshly ground
- 8–10 basil leaves
- 3 tbs vegetable oil (preferably good-quality olive oil)
- Salt to taste

## Method

- Heat the oil in a pan and add the garlic and onions, and cook for 5 minutes.
- Add the eggplant cubes and allow to soften and brown slightly before adding the zucchini and bell pepper cubes.
- Add the tomato concasse, red chilli flakes and freshly ground pepper, and cover and cook for 10 minutes on low heat.
- Add salt to taste and cook for another 15 minutes, stirring occasionally.
- Once the vegetables have cooked, add the dried thyme and fresh basil.
- Serve warm with pasta or a slice or two of crusty bread.

## Nutritive value per serving

- Energy: 205.34 kcal
- CHO: 17.16 gm
- Protein: 6.50 gm
- Fat: 12.34 gm
- Sodium: 45.74 mg
- Potassium: 696.62 mg
- Calcium: 56.33 mg
- Iron: 2.27 mg

- Vitamin A: 79.42 mcg
- Vitamin C: 97.91 mg

> 'Whenever I cook brinjals, I know that a lot of oil will be utilized—be it bharta or any other preparation. I followed this recipe exactly as mentioned and a lot less oil was used because of the GHA tip to toss the brinjal bits in salt, lemon and cornflour for some time. A very healthy dish'
>
> —Beena Ghosh, Kolkata

## EGGPLANT PICKLE

This pickle has its origins in Goa, a state better known for its prawn balchao, dried fish pickles, pickled meat, sausages and xacuti. I've used recheado masala here—a paste that is generally used to stuff mackerels and pomfrets or used as a marinade for prawns, mandeli or slices of king fish, rawas or salmon before they are grilled or pan-fried. The taste of just 1 teaspoon of this pickle will get you hooked to it for life!—*Charmaine*

*Preparation time* 1 hour
*Cooking time* 25 minutes
*Serves* 25

*Ingredients*

- 1 kg eggplant, cubed, with the peel
- 4 tbs vegetable oil
- Salt to taste

*For the recheado masala*

- 30 Kashmiri red chillies
- 20 cloves of garlic
- 2-inch piece of ginger, with the peel
- 1 tbs cumin seeds
- 10 cloves
- 2 sticks of cinnamon, 2 inches long
- 10 black peppercorns
- 250 ml vinegar
- 1 onion, finely chopped
- Salt to taste
- Jaggery to taste

*Method*

*For the recheado masala*

- Soak the chillies, garlic cloves, chopped ginger, cumin, cinnamon sticks, cloves and peppercorns in vinegar for 45 minutes. If you want to hasten the process, just warm the vinegar.
- Grind the spices along with the onion and gradually incorporate the vinegar until it is a fine paste.
- Add salt to taste and some jaggery to cut down the spiciness.
- If you want to store this masala for some time, you can fry it in some oil until the colour changes, cool and store in the refrigerator in a clean glass bottle.

*For the eggplant pickle*

- Sprinkle salt on the eggplant cubes and set aside. There is no need to add lemon juice and rice flour here.

- Heat the oil in a pan and sauté the eggplant cubes until the colour just begins to change.
- Add 6–8 tablespoons of the recheado masala (as per your taste).
- Mix well and add more salt, if needed.
- Transfer into a clean glass jar, cover and allow the pickle to mature on your kitchen windowsill or wherever there is sunlight, for a week.
- Store in your pantry or in the refrigerator.

*Nutritive value per serving*

- Energy: 41.37 kcal
- CHO: 2.92 gm
- Protein: 1.1 gm
- Fat: 2.81 gm
- Sodium: 3.64 mg
- Potassium: 584.85 mg
- Calcium: 19.79 mg
- Iron: 0.51 mg
- Vitamin A: 17.39 mcg
- Vitamin C: 1.13 mg

'I am not a lover of brinjal (with the exception of crisp-fried baingan bhaja) and I was reluctant to try out this recipe for the GHA trial. So my husband tried his hand at it and the result was excellent. He has saved some of the recheado masala to make Goan fried fish this weekend. This is a yummy pickle and, hopefully, a yummy fish treat soon!'

—Anju Bhattacharya, Patna

## EGGPLANT AND TOFU STACKS

These make for an exciting party snack/hors d'oeuvre simply because you can use different veggies for the filling and always end up with a winning entrée. Plus, it is so simple to make that you can leave it for a child to put together while you laboriously slave over the rest of the buffet dishes. An adult may just have to help with the pan searing. It is also a great way to get children interested in cooking.—*Charlyene*

*Preparation time* 20 minutes
*Cooking time* 10 minutes
*Serves* 10

*Ingredients*

- 500 gm elongated eggplant with the peel (easier when serving as a snack, but you can also use large eggplants)
- 4 tomatoes, with the peel and seeds (approximately the diameter of the eggplants)
- 2 avocados, firm and ripe (they should not be soft and mushy)
- 4 tbs lime juice (save the lime zest for this recipe itself)
- 1 tbs lime zest, grated
- 250 gm tofu or paneer, firm
- 3 tbs olive oil
- 1 tbs garlic, minced
- Salt to taste
- Sesame and pumpkin seeds, toasted, to garnish

*Method*

- Cut each eggplant into 1-inch rounds, add salt and leave aside.

- Cut the tomatoes into 1-inch rounds and refrigerate.
- Cut each avocado into half, remove the seed and the peel, and chop each half into 1-inch slices. Coat the avocado slices with lemon juice and zest, and keep aside.
- Cut the tofu or paneer into 1-inch slices so that each slice fits on the slices of the eggplant, tomato and avocado.
- Brush some oil and some of the minced garlic on to the eggplant slices and lightly sear on a greased pan for 3–4 minutes per side.
- Repeat the process for the tofu or paneer slices.
- Over each slice of grilled eggplant place 2–3 slices of avocado, a slice of paneer or tofu and a slice of tomato.
- Sprinkle the toasted sesame or sunflowers seeds, and season with a little salt.
- Pierce a wooden toothpick through to hold each stack in place (optional).
- Serve immediately.

*Nutritive value per serving*

- Energy: 116.03 kcal
- CHO: 4.3 gm
- Protein: 4.3 gm
- Fat: 9.07 gm
- Sodium: 9.37 mg
- Potassium: 331.69 mg
- Calcium: 40.43 mg
- Iron: 0.83 mg
- Vitamin A: 44.21 mcg
- Vitamin C: 12.45 mg

'A nice, crisp, clean hors d'oeuvre that looks as good as it tastes'

—Alexandra Barry, Toronto, Canada

## RAVAIYA

These green-chutney-stuffed baby eggplants are a dish that both Parsees and Gujaratis claim as their invention. We have many Bawi friends and an equal number or more of Gujju friends. So when it came to this particular recipe, we spoke to people from both communities. Not only did we receive many recipes for ravaiya but we also received dabbas of Parsee and Gujarati ravaiya to sample, savour and use as inspiration for our special ravaiya. Hope your taste buds are tickled by this dish, just as ours were.—*Savlyene*

*Preparation time* 15 minutes
*Cooking time* 25 minutes
*Serves* 5

*Ingredients*

*For the ravaiya*

- 20 medium round baby brinjals, with the peel and stems
- 1 tbs turmeric powder
- 1 tsp pepper powder
- 1 tbs vegetable oil
- Salt to taste

*For the green chutney stuffing*

- 1 cup coconut, grated
- 1/2 cup fresh coriander, chopped, with the stalks
- 1/4 cup mint, chopped, with the stalks
- 5 green chillies
- 10 cloves of garlic
- 1 tbs ginger, chopped, with the peel
- 6 tbs lemon juice
- Salt and sugar to taste

*Method*

*For the green chutney*

- Blend the coconut with the chopped coriander and mint.
- Add the chillies, garlic cloves and chopped ginger, and grind to a fine paste using a small amount of water if required.
- Add the lemon juice and mix well.
- Add salt and sugar to taste.
- This chutney can be stored for up to 1 week in the refrigerator. It can be used to make the yummiest chutney sandwiches, stuffed into a pomfret and fried, or diluted to make a lovely dip for all things snacky!

*To prepare the ravaiya*

- Wash the brinjals well and pat dry.
- Make 2 lengthwise slits, starting at the opposite end of the stem but not going all the way down.
- Sprinkle turmeric powder, pepper powder and salt (and some lemon juice and rice flour to prevent excessive absorption of oil) and keep aside for 10 minutes.

- Pick each baby brinjal by its stem and gently stuff about 2 teaspoons of green chutney into it, taking care not to overstuff.
- Leave aside to marinate for another 10 minutes.
- In a broad-based pressure cooker, heat the oil.
- Gently place the stuffed brinjals sideways into the cooker.
- Allow the skin to sear on one side and then move them over.
- Add the remaining green chutney and allow it to darken a bit but not burn.
- Add a small teacup of hot water and pressure-cook over 1 whistle.
- When the cooker cools down completely, remove the lid and adjust the consistency and the salt.
- Serve hot.

*Nutritive value per serving*

- Energy: 293.07 kcal
- CHO: 14.53 gm
- Protein: 6.74 gm
- Fat: 23.11 gm
- Sodium: 20.34 mg
- Potassium: 1006.24 mg
- Calcium: 90.14 mg
- Iron: 4.68 mg
- Vitamin A: 199.24 mcg
- Vitamin C: 21.30 mg

'Born to a Parsee mother and a Gujarati father, I will not say who makes the better version of this dish. I did make the GHA version, though, and I am very happy with the almost-oil-free version. Both parents relished it but chose not to comment!'

—Z.P. Desai, Vadodara

# RED PUMPKIN (LAAL KADDU)

This nutrient-dense vegetable/fruit from the Cucurbitaceae family is a veritable powerhouse of vitamins and minerals, and not just a Halloween decoration or a pie filling for Thanksgiving! Topping the list of the minerals it packs is potassium, for blood pressure stabilization, reduction of stroke risk, protection against muscle-mass loss, preservation of bone-mineral density and reduction in the formation of kidney stones. The iron present can boost fertility in women, while the zinc helps improve overall sexual health and testosterone levels in males. Pumpkin seed oil is known to safeguard prostate health. Its vitamin A and C content boosts immunity. Apart from this, the beta carotenes (precursors to vitamin A) in red pumpkin augment eye health, decreases the risk of age-related macular degeneration, reduces the risk of developing cancers of the colon and the prostate gland, protects against asthma, helps prevent heart disease, and helps form and maintain healthy skin, teeth and bones. Their fibre content helps maintain proper digestive health and prevents constipation. It also helps you feel fuller for longer and keeps hunger pangs at bay. Pumpkin seeds are full of nutrients and make for an interesting, satiating snack. They are rich in tryptophan, an amino acid that helps the body make serotonin, the feel-good neurotransmitter hormone that helps you relax and sleep better.

Consuming just 1 cup of cooked pumpkin every day will provide over 100 per cent of your daily requirement of vitamin A! Apart from this, you will get 20 per cent of the daily value of vitamin C, 10 per cent of vitamin E, riboflavin, potassium, copper and manganese, and at least 5 per cent of thiamin, vitamin B6, folate, pantothenic acid, niacin, iron, magnesium and phosphorus. So the next time someone calls you a pumpkin/kaddu/bhopla, please take it as a compliment!

So make a lip-smacking pumpkin curry or sabji, oven-roast cubes of pumpkin to make a hearty soup, add steamed and grated pumpkin to your rotis, theplas, parathas, raitas and salads, puree cooked pumpkin and combine it with herbs/yoghurt to make an interesting dip or sandwich spread. You can even add it to a smoothie, along with soya milk or coconut milk and some chia seeds.

*Pro-tip:* A pureed pumpkin face pack will provide an instant glow to your skin and fetch you many compliments. All you need to do is mix 4 tablespoons of red pumpkin puree with a teaspoon of honey and a teaspoon of rice flour. Apply this on your face and relax for 30 minutes. Wash off with cold water and apply an ice cube all over your face in circular movements. Pat dry and smile!

## RED PUMPKIN COOKIES

The first time I tasted these little morsels of deliciousness, my aunt had left out the fact that the main ingredient was bhopla! She was waiting to see my reaction to the cookie before she told me that she had very expertly made use of the extra pumpkin puree we had made for Thanksgiving dinner. They were moist, chewy and so very tasty. I love to bake and just had to try these out. Over the years I've experimented a lot, and today I will share the recipe that is the healthiest. Don't call them red pumpkin cookies if you have fussy eaters at home—just call them 'magic morsels' and the kids will happily gobble them up. If you undercook these a tiny bit and leave them to cool on a wire rack, they will stay soft and moist on the inside and a bit crunchy on the outside.—*Savlyene*

*Preparation time* 20 minutes
*Cooking time* 20 minutes
*Serves* 30 (2 cookies per serving)

*Ingredients*

- 200 gm red pumpkin puree (I usually steam, puree and then refrigerate a kilo at a time)
- 120 gm wholewheat flour
- 130 gm maida
- 150 gm pumpkin seeds, roasted and coarsely ground
- 1 cup raw cane sugar or 1-1/4 cup jaggery sugar
- 100 ml honey or date syrup
- 2 eggs (you can use flax meal or chia seeds instead)
- 2 tsp cinnamon powder
- 2 tsp nutmeg powder
- 1 tsp ginger powder
- 2 tsp baking soda
- 1/2 tsp salt
- 150 ml vegetable oil

*Method*

- Preheat the oven to 180 degrees.

- Sift together the wheat flour, maida, spice powders, baking soda and salt, and keep aside.
- Beat the eggs well (skip if you are using flax meal or chia seeds as a replacement).
- Add the oil, sugar and pumpkin puree, and continue beating until light and fluffy.
- Gently stir in the coarsely ground pumpkin seeds and spoonfuls of the sifted dry ingredients.
- Add the honey or date syrup to form a smooth, soft dough (you may need to add some cold milk).
- Place teaspoonfuls of this dough on to a lightly greased baking tray and bake for about 12 minutes.
- Cool on a wire rack. They may seem undercooked at first, but as they cool down, the outside will harden, leaving a warm, soft centre.
- Store in an airtight container.

*Nutritive value per serving*

- Energy: 107.1 kcal
- CHO: 10.41 gm
- Protein: 2.51 gm
- Fat: 6.27 gm
- Sodium: 124.68 mg
- Potassium: 64.96 mg
- Calcium: 13.54 mg
- Iron: 0.78 mg
- Vitamin A: 5.77 mcg
- Vitamin C: 0.55 mg

'I used flax eggs for this recipe, and they turned out great! Do not expect a very crunchy cookie, but taste-wise they are comparable to any good, rich cookies. You must leave them to cool for longer than you would regular cookies. This gives them time to harden on the outside and have a soft heart!'

—Myra Lobo, Goa

## ROASTED RED PUMPKIN SOUP

There is nothing that fills you with more warmth than a bowl of hot soup on a cold winter evening. When that soup is a roasted red pumpkin one, its robust flavour just warms the cockles of your heart. A family favourite made by my aunt, whose kitchen always smells so inviting on a chilly evening in Toronto, the recipe has been replicated many times in our home, even though Mumbai, sadly, lacks a boast-worthy winter. We make a whole batch of this and freeze it—and it tastes delicious each and every time we eat it. Do not just take my word for it—go ahead and make some today.—*Charlyene*

*Preparation time* 20 minutes
*Cooking time* 30 minutes
*Serves* 8

*Ingredients*

•   500 gm red pumpkin cubes (save the seeds and peel to make a crunchy roasted snack later)

- 10 spring onions, roughly chopped, with their green stalks
- 4 onions, roughly chopped
- 4 red bell peppers, cubed, with the inner core and seeds
- 20 cloves of garlic, cleaned and trimmed
- 1 tbs sugar (to hasten the roasting process, but optional)
- 6 cups vegetable stock (we always save the water we boil veggies in. Cool, add salt and refrigerate in glass bottles)
- 1 tsp nutmeg powder
- 1 tsp pepper powder
- 10 basil leaves, fresh
- 2 tbs vegetable oil
- Salt to taste

*Method*

- Preheat the oven to 225 degrees.
- Place the red pumpkin cubes, chopped onions and spring onions, garlic cloves and the chopped red bell peppers on a baking tray.
- Sprinkle salt and sugar on the veggies and coat with oil.
- Roast until the veggies have browned or the onions have caramelized and are very soft. You will need to toss them around occasionally so they brown evenly.
- Once the flesh of the pumpkins is so soft that it can easily be pierced with a fork, remove the tray from the oven and inhale the delicious aroma. No one will fault you if you spoon some into a bowl and quietly polish it off!
- Once cool, transfer into a blender, making sure you do not leave even a tiny drop of liquid on the baking tray.
- Blend until smooth.
- At this stage, you may choose to freeze the puree and save it for later use.

- If not, pour it into a deep pan, add the vegetable stock and bring to a gentle boil.
- Cook until you get the consistency you desire and then add the pepper, nutmeg, basil and some salt.
- Serve piping hot with some garlic bread.

*Nutritive value per serving*

- Energy: 357.9 kcal
- CHO: 37.23 gm
- Protein: 15.03 gm
- Fat: 16.54 gm
- Sodium: 922.64 mg
- Potassium: 1938.6 mg
- Calcium: 134.46 mg
- Iron: 3.35 mg
- Vitamin A: 114.91 mcg
- Vitamin C: 142.73 mg

'This is just right for the monsoons, and I'm sure for the winters too. I love that I can make this soup in advance and freeze it for later use. Super recipe. Thanks'

—Jivika K., Kolhapur

## RED PUMPKIN BHAJI

I use our traditional east Indian bottle masala for the dish. This magical aromatic blend of more than fifty ingredients is a must-have in all east Indian homes. In the good old days, just before the monsoons arrived in the city, on the hottest days in May, professional masala makers would come to east Indian homes and start the process of sun-drying, roasting and vigorously hand-pounding the various spices in a rhythmic manner. They would sing songs while pounding the spices using a metal-tipped long wooden pestle and a stone mortar. This job was laborious and, if an east Indian family had many young, robust female members, they would pound the spices themselves and not hire professionals. Once the masala was ready, it would be tightly packed in clean beer or alcohol bottles, hence the moniker 'bottle' masala. Each family had a secret recipe that was passed down the generations with the solemn promise of never sharing it with others. So my lips are sealed here because I wish to stay alive and not receive death threats! Just joking, folks. The masala is now easily available, so do try to get some to use here, else you can use a basic combination of red chilli powder, dhana jeera powder, and turmeric, pepper and saunf powder. It will not taste as delicious, though.—*Charmaine*

*Preparation time* 15 minutes
*Cooking time* 25 minutes
*Serves* 4

*Ingredients*

- 500 gm red pumpkin cubes
- 4 tbs east Indian bottle masala
- 2 large onions, finely chopped
- 1 tbs mustard seeds
- 2 sprigs of curry leaves
- 4 tbs coconut, freshly grated
- 1 tbs tamarind paste
- 2 tbs vegetable oil
- Salt to taste

*Method*

- Heat the oil in a pan and temper the mustard seeds and curry leaves.
- Add the chopped onions and cook until translucent.
- Once the onion has softened, add the bottle masala and fry until the masala has browned a bit.
- Add the pumpkin cubes, cover and cook for 5 minutes.
- Add a mug of hot water and continue until the vegetable has cooked.
- Add the grated coconut next. Cook for 5 more minutes.
- Add salt to taste and, just before you remove the pan from the flame, add the tamarind paste and give it a good stir.
- Serve hot with chapatis and yoghurt.

*Nutritive value per serving*

- Energy: 290.01 kcal
- CHO: 22.61 gm
- Protein: 5.23 gm
- Fat: 19.85 gm
- Sodium: 19.41 mg
- Potassium: 550.37 mg
- Calcium: 134.07 mg
- Iron: 4.2 mg
- Vitamin A: 63.26 mcg
- Vitamin C: 15.49 mg

'Made this twice, once with east Indian bottle masala and then with garam masala powder. We liked the east Indian bottle masala version better'

—Sonal Sheth, Nagpur

## RED PUMPKIN SEED AND PEEL MUNCHIES

If snack times are a challenge at home, please try making these munchies. The process may be long, especially while prepping the slippery red pumpkin seeds—and there are times you may just want to give up and give in to cravings for spicy, highly salted, nutrient-depleted packaged nonsense—I assure you that the end result will be tasty, crunchy and healthy, plus you will also be making good use of food 'scraps', which is the reason you have bought our *Good Health Always Cookbook* in the first place.—*Charmaine*

*Preparation time* 30 minutes
*Cooking time* 30 minutes
*Serves* 8

*Ingredients*

*For the red pumpkin peel munchies*

- 1 cup 'saved' red pumpkin peels, cut into 1/2-inch squares
- 1/2 tsp mustard seeds
- 10 curry leaves
- 1/2 tsp white sesame seeds
- 1/2 tsp poppy seeds (optional)
- 1/4 tsp turmeric powder
- 1/4 tsp pepper powder
- 1/2 tsp red chilli powder
- 1 tbs vegetable oil
- Salt to taste
- Sugar to taste (optional)

*For the red pumpkin seed munchies*

- ◆   1 cup 'saved' pumpkin seeds
- ◆   1 tbs vegetable oil
- ◆   Salt to taste

*Method*

- ◆   Place the pumpkin seeds, along with the orangish fibrous pith, in a bowl of ice-cold water and leave aside for 10 minutes.
- ◆   Wash thoroughly with cold water. You will have to pinch away the fibrous pith.
- ◆   Dry the seeds on a kitchen towel. Set aside to dry completely.
- ◆   In the meantime, heat a tablespoon of oil in a pan and temper the mustard seeds, curry leaves, white sesame seeds and poppy seeds.
- ◆   Add the turmeric, red chilli and pepper powders, and switch off the heat.
- ◆   Heat the oven to 250 degrees.
- ◆   Toss the red pumpkin peels in the masala pan and mix well.
- ◆   Arrange them on a lightly greased baking tray or a sheet of parchment paper.
- ◆   By now, the red pumpkin seeds will have air-dried. Toss in the oil and salt, and place on another baking tray.
- ◆   Place both baking trays in the heated oven, with the seed tray on top and the peel tray below.
- ◆   Roast until brown. You will have to check and move them around every 10 minutes.
- ◆   The peels brown first, so bring them out and allow the seeds to continue roasting.

- Once the peel tray is out, sprinkle salt and sugar on it (if desired).
- Place the roasted seeds on a wire rack and allow them to cool completely.
- You can choose to mix the two or serve them separately.
- Variations for the plain salted roasted red pumpkin seeds could be a sprinkling of paprika, or honey and pepper, chaat masala or even maple syrup.
- Store in airtight containers.

*Nutritive value per serving*

- Energy: 133.08 kcal
- CHO: 2.3 gm
- Protein: 5.12 gm
- Fat: 11.56 gm
- Sodium: 7.66 mg
- Potassium: 61.41 mg
- Calcium: 19.62 mg
- Iron: 1.21 mg
- Vitamin A: 13.01 mcg
- Vitamin C: 1.54 mg

'I loved the red pumpkin skin munchies and so did my husband, Ramesh. The boys refused to touch them but thoroughly enjoyed the seed munchies. Their loss, our gain. Great to know that the peels and seeds can be utilized in innovative ways'

—Dina R. Sinha, Delhi

# RIDGE GOURD (TURIYA)

This mineral-, vitamin- and fibre-rich, low-calorie vegetable with soft seeds and a pulpy white core is a natural laxative. If you can procure the leaves, flowers and fruits of this vegetable, please make use of them too. The leaves have components that protect against small-cell lung carcinomas. The leaves and flowers are rich in bioflavonoids, Apigenin 7-glucoside and Lutein 7-glucoside. The fruit has ethanol extract for liver protection. If you have diabetes, high LDL cholesterol, ulcers, issues with bowel regularity, piles, haemorrhoids, etc., you will benefit from eating ridge gourds. Diabetics benefit by balancing their blood sugar because of the insulin-like peptide present in ridge gourds. Use the seeds too in sabjis, dals and soups for their anti-inflammatory and analgesic properties.

*Pro-tip:* If you are growing ridge gourds in your garden, leave a few unplucked on the plant to dry naturally in the hot summer sun. Once they have dried, peel off the outer skin, and the inner fibrous network will act as a natural loofah to scrub off dead skin cells.

## RIDGE GOURD CHUTNEY

Beerakaya pachadi is a basic chutney that is a favourite in Andhra Pradesh. I conduct a number of wellness programmes in Hyderabad. This recipe was shared by a fitness trainer from Begumpet. Being a typical Andhraite, he had a preference for spicy food. When I tried making it at home, the only person who relished it was my husband. Subsequently, I toned down the spiciness and used our milder green chillies instead of the fiery hot Andhra ones.—*Charmaine*

*Preparation time* 10 minutes
*Cooking time* 20 minutes
*Serves* 4

*Ingredients*

- 200 gm ridge gourd, chopped (just scrape off the veins and leave the skin, pith and seeds intact)
- 4 small green chillies, slit lengthwise
- 2 large tomatoes, diced, with the peel and seeds
- 1 tbs white sesame seeds
- 1 tbs channa dal
- 1 tsp urad dal
- 1/2 tsp turmeric powder
- 2 tsp vegetable oil
- Salt to taste

*For tempering*

- 10 curry leaves
- 1 clove of garlic, crushed
- 1 tsp mustard seeds
- 1 tsp urad dal
- A pinch of asafoetida
- 2 tsp vegetable oil

*Method*

- ◆ Dry-roast and cool the sesame seeds, channa dal and urad dal.
- ◆ Heat the oil and fry the green chillies.
- ◆ Add the ridge gourd cubes and cook partially.
- ◆ Add the tomatoes, turmeric powder and salt, and cook until the tomatoes soften.
- ◆ Dry-grind the roasted sesame seeds, and the channa and urad dal.
- ◆ Add the cooked ridge gourd, tomatoes and chillies, and grind to a fine paste.
- ◆ Place in a bowl or a jar if you want to store it.
- ◆ Temper the garlic, mustard seeds and urad dal in hot oil.
- ◆ Add the curry leaves and fry until crisp.
- ◆ Add the asafoetida.
- ◆ Pour this tempering over the ridge gourd chutney.
- ◆ Serve with hot chapatis or with dal and rice. This will stay in the refrigerator for up to three days.

*Nutritive value per serving*

- ◆ Energy: 109.93 kcal
- ◆ CHO: 6.83 gm
- ◆ Protein: 3.62 gm
- ◆ Fat: 7.57 gm
- ◆ Sodium: 7.47 mg
- ◆ Potassium: 236.85 mg
- ◆ Calcium: 76.77 mg
- ◆ Iron: 1.96 mg
- ◆ Vitamin A: 96.85 mcg
- ◆ Vitamin C: 9.89 mg

'This is very easy to prepare. My family loved the taste, so I will be making it regularly'

—Priti S. Verma, Dubai

## RIDGE GOURD DRY CHUTNEY

Peechinga podi is a dry chutney powder that is a mealtime must-have in most homes in southern India. One of my classmates, Karthika, would always have a jarful of this dry chutney in her hostel room in college. Whenever we were served bland meals, which was almost every day, we would plead with her to share some of this podi. A minuscule amount was grudgingly placed on our plates and then the begging would start. I cannot blame the dear girl, because the rest of us had access to home-cooked dinners while her hostel-mess dinners were tasteless. Then one fine day, fed up of us feasting on her chutney, Karthika shared the recipe with us. She had got her eighty-six-year-old *achamma* to dictate it to her. Did we stop harassing her after that? No. We were shameless and we continued to bully her into parting with the podi. Years later, I found the recipe in an old notebook and tried it. It brings back fond memories of college life.—*Charlyene*

*Preparation time* 5 minutes
*Cooking time* 15 minutes
*Serves* 8

*Ingredients*

- 200 gm ridge gourd peel (preferably a day old)

- 1 tbs urad dal
- 1 tbs channa dal
- 2 tsp sesame seeds
- 1 tbs raw mango powder (amchur)
- 1 tbs jaggery powder
- 1 tbs red chilli powder
- A pinch of asafoetida
- 1 tbs vegetable oil
- Salt to taste

*Method*

- Heat a cast-iron pan and add the vegetable oil.
- Roast both dals well, until they change colour.
- Add the ridge gourd peel and sesame seeds, and roast until the peels get crisp.
- Add a pinch of asafoetida.
- Remove from the stovetop.
- Add the raw mango powder, jaggery powder, red chilli powder and salt to taste.
- Cool completely and powder until fine.
- Store in an airtight container.

*Nutritive value per serving*

- Energy: 59.77 kcal
- CHO: 6.44 gm
- Protein: 1.73 gm
- Fat: 3.01 gm
- Sodium: 35.58 mg
- Potassium: 173.05 mg
- Calcium: 36.04 mg

- Iron: 1.65 mg
- Vitamin A: 5.68 mcg
- Vitamin C: 11.63 mg

> 'A well-seasoned cast-iron pan makes all the difference to this podi. We loved it and did not realize that the cook had used peels of ridge gourd. Good way to get all of us to eat healthy'
>
> —Vijaya Mathur, Jabalpur

## RIDGE GOURD CURRY

The original recipe that I tried from the Internet had ash gourd as the key ingredient. Since I had just received some fresh ridge gourds from a neighbour's farm, I decided to replace the ash gourd with that. The spice mix also had khus and pine nuts, which gave it a nuttier taste and a gravy that split at the end. I worked on a few different spice mixes without the khus and the pine nuts. I love the combination I've shared here for the taste and also the way the thin gravy thickens once you incorporate the spice mix into it.—*Charmaine*

*Preparation time* 5 minutes
*Cooking time* 15 minutes
*Serves* 2

*Ingredients*

*For the vegetable curry*

- 400 gm ridge gourd, diced

- 2 small onions, finely chopped
- 2 large tomatoes, finely chopped, with the peel and seeds
- 2 green chillies, finely chopped
- 4 cloves of garlic, minced
- 15 curry leaves
- 1/2 tsp mustard seeds
- 2 tsp vegetable oil
- Salt to taste

*For the spice mix*

- 1 tbs channa dal
- 1 tbs urad dal
- 1 tsp red chilli powder
- 1 tsp turmeric powder
- 1 tsp cumin powder
- 1 tsp white sesame seeds
- 3–4 methi seeds
- 2 tbs coconut, desiccated

*Method*

- Dry-roast the spice mix ingredients.
- Cool completely and grind to a fine powder.
- Keep aside.
- Heat the oil in a pan and temper the mustard seeds and the curry leaves, followed by the minced garlic and green chillies.
- Add the onions and cook until translucent.
- Add the cubes of ridge gourd and cook for 5 minutes.
- Once partially cooked, add the tomatoes and mix well.
- Cover and cook on a low flame, stirring occasionally to prevent it from burning.
- Add some water.

- Once cooked, add the spice mix.
- Cover again and let the gravy thicken.
- Adjust the salt as per your taste.
- Serve with steamed rice and some yoghurt.

*Nutritive value per serving*

- Energy: 298.68 kcal
- CHO: 22.67 gm
- Protein: 10.15 gm
- Fat: 18.6 gm
- Sodium: 68.97 mg
- Potassium: 899.33 mg
- Calcium: 151.89 mg
- Iron: 5.34 mg
- Vitamin A: 278.48 mcg
- Vitamin C: 28.41 mg

---

'The spice mix for the recipe really made it taste so much better. In my opinion, even the most humble of vegetables can taste a hundred times better than expensive non-vegetarian food if cooked with love and care. This recipe is proof. Good health always to all'

—R.N. Goenka, Pune

---

## RIDGE GOURD THEPLAS

While doing research for this cookbook, I've tried to limit food waste. It was not very difficult once I started placing a small bowl on the kitchen counter to put food 'scraps' into. Mum was more interested in pictures of this bowl. Hence 'scraps' would be trimmed again and again to minimize wastage. The 'scrap' bowl for these theplas only had the veins of the ridge gourd and 2 green chilli stems.—*Savlyene*

*Preparation time* 10 minutes
*Cooking time* 20 minutes
*Serves* 4

*Ingredients*

+ 250 gm ridge gourd
+ 300 gm wholewheat flour
+ 1 tsp cumin seeds
+ 1 tsp red chilli powder
+ 1/2 tsp turmeric powder
+ 1/2 tsp asafoetida powder
+ 2 small green chillies, finely chopped
+ 1 tsp ginger, grated, with the peel
+ 4 tbs yoghurt
+ 3 tbs vegetable oil
+ Salt to taste

*Method*

+ In a large bowl, add salt to the grated ridge gourd and leave aside for about 10 minutes for the release of vegetable water.
+ Remove the water and keep aside.
+ Add the wholewheat flour to the grated ridge gourd, along with the cumin seeds, red chilli powder, turmeric powder, asafoetida, green chillies and ginger.
+ Add the whisked yoghurt, 1 tablespoon vegetable oil and the vegetable water.

- Knead to make a soft, pliable dough. You may need to add some more water and some salt.
- Cover the dough and keep aside for 15 minutes.
- Divide the dough into 8 equal portions and form balls.
- Roll out each ball into 6-inch discs using dry flour to prevent the disc from sticking to the board.
- Heat a griddle over high heat.
- Place the thepla on the hot griddle and cook on medium heat until brown spots appear on both sides.
- Apply 1/2 teaspoon oil on each side of the thepla and cook until the spots darken.
- Store in a covered container.
- Serve hot with pickle and plain yoghurt, or some chilled raita.

*Nutritive value per serving*

- Energy: 367.23 kcal
- CHO: 51.13 gm
- Protein: 9.92 gm
- Fat: 13.67 gm
- Sodium: 16.89 mg
- Potassium: 357.02 mg
- Calcium: 73.5 mg
- Iron: 3.97 mg
- Vitamin A: 37.26 mcg
- Vitamin C: 4.63 mg

'My advice to you is make double and triple the amount. This is simply great as an on-the-go snack. Lovely'

—Sneha, Madurai

# SPINACH (PALAK)

This is a nutrient-dense leafy vegetable belonging to the amaranth family. It shares its lineage with beetroot and quinoa. It has a host of health-boosting properties, which vary from blood pressure management and cancer prevention to improvement in eye health, digestive health and general well-being. However, you should limit your intake of spinach if you have a propensity for developing kidney stones (high calcium oxalate content) or if you are taking blood thinners (high vitamin K1 content).

*Pro-tip:* Antinutrients, substances naturally found in leafy vegetables, beans, seeds, nuts and whole grains, can reduce the nutritive value of the food we eat by decreasing their availability to the human body. Fortunately, the simple act of cooking foods such as grains and beans, or adding lemon juice to leafy greens, helps reduce this antinutrient content and improve the availability of nutrients. Research now shows that these antinutrients have anti-inflammatory properties, preventing diabetes, arthritis, heart disease and cancer. So don't be anti-antinutrients! The different kinds of antinutrients in food include:

- Oxalates (in leafy greens such as methi and spinach), which interfere with the body's absorption of calcium present in these foods.
- Phytates (in legumes, nuts, seeds and grains), which impair the absorption of iron, zinc and calcium.

-   Lectins and trypsin inhibitors (in lentils and soya beans), which prevent normal digestion.

So what can you do?

-   Add vitamin C in the form of lemon juice or citrus fruits to foods with high iron content, such as meats, beans and dark leafy greens, to improve iron absorption.
-   Steam greens for a short while to reduce antinutrients.
-   Decrease your consumption of phytate-rich wheat bran, because it can interfere with iron absorption.
-   When baking, use lemon juice, dahi or chaas, if the recipe calls for wholewheat flour. This removes phytates.

## SPINACH BROWNIES

Shh . . . Mum's the word if you are serving these to young children or to fussy adults! Just call them chocolate brownies, and everyone will love them. This is not sneakiness but loving deception. For reasons unknown, the minute you say 'spinach', most people make gagging sounds! Bake them once and you will get so many compliments about your baking prowess that you will use this recipe again and again. And I won't blame you—these brownies have fooled everyone, every single time I've baked them. As much as your family may want to eat them straight out of the oven, distract them with other stuff. The flavour of spinach disappears when the brownies have cooled completely. So get them to run errands for you, give you a head massage, tidy up their rooms with the promise of a scrumptious reward only once they have completed the tasks you've set for them!—*Savlyene*

*Preparation time* 15 minutes
*Cooking time* 40 minutes
*Serves* 12

*Ingredients*

- 100 gm oat or ragi flour
- 80 gm maida
- 200 gm spinach puree, with the stalks (add a teaspoon of lemon juice to reduce the oxalate content)
- 4 tbs carrot puree, with the peel
- 100 gm cooking chocolate (or carob chips, if you want the brownies to be healthier)
- 100 gm raw sugar
- 2 tbs butter
- 4 tbs cocoa powder
- 3 egg whites
- 1 egg yolk
- 1 vanilla bean
- 1/2 tsp baking powder
- 1/2 tsp salt

*Method*

- Preheat the oven to 200 degrees.
- Grease an 8-inch square or round baking dish with some butter or oil.
- Melt the chocolate or carob chips in a large bowl over a double boiler.
- Sift the oat or ragi flour and maida with the cocoa powder, salt and baking powder.

- Add the raw sugar, spinach and carrot purees to the bowl containing the melted chocolate, and quickly whisk them together (keep everyone away during this step!).
- Everyone can get back into the kitchen to add the butter, egg yolk and the extract from the vanilla bean, and to whisk the egg whites and add them in too.
- Gradually spoon in the dry sifted ingredients and gently stir.
- Pour the batter into the pan and bake for 30–35 minutes, until an inserted toothpick comes out clean.
- Shoo everyone out of the kitchen and assign them their chores! Your brownies will cool and automatically lose that spinach flavour.
- Once cooled completely, cut into 12 equal squares.

*Nutritive value per brownie*

- Energy: 179.7 kcal
- CHO: 26 gm
- Protein: 4.18 gm
- Fat: 6.56 gm
- Sodium: 72.91 mg
- Potassium: 232.46 mg
- Calcium: 54.79 mg
- Iron: 2.05 mg
- Vitamin A: 99.86 mcg
- Vitamin C: 5.38 mg

'Ingeniously simple! Incredibly healthy! Sinfully delicious! I give this recipe 5 stars!'

—Radhika Goel, Delhi

## SPINACH CHANNA DAL SABJI

Basic, easy to prepare, tasty and healthy. Well, isn't that what cooking should be all about? Serve this no-fuss dish with a side of kachumber and mixed grain rotis, all washed down with a glass or two of spiced buttermilk.—*Charmaine*

*Preparation time* 20 minutes
*Cooking time* 20 minutes
*Serves* 4

*Ingredients*

- 3 large bunches of spinach, with the stalks
- 150 gm channa dal
- 2 large onions, finely chopped
- 5 cloves of garlic
- 2 green chillies, finely chopped
- 1 tsp pepper powder
- 1 tsp turmeric powder
- 1 tsp kalonji seeds
- 2 tbs lemon juice
- 2 tbs vegetable oil
- Salt to taste

*Method*

- Soak the channa dal in water for 20 minutes, wash well and pressure-cook with some salt over 1 or 2 whistles. Cool, strain, save the cooking water and leave the cooked dal aside.
- Trim the ends of the spinach leaves and remove the leaves that have been eaten by insects.
- Soak the leaves, along with the stalks, in cold, salted water.

- Remove and finely chop both leaves and stems.
- Heat oil in a pan and temper the kalonji.
- Add the onion, garlic and green chillies.
- Allow the onion to soften and add the turmeric and pepper powders.
- Add the spinach and let it steam-cook for 5 minutes without stirring it.
- Add the channa dal and cook for 2 more minutes.
- The reserved channa dal cooking liquid can be added next.
- Add salt to taste.
- Add the lemon juice and remove from the stovetop.
- Serve hot.

*Nutritive value per serving*

- Energy: 230.15 kcal
- CHO: 22.99 gm
- Protein: 10 gm
- Fat: 10.31 gm
- Sodium: 370.4 mg
- Potassium: 844.4 mg
- Calcium: 94.02 mg
- Iron: 25.79 mg
- Vitamin A: 283.77 mcg
- Vitamin C: 25.04 mg

'I am so happy to have used the stems, stalks and parts of the vegetables that we would normally have wasted. This is a great concept of working on recipes to reduce food waste. Be blessed'

—Diana K., Mumbai

## SPINACH AND CORN BAKE

When I was in Grade VIII, my class teacher announced on a Thursday that we would have to get a baked dish for a bake sale on Friday. School fundraisers were for special stuff such as kits for visually impaired students of the school or for the children's ward at a nearby hospital. Hence we would very enthusiastically participate. As luck would have it, Dad was offshore, Mum was in Delhi and my sister was busy with her college exams. So this is what I made, and this is what nearly garnered the most funds.—*Savlyene*

*Preparation time* 25 minutes
*Cooking time* 12 minutes (because I use individual ramekin/cupcake moulds)
*Serves* 8

*Ingredients*

*For the white sauce*

- 3 tbs wheat flour
- 2 tbs butter
- 300 ml milk
- 1 tsp pepper powder
- Salt to taste

*For the spinach–corn mixture*

- 3 cups spinach, chopped, with the stalks
- 1 cup corn, cooked
- 1 cup onions, finely chopped
- 8 cloves of garlic, minced
- 1 tbs vegetable oil or butter

- 2 tsp pepper, freshly ground
- 1 tsp smoked paprika powder
- Salt to taste
- Breadcrumbs or coarsely ground pumpkin seeds, and grated cheese or crumbled paneer for gratinating.

## Method

### For the white sauce

- Heat the butter in a pan, add the wheat flour and brown slightly on a low flame.
- Add the cold milk and stir well to prevent lumps from forming. I use a metal whisk.
- Continue cooking until it reaches a consistency that will coat the back of a spoon.
- Add the pepper powder and salt to taste, and set aside.

### For the spinach–corn mixture

- Heat the vegetable oil or butter in another pan and sauté the minced garlic for 30 seconds.
- Add the chopped onions.
- Add the chopped spinach and boiled corn, and cook lightly.
- Season with salt, smoked paprika powder and freshly ground pepper, and turn off the flame.
- Add this mixture to the white sauce and stir well.
- Preheat the oven to 180 degrees.
- Spoon out the mixture on to a greased baking dish, individual ramekins or cupcake moulds.
- Top with breadcrumbs or coarsely ground pumpkin seeds, and grated cheese or crumbled paneer.

- Bake for 8–10 minutes, until it gets golden-brown on top.
- Serve hot or cold. Both will taste equally good.

*Nutritive value per serving*

- Energy: 138.67 kcal
- CHO: 12.79 gm
- Protein: 4.49 gm
- Fat: 7.75 gm
- Sodium: 72.48 mg
- Potassium: 519.76 mg
- Calcium: 121.66 mg
- Iron: 2.43 mg
- Vitamin A: 251.87 mcg
- Vitamin C: 20.88 mg

'My dad made two bowls of this bake, and it was so good. He did add more smoked paprika and some grated cheese to the spinach and corn mixture to bind it better. We loved it'

—Christopher Fernandes, Toronto, Canada

## DESI SPINACH OMELETTE

A part of my case studies had to be from rural areas to understand why farmers and farm hands who were exposed to so much sunlight every day still had a vitamin D deficiency. Sadly, their nutrient-depleted status had ramifications on the health of their bones, their immunity, their fertility, their cardiac health and their mental health. If the diet is lacking and the liver is not functioning properly, there is no way the body will produce active forms of various nutrients. Egg yolks and cheese are rich in precursors to vitamin D but getting the workers to eat a fancy cheese omelette was neither practical nor palatable to them. So our desi spinach omelette, loaded with masalas, soon became their breakfast staple. You can use besan to make a vegetarian version.—*Charlyene*

*Preparation time* 20 minutes
*Cooking time* 10 minutes
*Serves* 4

*Ingredients*

- 8 eggs or 150 gm Bengal gram flour
- 3 cups spinach, finely chopped, with the stalks
- 1 medium onion, finely chopped
- 2 tbs methi, finely chopped, with the stalks
- 2 tbs coriander, finely chopped, with the stalks
- 2 tbs mint, finely chopped, with the stalks
- 4 green chillies, finely chopped
- 6 cloves of garlic, finely chopped
- 1 tbs ginger, freshly grated, with the peel
- 1 tsp turmeric powder
- 1/2 tsp pepper powder
- 1/2 tsp jeera powder
- 2 tbs vegetable oil
- Salt to taste

*Method*

- Beat the eggs, along with 1/2 cup water, until light and frothy. For the egg-free version, mix the Bengal gram flour with water.

- ◆ Add the remaining ingredients, except the oil.
- ◆ Mix well.
- ◆ Heat a large frying pan, add the oil and move the pan around so the oil evenly coats the pan.
- ◆ Depending on the size of the pan, you can either pour in the entire amount of mixture or cook in smaller batches.
- ◆ Cover the pan and cook on low to medium heat until the base is cooked.
- ◆ Flip the omelette over and cook until done.
- ◆ Serve hot.

*Nutritive value per serving*

- ◆ Energy: 208.71 kcal
- ◆ CHO: 6.31 gm
- ◆ Protein: 13.52 gm
- ◆ Fat: 14.4 gm
- ◆ Sodium: 130.42 mg
- ◆ Potassium: 1025.99 mg
- ◆ Calcium: 166.94 mg
- ◆ Iron: 6.91 mg
- ◆ Vitamin A: 717.33 mcg
- ◆ Vitamin C: 40.77 mg

'My boys and wife ate a "desi" omelette with the greens for the first time. They didn't miss tomatoes and cheese. I am going to try this once again with the Bengal gram flour instead of eggs. Good one!'

—Chelston Fernandes, Toronto, Canada

# SWEET POTATO (SHAKARKHAND)

Native to Central and South America, sweet potatoes are one of the oldest vegetables known to man. They were brought to India by the Portuguese in the sixteenth century. These tuberous roots are very nutritious. They are the unsung heroes of a balanced diet for many reasons. They are rich in antioxidants such as beta carotene and vitamins A, D, E and C, which are all necessary to delay ageing, protect against asthma and maintain the health of our skin, bones, teeth, heart, nerves and the thyroid gland. They are a source of vitamin B6, which helps lower blood homocysteine levels. Homocysteine is a chemical associated with degenerative heart disease. They are also a good source of minerals such as manganese, calcium, phosphorus, zinc and iron, which are all needed for maintaining immune function, forming red and white blood cells and metabolizing proteins. Due to their iron and vitamin A content, sweet potatoes help increase fertility and are essential for balancing hormones during pregnancy and lactation. Since they are high in potassium, they help lower blood pressure by removing excess sodium from the body. Potassium also helps regulate the heartbeat and the fluid balance in the body, protect the kidneys, relax muscular contractions and reduce swelling. They are an excellent source of magnesium, which is an anti-stress mineral that helps relax muscles, calm the nerves and relax the body. The natural sugars in sweet potatoes are slowly released into the bloodstream, ensuring a regular and balanced source of energy without any blood sugar spike, which is usually linked to fatigue and weight gain. This makes them a good snack food for diabetics. They help prevent cancers of the mouth, breast, lung, skin and colon. They have a high fibre content, are easily digestible and are an excellent food choice for people with oral ulcers, inflamed colons, digestive disorders and constipation. Beta-cryptoxanthin in sweet potatoes lowers the risk of arthritis. Phytochelatins, also present in sweet potatoes, bind with heavy metals such as lead, mercury, copper and cadmium, and safely remove them from the body. Folate in sweet potatoes helps develop cells and tissues of a foetus in the mother's womb.

*Pro-tip:* If you take beta blockers for heart disease, limit your consumption of potassium-rich sweet potatoes. Beta blockers can increase blood potassium levels. People with impaired kidney function need to know that too much potassium can be harmful, as the kidneys are unable to remove the excess potassium from the blood.

## SWEET POTATO BEBINCA

This adaptation of the traditional Goan dessert of flour, coconut milk, eggs and jaggery may not be as popular as the cloyingly sweet seven-layered Goan delicacy but it is nutrient-dense and soul-satisfying. Most sweet potato bebinca recipes call for the entire pudding ingredients to be baked together to make it a less laborious task. But I tried a layered version by baking a pancake-thin layer, drizzling some melted butter over it, then baking the next layer, repeating the butter drizzle, then the third layer and so on. It is time-consuming and super-rich, but received a nod of approval from a grouchy Goan uncle— so I was on the right track. This is a mock bebinca that will

tug at your heartstrings and serve as a memory of all things
Goan.—*Charmaine*

*Preparation time* 30 minutes
*Cooking time* 1 hour 10 minutes
*Serves* 12

*Ingredients*

* 600 gm sweet potatoes, with the peel
* 150 gm wholewheat flour
* 8 eggs
* 400 ml coconut milk, thick (save the coconut meal for
  chutneys, cookies, etc., and also to thicken gravies)
* 400 gm jaggery, grated
* 100 gm butter, melted
* 1 tsp nutmeg, freshly grated
* Salt to taste

*Method*

* Preheat the oven to 250 degrees.
* Thoroughly wash the sweet potatoes, pat dry and poke a
  couple of holes in them with a fork.
* Roast them on a greased baking tray until soft, for
  approximately 30 minutes. Then remove them from the
  oven and cool completely.
* Once cooled, peel them and puree in a blender.
* The skins can be eaten as is, to get your daily dose of fibre.
* Whisk the sweet potato purée, together with the melted
  butter and whole eggs.
* Once light and fluffy, add the grated jaggery and gradually
  incorporate spoonfuls of the flour.

- Add the coconut milk, grated nutmeg and a pinch of salt to form a thick batter.
- Heat the oven to 200 degrees.
- Pour the batter on to a greased, deep-set baking pan (preferably a springform pan).
- Bake for an hour, until the bebinca pudding is firm to the touch and has a light golden-brown edge.
- Remove from the oven and cool the pan on a wire rack.
- It tastes better if the pan is subsequently covered and left to set overnight in the refrigerator.
- For the layered version, you will need a lot more butter or ghee. Pour a ladleful of batter into your prepped baking pan and bake until you see golden-brown bubbles form on top. Pour some melted butter or ghee over this layer and pour another ladleful of batter. Cook until golden-brown bubbles form. Repeat the butter/ghee layer and the subsequent layers of batter. You should get 7–8 layers, depending upon the size of your baking pan.

*Nutritive value per serving*

- Energy: 345.63 kcal
- CHO: 49.15 gm
- Protein: 5.69 gm
- Fat: 15.15 gm
- Sodium: 125.83 mg
- Potassium: 393.64 mg
- Calcium: 64.1 mg
- Iron: 2.83 mg
- Vitamin A: 41.93 mcg
- Vitamin C: 11.1 mg

'Ah! Goa! Subtle hints of nutmeg, jaggery and butter make this version of the Goan delicacy "health on a plate" instead of a "heart attack on a plate"! Kudos!'

—Rahul A., Dubai

## SWEET POTATO CHACH

Not to be confused with chaas, which is a salted/spiced buttermilk, this chach is comfort food when you need it the most—like when you were four, and your parents scolded you for breaking your baby sister's favourite doll and you ran to your grandma next door to complain about the 'apple of her eye', your dad! She promised that she would shout at him and rushed to make you a bowl of chach. Most east Indian mums and grandmas use chach to bribe young children to study, finish their homework, eat their greens, dust the furniture . . . you get the drift! I've even tried making chach in our Crockpot overnight, and the kitchen smells dizzyingly sweet the next morning.—*Charlyene*

*Preparation time* 15 minutes
*Cooking time* 15 minutes
*Serves* 4

*Ingredients*

- 700 gm sweet potatoes, with the peel
- 150 ml milk
- 300 ml coconut milk (freshly extracted or you can thin down packaged coconut milk)

- 4 tbs jaggery sugar
- 1 tsp cardamom powder
- Salt to taste

## Method

- Thoroughly wash the sweet potatoes, ensuring that you remove the soil from it.
- Trim the ends and cut into 1/8-inch thick roundels.
- Place them in a pressure cooker along with the rest of the ingredients (except the cardamom powder).
- You may need to add water, so the roundels are properly soaking in the liquid.
- Pressure-cook over 3 whistles. Cook and remove the lid.
- Bring to a slow simmer and further cook for 5 minutes uncovered to reach the consistency you desire.
- Adjust sweetness as desired and add the cardamom powder.
- Serve warm.

## Nutritive value per serving

- Energy: 402.09 kcal
- CHO: 58.93 gm
- Protein: 4.76 gm
- Fat: 16.37 gm
- Sodium: 83.11 mg
- Potassium: 707.85 mg
- Calcium: 115.65 mg
- Iron: 2.08 mg
- Vitamin A: 4.14 mcg
- Vitamin C: 39.60 mg

> 'This is a warm, hearty dish with a hint of cardamom and the creaminess of coconut—but the star of this bowl was the sweet potato. Yum!'
>
> —Tilak Shetty, Mangalore

## SWEET POTATO CHIPS

Chips make me happy and sweet potato chips double my joy. Well, that's because sweet potatoes help the brain release endorphins or 'feel good' hormones such as serotonin and epinephrine. There is nothing better than these endorphins to elevate my mood when I am missing my friends during these quarantine times.—*Savlyene*

*Preparation time* 30 minutes
*Cooking time* 50 minutes
*Serves* 4

*Ingredients*

- 300 gm sweet potatoes, with the peel
- 2 tbs olive oil
- 1 tbs white vinegar
- Salt and pepper to taste

*Method*

- Wash the sweet potatoes thoroughly to remove all adhering soil.

- Dry them well and leave the peels on.
- Slice thinly using a sharp knife or a slicer or a mandolin. The thinner the slice, the crispier the chip!
- Soak the slices along with the white vinegar in a bowl of ice-cold water for 20 minutes.
- Remove from the water and pat dry.
- Lightly coat the slices with olive oil and place them in a single layer in the air fryer. You will need to do this in small batches.
- Cook each batch for 7–8 minutes, checking to see if they are sticking together.
- Once done, remove them from the airfryer, add a sprinkling of salt and pepper, and patiently wait for them to cool and crisp.
- Repeat the same process with the rest of the batches.
- Alternatively, you can bake them for an hour or so, on the centre rack of an oven, heated to 125 degrees.

*Nutritive value per serving*

- Energy: 205.01 kcal
- CHO: 33.04 gm
- Protein: 1.07 gm
- Fat: 7.74 gm
- Sodium: 54.93 mg
- Potassium: 246.82 mg
- Calcium: 21.77 mg
- Iron: 0.69 mg
- Vitamin A: 1.39 mcg
- Vitamin C: 16.65 mg

'I have used my air fryer for potato chips but never for sweet potato chips. But it was so easy, crunchy, healthy and tasty! And that's expected, when the recipe is from GHA'

—Sunita Rathi, Kochi

## SWEET POTATO CUTLETS

Everyone loves aloo tikkis, but once you've sampled a sweet potato tikki/cutlet—crispy on the outside and creamy inside—you will never want to eat an aloo tikki again. A big shoutout to all chaat lovers: 'Try this today.' They taste just as good cold as piping hot, or even at room temperature. I always add rice flour to the sweet potato mix to prevent it from falling apart, and then some more to toss the uncooked tikkis in, to ensure a crispy covering. To further up the nutrition quotient, I add some coarsely ground mixed seeds to the rice flour. You may want to add some salt to the rice flour being used to coat the tikkis. Have fun making and eating them. They also store well in the freezer—but ours never make it beyond the dining table!—*Savlyene*

*Preparation time* 15 minutes
*Cooking time* 20 minutes
*Serves* 4

*Ingredients*

- 4 medium sweet potatoes, pressure-cooked, with the peel (or save the skins to bake in the oven, brushed with butter.

Once crisp, bring them out and sprinkle salt, pepper and chaat masala)

- 2 tbs celery stalks, finely chopped, with the leaves
- 1 tbs dhana jeera powder
- 4 green chillies, finely chopped
- 4 tbs coriander, freshly chopped, with the stalks
- 1 tsp amchur powder
- 1 tsp garam masala powder
- 2 tbs vegetable oil
- Salt to taste
- Mixed seeds, coarsely ground, and rice flour, as required, to crumb

## Method

- Once the sweet potatoes have cooled, mash them with a fork.
- Add the rest of the ingredients, except the oil, and bind together. You may want to add some rice flour at this stage to help with the binding process.
- Divide into 8 portions and shape into ovals or rounds.
- Coat with some lightly salted rice flour and some coarsely ground mixed seeds.
- Heat the oil in a pan and fry the tikkis until golden-brown on both sides. Or you may want to air-fry or bake the tikkis.
- Serve with avocado-mint chutney, sweet-and-sour imli chutney or a spicy yoghurt dip.

## Nutritive value per serving

- Energy: 192.3 kcal
- CHO: 25.4 gm

- Protein: 2.74 gm
- Fat: 8.86 gm
- Sodium: 32.445 mg
- Potassium: 402.9 mg
- Calcium: 57.72 mg
- Iron: 2.17 mg
- Vitamin A: 102.76 mcg
- Vitamin C: 26.17 mg

'Sweet potatoes are the new superfood. Double thumbs up for this cutlet recipe'

—Neha G., Ahmedabad

# TOMATO

Even though a tomato is botanically a fruit, we have added it in our vegetable section. After all, knowledge is knowing that tomato is a fruit and wisdom is not putting it in a fruit salad! Tomatoes belong to the Solanaceae (nightshade) family. They are an excellent source of vitamin A—in the form of the antioxidant phytochemical lycopene—vitamins C and K, potassium and folic acid. The lycopene content in cooked tomatoes is much higher than in the fresh ones. So you can choose a home-made tomato curry/gravy/sabji/sauce/ketchup/cooked paste over tomatoes found in a salad for better absorption of its nutrients, and also if you want to up your vitamin A level. Lutein in tomatoes is an antioxidant that protects the retina from free-radical damage. Chlorogenic acid, the powerful antioxidant found in tomatoes, can help stabilize blood pressure. Tomatoes can protect against certain types of cancers, such as cancer of the prostate gland, and also against heart disease. Since the leaves of the tomato plant contain the neurotoxin solanine, please avoid eating them. Although allergies to tomatoes are rare, individuals with a latex allergy can experience it. You can safely eat tomato seeds, because their oxalate content is too little to contribute to the formation of kidney stones.

*Pro-tip:* If you have decided to grow tomatoes in your balcony, remember to choose a spot that receives a lot of sunshine. Water your plants well, because those big, sweet, juicy tomatoes need to be well hydrated. Cracked eggshells added to the soil will boost the calcium content. Grow basil, chives and garlic in nearby pots, because, together, they not only make great companions on your chopping board but also repel pests in your kitchen garden. Ripen tomatoes on the plant itself or harvest them early and continue the ripening process in paper bags. There is nothing more satisfying than looking at that huge red fruit and bragging to all and sundry that 'I grew that beauty'.

## TOMATO CONCASSE

I get back from school hungry, there is no one at home, I do not have the option of going out to buy a snack and I cannot order in. Please remember that we grew up at a time when Swiggy and Zomato were not on our speed dial. So I look around for some sliced bread, leftover chapati, toast or a packet of tasteless crackers, and poke my head into the fridge. Ninety-nine per cent of the time I would end up with a jar of what we liked to call 'Mum's magic potion' or tomato concasse. She always stocked a big jar of this in the fridge for emergencies—such as running out of tomatoes for a sabji, wanting to jazz up a bharta, or making a quick toastie, a bread pizza or a baked entree with cheese. Much later, when I tried my hand at making it, from *Larousse*, that bible of French cuisine, I was upset that it wasn't a patch on what my mum makes. When I told her about it, she grinned sheepishly—a sure sign that she had not been using an authentic recipe. Today I'm sharing that magic recipe and I do hope you find as much joy eating it as I did, and still do.—*Savlyene*

*Preparation time* 15 minutes
*Cooking time* 30 minutes
*Serves* Unlimited hungry people

*Ingredients*

- 2 kg diced red tomatoes, with the peels and seeds
- 1 kg carrot puree, with the peels (simply wash well, trim the edges, chop and puree)
- 200 gm red pumpkin puree (save the peels and seeds to make baked munchies)
- 20 cloves of garlic, minced
- 25 basil leaves, fresh (or 1 heaped tbs basil, dried)
- 1 tbs oregano, dried
- 1 tbs pepper powder
- 4 tbs vegetable oil
- 1 tbs jaggery sugar
- Salt to taste

*Method*

- Heat the oil in a large pan and cook the garlic until soft.
- Add the carrot and red pumpkin purees, and cook well.
- Place the diced tomatoes and cover with a well-fitted lid.
- Stir occasionally and allow the tomatoes to cook in the water they will release.
- Once the tomatoes have fully softened and the vegetable purees have been well incorporated in the sauce, add the herbs, pepper, jaggery sugar and salt to taste.
- Add some more jaggery to reduce the tartness if necessary.
- Cool and store in a clean glass jar.
- Keeps well for up to two weeks when refrigerated.

*Nutritive value per tablespoon serving*

- Energy: 19.56 kcal
- CHO: 2.23 gm
- Protein: 0.41 gm
- Fat: 1 gm
- Sodium: 12.39 mg
- Potassium: 95.36 mg
- Calcium: 9.35 mg
- Iron: 0.18 mg
- Vitamin A: 137.18 mcg
- Vitamin C: 8.45 mg

> 'Such a simple recipe to make—a sauce that can be used for so many different dishes, from pizza to pasta to wraps, rolls, burgers and sandwiches. You can even just have it with dal-chawal. Loved the hidden vegetables. It makes the sauce thicker and more nutritive'
>
> —Neesha Nihalani, Mumbai

## TOMATO SPAETZLE

This pasta is generally had in Switzerland, Austria, Germany and Hungary. It is made using flour, eggs, salt and water. I remember eating a bowl of spaetzle in Germany as an accompaniment to Bavarian meatballs. I also remember shoving the meatballs on to Dad's plate and polishing off the spaetzle with just the tomato sauce. YUM! If you want to use eggs for this pasta, the thumb rule is to use one more egg than the total number of people eating the pasta—so five eggs for a family of four hearty eaters. I've avoided the egg here and used tomato paste instead. It binds the dough well and the taste is so much better.—*Charlyene*

*Preparation time* 15 minutes
*Cooking time* 15 minutes
*Serves* 4

*Ingredients*

* 120 gm tomato paste
* 225 gm wheat flour
* 2 tsp salt
* 1 tbs olive oil

*Method*

* In a large bowl, mix the wheat flour, tomato paste and salt with some warm water to form a soft dough.
* Let the dough rest for 10 minutes.
* Boil water in a large pot.
* When it begins to bubble, add salt and lower the flame.
* Set a large bowl of ice water on the kitchen counter.
* Press the dough through a colander or sieve directly into the boiling water to form the spaetzle.
* Remember to keep the colander or sieve at least 6 inches above the water.
* About 3 minutes later, the spaetzle will rise to the top of the boiling water.
* Remove and drain, and immediately put the spaetzle into the ice bath to prevent further cooking.
* Rinse well in the cold water, drain and toss with olive oil.

- Serve with tomato concasse or tomato coconut curry sauce (p. 229).

*Nutritive value per serving*

- Energy: 221.05 kcal
- CHO: 38.47 gm
- Protein: 6.42 gm
- Fat: 4.61 gm
- Sodium: 975.92 mg
- Potassium: 174.97 mg
- Calcium: 17.44 mg
- Iron: 2.67 mg
- Vitamin A: 1 mcg
- Vitamin C: 4.29 mg

---

'I have never made any pasta or noodles from scratch, so I kept messaging Charlyene for instructions. The results were very good, and I'm ready to try more GHA recipes. This tomato spaetzle was the base for my husband Ravi's tomato coconut curry sauce. An easy yet delicious combo'

—Anu Karnani, Kuwait

---

## TOMATO COCONUT CURRY SAUCE

This sauce can be made in large quantities and used as a base for many dishes, both vegetarian and non-vegetarian. Think green peas, cauliflower, mushrooms, broccoli, snow peas, French beans, carrots, paneer or a medley of all this for vegetarian options. If you eat meat, this is a good curry base for chicken, eggs, lamb or prawns. However, if you want to eat it without any additions, just serve it with steamed basmati rice and a dollop of mango pickle, or with tomato spaetzle and some salad. Do let us know how you like it.—*Charlyene*

*Preparation time* 20 minutes
*Cooking time* 30 minutes
*Serves* 8

## Ingredients

* 250 gm coconut, desiccated
* 8 large tomatoes, chopped, with the peels and seeds
* 4 small onions, diced
* 2 tbs garlic, chopped
* 2 tbs ginger, chopped, with the peel
* 2 tbs curry powder
* 2 tsp red chilli powder
* 1 tbs cumin powder
* 4 stalks lemongrass, cut into 1-Inch pieces (optional)
* 2 cups coconut milk
* Grated zest of 2 lemons (saved from previously used lemons)
* Salt to taste
* 2 tbs vegetable oil

## Method

* Toast the coconut and set aside.
* Roughly puree the tomatoes in a blender to form a chunky sauce.
* Heat with the oil in a pan and cook the onions, garlic and ginger for 5 minutes.

- Add the toasted coconut and mix well.
- Cook for another 5 minutes, along with the tomatoes, curry powder, chilli powder, cumin powder, lemongrass and lemon zest.
- Add the coconut milk and salt to taste.
- Cook until it becomes a thick sauce. This sauce will stay well in the refrigerator for five days.

*Nutritive value per serving*

- Energy: 334.39 kcal
- CHO: 9.06 gm
- Protein: 4.36 gm
- Fat: 31.19 gm
- Sodium: 23.64 mg
- Potassium: 457.7 mg
- Calcium: 63.06 mg
- Iron: 2.39 mg
- Vitamin A: 109.1 mcg
- Vitamin C: 13.46 mg

'This curry sauce paired fabulously with the tomato spaetzle my wife made. Both are great recipes. Good luck with the rest of the recipe trials, Charmaine'

—Ravi Karnani, Kuwait

## TOMATO ROGAN JOSH

Rogan josh is an aromatic lamb dish of Persian and Kashmiri origin, very rarely cooked in our home because Savio, my

hubby, feels lamb in our country doesn't taste right—he can smell and taste grass when eating lamb! The girls will skip the meat and only have the gravy with roti. I, too, am not a lover of lamb or mutton. We usually substitute the lamb with mushrooms, paneer or eggplant because the thick, fiery red sauce is something we love to indulge in. A couple of months ago, the sauce was already cooking on the stovetop when I realized that there weren't any mushrooms, eggplant or paneer cubes in the refrigerator. The available options were not too appealing—eggs and corn! Luckily, I spotted some large greenish red tomatoes that Savio had purchased from an organic farmers' market and, as they say, the rest is history! Culinary history from our home to yours. Enjoy!
—*Charmaine*

*Preparation time* 15 minutes
*Cooking time* 45 minutes
*Serves* 4

*Ingredients*

+ 1 kg large greenish tomatoes, with the peels and seeds, cut into quarters (please avoid the soft, mushy ones)
+ 2 large onions, thinly sliced
+ 5 cloves of garlic, finely chopped
+ 2 inches of ginger, finely chopped, with the peel
+ 4 green chillies, finely chopped
+ 10 green cardamom, lightly crushed
+ 1 tsp cumin seeds
+ 1 tsp nigella seeds
+ 1/2 tsp turmeric
+ 2 tsp garam masala powder

- 2 tbs vegetable oil
- Salt to taste

*For the garnish*

- 2 tbs coriander, freshly chopped, with the stalks

*Method*

- Heat the oil in a deep saucepan and temper the cardamom pods, and cumin and nigella seeds until they start to pop.
- Add the sliced onions and fry until light brown.
- Stir in the garlic, ginger, green chillies, turmeric and 1 teaspoon of garam masala powder.
- Pour in a third of the tomatoes, along with 1 cup of water, and cook for about 10 minutes or until the tomatoes soften.
- Add salt to taste.
- Add the remaining tomatoes and simmer over a gentle heat, uncovered until the tomatoes are tender.
- Remember to stir occasionally.
- Season with the remaining garam masala and the chopped coriander.
- Serve with rotis or a simple jeera pulao.

*Nutritive value per serving*

- Energy: 182.9 kcal
- CHO: 16.78 gm
- Protein: 5.59 gm
- Fat: 10.38 gm
- Sodium: 40.88 mg

- Potassium: 673.92 mg
- Calcium: 111.08 mg
- Iron: 23.13 mg
- Vitamin A: 14.64 mcg
- Vitamin C: 47.48 mg

'Juicy tomatoes and the rogan josh masala make this a lip-smacking dish. The firmer the tomatoes, the better the dish'

—Aditi Dani, Kolhapur

# FRUITS

Fruits are naturally sweet, energy-boosting promoters of good health. Generally eaten uncooked, they cleanse the system, provide energy and supply good carbohydrates and natural sugars, soluble and insoluble fibres, vitamins, minerals and free-radical-removing antioxidants. People who eat a minimum of five servings of fruit every day are less likely to suffer from ill health. They are able to lower their risk of developing kidney stones, osteoporosis, type 2 diabetes, cardiac diseases, hypertension, some types of cancer—such as of the mouth, throat, ovaries, bladder and colon—diverticulosis, diseases of the gums and even dental caries.

If you have diabetes or hypertriglyceridemia, you should consult a qualified nutritionist and dietitian to figure out exactly which type of fruits you are allowed to eat, as well as the amounts you can. You will also be given guidance on how often and at what time you should be eating fruit. A qualified healthcare practitioner will go through the list of medicines you are taking and be able to let you know which foods will impact your medicines in a negative way. Grapefruit, for example, can affect the way some statins work in your body and make their side effects more pronounced. Cranberries, mangoes and grapefruit can alter the effects of the blood thinner warfarin.

# APPLE

The most popular fruit in the world has multiple health benefits. Apples are best eaten raw and are a good source of fructose, glucose and sucrose. Despite the presence of these simple sugars, apples have a low GI. This is attributed to their high fibre and polyphenol content. To derive maximum health benefits, eat apples with their peel. The peel has half the total fibre content and is a concentrated source of polyphenols. Polyphenols are a good source of antioxidants such as catechin, chlorogenic acid and quercetin, all of whose possible health benefits include lower blood sugar levels, weight loss, better muscle and brain function and anti-depressant, anti-cancer, anti-inflammatory and anti-viral effects. This fruit is known for its pectin content, a type of fibre that acts as a prebiotic, feeding good gut bacteria. People who eat apples regularly may be protected from diabetes, cardiovascular disease and cancer.

*Pro-tip:* People with irritable bowel syndrome, or IBS, may need to limit their apple intake or omit it altogether, because apples contain FODMAPS (Fermentable Oligosaccharides, Disaccharides, Monosaccharides, and Polyols). These are types of fibres that might cause digestive distress, characterized by bloating, gas, flatulence and abdominal pain in susceptible individuals. Apart from this, those who are intolerant to the fruit sugar fructose should also limit their intake of apples.

## SPICED APPLE BUTTER

You are forgiven for thinking you need butter to make apple butter. The first time I tasted it at a college organic farmers' market event, I was told that the tartness came from the Granny Smith apples used. Since this variety of apples is not widely available in India, I have added a little more apple cider vinegar than what the recipe called for. It is easy to make, needs no peeling or coring of the fruit—you do not want to lose out on the pectin from the core, nor the flavour from the peels. You can leave it in a slow cooker or a Crockpot to cook overnight or make it on the stovetop. Our GHA spiced version has the usual cinnamon and cloves, but also calls for our favourite spice—star anise!—*Charlyene*

*Preparation time* 15 minutes
*Cooking time* 45 minutes, or overnight in a Crockpot
*Serves* 50 tablespoons

*Ingredients*

- 1 kg apples, cut into quarters (without discarding the peel and the core)
- 300 gm jaggery or coconut sugar
- 100 ml apple cider vinegar
- 1 tsp cinnamon powder
- 1/4 tsp clove powder
- 1/4 tsp star anise powder
- Juice and zest of 2 limes
- A pinch of salt

## Method

- Bring 2 cups of water to a boil in a large pan and add the apple quarters along with the apple cider vinegar.
- Cook for around 15 minutes, until the apples are soft.
- Puree the cooked apples, strain through a muslin cloth or conical chinois strainer and force out most of the pulp into another pan. The strainer or muslin cloth should barely have any residue left.
- Add the jaggery sugar, a pinch of salt, the spices and the lime zest and juice.
- Cook on the stovetop on low heat for about 20 minutes, stirring regularly until it thickens.
- To test for thickness, pour a teaspoon of the butter on to a freezer-chilled saucer. It should be thick, not runny.
- Pour the spiced apple butter into clean airtight glass jars and refrigerate.
- Pairs well with toast, crackers and rusks.

## Nutritive value per serving

- Energy: 33.35 kcal
- CHO: 7.82 gm
- Protein: 0.18 gm
- Fat: 0.15 gm
- Sodium: 17.41 mg
- Potassium: 54.34 mg
- Calcium: 10.75mg
- Iron: 0.35 mg
- Vitamin A: 0.1 mcg
- Vitamin C: 0.72 mg

'An amazing and very refined MasterChef-quality taste and recipe'

—Nitya Malani, Hyderabad

## APPLE PIE

This is my dad's secret recipe, something he uses to bake the most delicious apple pies for his favourite girl—me! I had to twist his arm to have him share the recipe with me, when I was doing recipe trials for our cookbook. After much cajoling, he finally relented. The secret lies in using different types of apples and cooking them with a tablespoon or two of our spiced apple butter (p. 238). The different types of apples taste and cook differently. So you will end up with a pie that has so much more texture and flavour. Try it out someday. It is the best home-made apple pie you will have ever tasted—and then this pie and you will live apple-y ever after!—*Savlyene*

*Preparation time* 1 hour, 10 minutes, plus 2 hours pie-crust-resting time
*Cooking time* 45 minutes
*Serves* 8

*Ingredients*

*For the 8-inch pie crust*

- 400 gm wholewheat flour
- 200 gm butter
- 80 gm vegetable oil
- 2 tbs white vinegar
- A pinch of salt

- Sugar, if needed
- 240 ml ice-cold water
- Cold milk for the wash

## For the filling

- 1.2 kg apples, with the peel (preferably of different types)
- 2–3 tbs spiced apple butter (optional) (p. 238)
- 4 tbs lime juice
- 100 gm jaggery sugar or coconut sugar
- 3 tbs wheat flour, to dust the apple slices
- 1–2 tsp cinnamon powder

## Method

### For the pie crust

- Sift the flour and the salt, and put it into a large mixing bowl.
- Add sugar if you want a slightly sweet pie crust.
- Cut the butter into cubes and add it to the flour, along with the oil.
- Mix together, preferably with your fingertips, until it resembles coarse crumbs.
- Add the vinegar to the ice-cold water and gradually incorporate it into the flour, mixing lightly.
- Divide the dough and knead each portion well, until the dough is smooth.
- Refrigerate for 2 hours.

### For the filling

- Chop the apples into slices of even thickness and place in a bowl.

- Add the spiced apple butter or the lime juice to the apple slices.
- Sift the wheat flour with the cinnamon powder and add the jaggery sugar.
- Dust the flour mixture over the apple slices and toss, so that it is well coated.
- Leave aside for 10 minutes.

*To assemble the apple pie*

- Preheat the oven to 180 degrees.
- Roll out 2 dough discs of even thickness, one approximately 8.5–9 inches for the top and the other around 12 inches for the base and the sides. Dust the board with flour.
- Line an 8-inch pie tin with the base dough disc and press down. Save the other rolled disc for the top covering.
- Arrange the apple slices neatly in a circular fashion all over the base of the pie tin, leaving no space unfilled.
- Cover with the second dough disc and press down tightly.
- Brush with cold milk.
- Cut serrations or vents on top to let off steam.
- Bake until the crust is golden-brown. You will see the apple juices bubbling out.
- Cool on a wire rack.
- Serve warm.

*Nutritive value per serving*

- Energy: 577.99 kcal
- CHO: 66.29 gm
- Protein: 6.42 gm
- Fat: 31.9 gm

- Sodium: 248.71 mg
- Potassium: 406.66 mg
- Calcium: 93.69 mg
- Iron: 3.62 mg
- Vitamin A: 4.42 mcg
- Vitamin C: 10.22 mg

'Having baked apple pies for years now, I have to admit that the secret of this particular apple pie has to be in the use of the GHA apple butter. This made the pie so buttery, moist and so much tastier. I served it with a frozen yoghurt ice-cream and my family wiped it all off—not even a crumb was left'

—Juhi Shah, Boston, the US

# BANANA

This globally popular fruit is high in potassium, pectin, fibre, magnesium, and vitamins C and B6. Its B6 content helps strengthen the nervous system and its tryptophan content gets converted to the mood-enhancing brain neurotransmitter serotonin in the body. Therefore, bananas are also recommended in helping patients combat depression, to relax and to sleep better. A banana a day truly keeps the blues away. The ripened fruit is packed with potassium and is low in sodium, hence it is good for lowering blood pressure and improving heart health. Although not a very high source of calcium, bananas help improve bone health. This is because their fructooligosaccharides serve as probiotics and increase calcium absorption. The resistant starch in bananas helps improve blood sugar levels and gut health. Athletes fare much better when they refuel on a banana and plenty of water. The serotonin and dopamine from the banana help reduce oxidative stress and improve overall performance.

*Pro-tip:* Bananas ripen at room temperature. We have not only read frightening reports of the fruit being hastily ripened in calcium carbide but also seen truckloads of the raw dark green fruit being unloaded into a warehouse and a few hours later being loaded into the same truck in all its ripened glory. SCARY! The best thing to do is to buy the raw fruit and let it ripen naturally in your kitchen. To hasten the ripening process, you can put the bunch in a brown paper bag.

## BANANA CUCUMBER BREAD

Since the start of the lockdown, banana bread has risen to the top of everyone's frequently baked list and is the most posted pic on Instagram. We just had to give this delicious bread an east Indian/Goan twist as a tribute to our heritage. The traditional cucumber cake is steamed over hot coals and calls for a large, elongated cucumber called 'tavsa' in east Indian Marathi and 'tavshe' in Konkani. Our GHA banana cucumber bread can be baked in a loaf pan or in a cake dish. It is dense, moist and yummy.—*Savlyene*

*Preparation time* 15 minutes
*Cooking time* 25 minutes
*Serves* 6

*Ingredients*

- 3 large ripe bananas, mashed (use the peel to make a sabji or a thoran)
- 150 gm cucumber, grated, with the peel
- 90 gm oat flour
- 80 gm coconut, desiccated
- 120 gm jaggery powder
- 20 gm cashew, chopped
- 1 tsp coconut oil

*Method*

- Preheat the oven to 175 degrees.
- In a mixing bowl, mix the mashed bananas with the grated cucumber, oat flour, desiccated coconut, jaggery and chopped cashew.

- The batter must have a medium consistency and without any lumps. Add some milk or coconut milk if needed to adjust the consistency.
- Grease a loaf tin or baking pan with coconut oil and pour the banana cucumber batter into it.
- Place the pan in a water bath and bake for 20–25 minutes, until the top is golden-brown and an inserted toothpick comes out clean.
- Remove from the oven and cool on a wire rack.
- Serve warm or cold.

*Nutritive value per serving*

- Energy: 316.39 kcal
- CHO: 46.05 gm
- Protein: 5.62 gm
- Fat: 12.19 gm
- Sodium: 9.77 mg
- Potassium: 477.25 mg
- Calcium: 41.95 mg
- Iron: 2.52 mg
- Vitamin A: 6.84 mcg
- Vitamin C: 4.86 mg

'Our favourite bakery item has been banana walnut bread, so our curiosity was piqued by this recipe, which included cucumbers in it. We tried it and found that it was dense, just like Savlyene had mentioned it would be—and yum too. I wanted my mom-in-law to try it too, so I shared the recipe with her and she loved it'

—Kavita Saini, Chandigarh

## BANANA PEEL THORAN

The peels used in this Kerala-style dish are from unripe bananas, but you can also use the peels of the ripened fruit and lessen the cooking time. Banana peels are not poisonous. You just have to wash them well in vinegar solution. They are packed with nutrients—the vitamins B6 and B12, fibre, protein, magnesium, potassium, polyphenols and carotenoids would all be wasted if you junked the peels. Turns out that the biggest risk from a banana peel is slipping on it. Ouch!—*Charlyene*

*Preparation time* 5 minutes
*Cooking time* 15 minutes
*Serves* 4

*Ingredients*

* Peels of 4 raw or ripe bananas (washed in vinegar solution)
* 2 large onions, finely chopped
* 4 tbs coconut, freshly grated
* 2 green chillies, finely chopped
* 1 tsp ginger, grated, with the peel
* 1/2 teaspoon jeera powder
* 1/2 tsp turmeric powder
* 1/4 tsp pepper powder
* 1 tbs vegetable oil plus 1 tsp to temper
* 10 curry leaves
* 1 tsp mustard seeds
* 1 whole red chilli, dried
* Salt to taste

*Method*

- Chop the peels into even-sized pieces and place them in a bowl of salted water.
- Heat 1 tablespoon vegetable oil in a pan, add the chopped onions and fry until soft.
- Add the chopped green chillies, grated ginger, jeera, turmeric and pepper powders, and continue to cook for 2 minutes.
- Remove the chopped banana peels from the water and add them to the pan.
- Sauté for 5 minutes (lesser for ripened banana peels).
- Add the grated coconut and 1/2 cup water, along with salt to taste.
- Cover and cook until the peels are cooked and the vegetable dish has very little moisture.
- In another small pan, temper the mustard seeds, curry leaves and whole red chilli in 1 teaspoon oil. Then add this to the thoran.
- Serve warm with rotis.

*Nutritive value per serving*

- Energy: 156.42 kcal
- CHO: 12.1 gm
- Protein: 2.39 gm
- Fat: 10.94 gm
- Sodium: 5.91 mg
- Potassium: 284.35 mg
- Calcium: 52.11 mg
- Iron: 1.61 mg
- Vitamin A: 55 mcg
- Vitamin C: 4.11 mg

'I made this on the day I made the banana cucumber bread and never told my kids what it was. Stuffed into roti rolls, it looked and tasted like any other sabji— and they ate it all. Will repeat with raw banana peels next time'

—Kavita Saini, Chandigarh

# GUAVA

This is a superfood with many health benefits. Its vitamin (A, C, E, B-complex and K) and mineral (potassium, copper, calcium, magnesium, manganese and zinc) content make the humble guava a powerhouse of nutrients. The copper in guavas helps maintain a healthy thyroid gland. This fruit is loaded with vitamin C (five times more than oranges), which is required to prevent scurvy and to produce collagen, a substance that keeps the skin supple, smooth and wrinkle-free! It contains high amounts of lycopene (vitamin A), which helps protect against cancers (especially of the lung and the oral cavity), macular degeneration, cardiovascular disease, different forms of bone degeneration such as osteopenia and osteoporosis, and changes in skin structure. Tomatoes are known for their lycopene content, but guavas have twice the amount! It has antioxidants that boost the immune system and protect against harmful infections. These antioxidants also help prevent cancers of the skin, lung, breast, prostate gland and large intestine. Since they have a high fibre and pectin content, they aid in laxative action and prevent constipation. Their soluble fibre content also stabilizes blood sugars. They are a good source of potassium and help normalize blood pressure.

*Pro-tip:* Guava leaves are also beneficial. If you have a nose bleed, just crush a guava leaf in the palm of your hand and inhale. The bleeding will magically stop. To cleanse the liver, improve digestion, soothe the gastric lining, and relieve nausea, diarrhoea and vomiting, boil 10 guava leaves in 2 litres of water. Add a sliver of ginger and drink the decoction through the day. You can also gargle using this, to get relief from toothaches, and heal bleeding gums, oral ulcers and sore throats. Avoid if you are pregnant or breastfeeding.

## AMRUD AUR KALONJI KI SABJI

When my daughters were younger, living in a cottage with a garden was a real blessing. The pink-fleshed guava tree right outside my kitchen window was always laden with fruit— fruit that the parrots would eat if it was allowed to ripen on the tree, else plucked by staff or by the hordes of children returning home from school. This sabji was first made when we knocked down a sack of semi-ripened guavas. It is still a hit, especially when we are hosting vegetarian friends. Since the vitamin C content of guavas is heat-sensitive, and the nutritive value of the tomatoes is enhanced after cooking them, I add the fruit only after the thick yoghurt-and-tomato-based gravy is prepared. That preserves some of the vitamin C content of the guavas and makes for a lip-smacking preparation.—*Charmaine*

*Preparation time* 15 minutes
*Cooking time* 30 minutes
*Serves* 8

*Ingredients*

- 800 gm guavas, semi-ripened, with the peel and seeds
- 200 gm tomatoes, chopped, with the peel and seeds

- 250 gm yoghurt, whisked
- 2 tbs coriander, freshly chopped, with the stalks
- 3 tsp nigella seeds
- 1 tsp cumin seeds
- 1 tsp turmeric powder
- 1/2 tsp pepper powder
- 1 tsp raw mango powder
- 1 tsp red chilli powder
- 2 tbs ghee
- Salt to taste
- Sugar or jaggery sugar to taste
- 2 tbs lime juice

*Method*

- Wash the guavas and keep aside.
- Heat the ghee in a pan and temper the nigella and cumin seeds.
- Add the chopped tomatoes and cover. Cook for 5 minutes.
- Next add the spice powders, turmeric powder and raw mango powder, and continue cooking the tomatoes.
- Once the tomatoes have reduced to a smooth paste, along with the masalas, add the salt, sugar and whisked yoghurt, and give it a good stir.
- Cook until the yoghurt melds well with the tomatoes and droplets of fat can be seen on top of the dish.
- Remove from the stovetop.
- Cut the guavas into small equal-sized pieces and add them to the gravy.
- Stir well, cover with a lid and set aside for 5 minutes.
- Add the lime juice and stir well.

- Garnish with chopped coriander.
- Serve with rotis.

*Nutritive value per serving*

- Energy: 128.02 kcal
- CHO: 13.39 gm
- Protein: 3.9 gm
- Fat: 6.54 gm
- Sodium: 174.13 mg
- Potassium: 347.62 mg
- Calcium: 101.95 mg
- Iron: 32.49 mg
- Vitamin A: 86.1 mcg
- Vitamin C: 228.86 mg

'Eating a guava always takes me back to my childhood spent in Mumbai, eating this fruit fresh from the trees with lots of salt and spicy red chilli powder. So this GHA guava sabji recipe with kalonji was a hit at home and so well worth the trouble of searching for guavas here in Whitby. Adding the guavas at the very end helps maintain that bite without them getting mushy'

—Allwyn Pinto, Toronto, Canada

## GUAVA BANANA SMOOTHIE

This was another good way to make use of the guavas from our tree, especially when the girls were looking to quench their thirst and the nutritionist in me wanted to boost their vitamin C. You need not stick to just bananas here—you can add mangoes, pineapple or any other fruit that you have at home. Only ensure that you serve it as soon as it is ready and that it is consumed immediately.—*Charmaine*

*Preparation time* 5 minutes
*Cooking time* 0 minutes
*Serves* 4

*Ingredients*

- 400 gm ripe guavas, chopped, with the peel and seeds
- 300 gm yoghurt, low-fat
- 2 bananas, sliced
- A pinch of paprika
- 3 cups ice cubes

*Method*

- Combine all the ingredients in a blender or a food processor.
- Cover and blend until smooth and frothy.
- Pour into tall glasses.
- Serve chilled.
- Consume as soon as it is made to derive the vitamin C benefits of the guavas.

*Nutritive value per serving*

- Energy: 201.14 kcal
- CHO: 31.16 gm
- Protein: 7.73 gm
- Fat: 5.12 gm
- Sodium: 55.02 mg
- Potassium: 499.5 mg
- Calcium: 159.77 mg
- Iron: 0.79 mg
- Vitamin A: 51.59 mcg
- Vitamin C: 225.57 mg

'The smoothie was very delicious and so very filling too'

—Megan Pinto, Toronto, Canada

# JACKFRUIT

Native to south India, this exotic fruit is the largest tree fruit in the world. Some fruits can weigh up to 30 kg. Since the texture of the raw fruit is very similar to that of shredded meat, jackfruit has found favour as a 'superfood' meat substitute by vegetarians and vegans the world over. Its protein content is higher than in other fruits. When you eat the flesh of jackfruit, its fibre will lower digestive rate and prevent spikes in blood sugar levels. Its carotenoid, flavanone and vitamin C content prevent inflammation in the body and reduce the risk of type 2 diabetes, dyslipidemia, hypertension and cancer. Jackfruit seeds are also edible and packed with nutrients. Just boil them, remove the outer skin and add them to gravies, or use them to make a smooth hummus.

*Pro-tip:* If you have bought the entire jackfruit and want to know when it is ready to eat, just go by your olfactory senses. A strong, pleasant fruity smell indicates that the fruit is ready to be cut up and eaten. The skin, at this point, will also be soft to the touch. Knocking on the fruit and hearing a dull, hollow sound will also indicate that the fruit has ripened. Apply a good amount of coconut oil to your hands before you cut open the jackfruit. This will prevent the gooey gum from sticking to your fingers. Alternatively, you can use disposable latex gloves. Be sure to spread out a plastic sheet on the work surface. Now cut the fruit into quarters. There will be sap and gum oozing out, which you can wipe off with a paper towel.

Remove the core to loosen up the edible flesh. Remove the seeds and chop off the bulbs and tendrils. The fruit of your labour will be really sweet.

## JACKFRUIT SEED CURRY

Summertime brings back fond memories of holidays spent scrambling around like monkeys in our backyard, eating fruit off trees, falling asleep on the hammock tied between two coconut trees, drinking lots of nimbu pani and waiting patiently for the whistles of the pressure cooker to go off. Why? Well, that was a signal that our meal was ready—our cue to go back indoors. At times, when the whistle would be heard mid-afternoon or early in the evening, it would only signal one thing—jackfruit seeds! Our cue to rush indoors at double speed! Here is a simple recipe from my childhood. I do hope it fills you with happiness.—*Charlyene*

*Preparation time* 10 minutes
*Cooking time* 25 minutes
*Serves* 4

*Ingredients*

- 2 cups jackfruit seeds (pressure-cook in salted water over 4–6 whistles, cool and remove the thin outer skin)
- 1 tsp mustard seeds
- 10 curry leaves
- 3 onions, finely chopped
- 2 tbs coconut, freshly grated
- 3 tbs east Indian bottle masala (or you can use garam masala powder with red chilli powder and dhania–jeera powder)
- 1/2 cup coconut milk

- 1 tbs vegetable oil
- Salt to taste

*Method*

- Heat the oil in a pan and temper the mustard seed until they sputter. Then add the curry leaves.
- Add the onions and let them sauté for about 5 minutes.
- Add the freshly grated coconut and the east Indian bottle masala and fry until it changes colour.
- Add the peeled jackfruit seeds.
- Add 1 cup warm water and cook for 10 minutes.
- Season with salt and, just before you remove the curry from the stovetop, stir in the coconut milk.
- Serve hot with steamed rice.

*Nutritive value per serving*

- Energy: 239.17 kcal
- CHO: 21.69 gm
- Protein: 7.21 gm
- Fat: 13.73 gm
- Sodium: 13.3 mg
- Potassium: 417.42 mg
- Calcium: 90.05 mg
- Iron: 2.55 mg
- Vitamin A: 6.53 mcg
- Vitamin C: 12.32 mg

'This is a great way to not waste the jackfruit seeds. They tasted just like meat in this curry'

—Sudha Kapoor, Behror, Rajasthan

# VEGAN JACKFRUIT 'PULLED PORK' BURGERS

Chefs the world over are using raw jackfruit in vegan cookery because the unripe flesh has a pork-like texture. The shredded fruit is a popular alternative to pulled pork and is now being used as a vegetarian pizza topping and a filling for tacos. It has a hard bite and absorbs the spices and flavours of a dish just like meat does. Try this recipe for our burgers. You will soon become a jackfruit convert. —*Savlyene*

*Preparation time* 30 minutes
*Cooking time* 20 minutes
*Serves* 4

*Ingredients*

- 4 wholewheat garlic buns (p. 39)

*For the jackfruit filling*

- 400 gm green jackfruit
- 2 tbs jaggery sugar or brown sugar
- 1 tbs garlic, finely minced
- 2 tsp smoked paprika powder (or red chilli powder)
- 1/2 tsp pepper powder
- 1/2 tsp star anise powder
- 2 tbs vegetable oil
- 1 cup BBQ sauce (preferably vegan, to be used for the filling as well as for serving)
- Salt to taste

*For the mixed vegetable slaw*

- 1 cup mixed vegetables, finely sliced (onions, cabbage with the outer leaves and inner core, carrots with the peel, and red, green and yellow bell peppers with the inner pith and seeds)
- 1 tbs jaggery or brown sugar
- 2 tbs lime juice
- 1 tsp pepper powder
- Salt to taste

*Method*

- In a large bowl, mix the ingredients for the mixed vegetable slaw thoroughly to ensure that the veggies marinate in the seasonings. You may need to add a tablespoon or two of water.
- Refrigerate.
- Mix the jackfruit with the rest of the filling ingredients (except the oil and the BBQ sauce) and toss them well to coat each bit.
- Keep aside for 5 minutes.
- Heat a pan and add the oil.
- Add the marinated jackfruit and cook for 5 minutes.
- Add 1/2 cup BBQ sauce and 1 cup water, and cook for about 15–20 minutes.
- Using 2 forks, shred the jackfruit as it cooks in the sauce.
- Once the shredded jackfruit has properly cooked, turn up the heat and cook for 2 more minutes. Then remove from the stovetop.

## To assemble

- Cut the wholewheat garlic buns in half and put 2 heaped tablespoons of the mixed vegetable slaw on the bottom buns.
- Top with a generous serving of the shredded jackfruit filling and cover with the other half of the bun. Alternatively, you can omit the slaw and just use thinly sliced onions and tomatoes.
- Serve with the remaining BBQ sauce.

## Nutritive value per serving

- Energy: 206.33 kcal
- CHO: 30.09 gm
- Protein: 3.29 gm
- Fat: 8.09 gm
- Sodium: 366.53 mg
- Potassium: 525.94 mg
- Calcium: 90.88 mg
- Iron: 1.51 mg
- Vitamin A: 3.83 mcg
- Vitamin C: 30.61 mg

'Having seen Savio's post on Facebook about how Charmaine had fooled him by replacing a pulled-pork burger with a pulled-jackfruit burger, I asked her for the recipe. My husband is a staunch non-vegetarian and I am elated to say that he, too, was fooled! The burger was hot, juicy and wonderful. Best of all, no fear of cholesterol and fat. No more pork for us, thanks to team GHA!

—Cheryl Lopes, Mumbai

# MANGO

The 'king of fruits' has a unique taste, flavour, texture and health-promoting properties. Mangoes are an amazing source of vitamins A, C, E and B-complex as well as flavonoids such as beta-carotene and alpha-carotene. As an anti-cancer food, they prevent oral, breast, prostate, lung, blood and colon cancers. They help prevent anaemia, insomnia, night blindness, strokes, heart disease, arthritis, cognitive disorders, and respiratory and kidney diseases. Their potassium content helps control the heart rate and blood pressure. Tartaric, malic and citric acids in mangoes alkalinize the body. The enzymes of this fruit are prebiotic and feed good bacteria in the gut. They have a relatively low GI and, if eaten in moderation, as a snack and not along with a main meal, they will not spike blood sugar levels. Restrict your intake of this fruit if you are on warfarin therapy. Since mangoes have a high vitamin A content, they could result in potentiation of warfarin activity and increased bleeding risk.

*Pro-tip:* If you are not sure whether the mangoes you have bought are organic or if they have been artificially ripened with calcium carbide, wash them thoroughly and leave them overnight in a bowl of water. If the mangoes sink, they are naturally ripened, if they float, they are artificially ripened.

## MANGO CHIA PUDDING

This mandatory tropical summer pudding has our GHA healthy twist of sabudana, or sago. We make this often and vary the fruits used according to the season. You can use purees or chopped bits of peach, apple, pear, guava, strawberries, blueberries, muskmelon, papaya or even a combination of two or more fruits. Just add more chia seeds if you want a pudding that is more firmly set.—*Charlyene*

*Preparation time* 20 mins
*Cooking time* 20 minutes
*Setting time* 5 hours
*Serves* 6

*Ingredients*

- 3 cups mango puree
- 1 cup soya or coconut milk
- 4 tbs sago, soaked overnight
- 10 tbs white chia seeds (soaked in 1 cup water for 20 minutes and then blended)
- Agave nectar or honey to sweeten, if needed
- A few slices of mango to garnish the pudding

*Method*

- Drain the sago and cook in 1 cup of water for 5 minutes.
- Add the coconut or soya milk and continue to heat until the sago is cooked.
- Stir constantly until the sago disintegrates and melds completely.
- When cooked, remove from the stovetop, add the blended white chia seeds and stir well to prevent lumps from forming.
- When cooled completely, add the mango puree and, if needed, sweeten with agave nectar or honey.

- Pour into a dessert bowl or individual serving cups.
- Allow it to set in the refrigerator.
- Garnish with mango slices and serve chilled.

*Nutritive value per serving*

- Energy: 214.35 kcal
- CHO: 27.38 gm
- Protein: 6.16 gm
- Fat: 8.91 gm
- Sodium: 5.02 mg
- Potassium: 207.71 mg
- Calcium: 170.12 mg
- Iron: 2.35 mg
- Vitamin A: 118 mcg
- Vitamin C: 24.47 mg

'I have an extremely fussy three-year-old who throws tantrums when food has too much texture. The smoothness of this pudding was such a surprise to me and to him, and he loved it so much! I used small dessert cups to set the pudding and covered each with cling film. So I have a ready stock of this mango chia pudding whenever my son wants more'

—Supriya Kanitkar, Mumbai

## MANGO CHIPOTLE JAM

The jalapeno chilli pepper is dried and wood-smoked to make chipotle. We grow these chilli peppers and when we get a good harvest, we dry them in the oven and use a DIY smoker to wood-smoke them on our sun deck, which is a basic incense pot filled with wood shavings, topped with the oven-dried chilli peppers on a wire mesh, covered with a dome-shaped lid. Heat the wood shavings and, a few hours later, the chipotle peppers are ready. This home-made chipotle is a wonderful addition to a number of dishes, and here we have added them to a basic Gujarati chundo to make a sweet, sour, spicy and smoked jam.—*Savlyene*

*Preparation time* 15 minutes
*Cooking time* 35 minutes
*Serves* 30 (1 tablespoon serving size)

*Ingredients*

+ 2 large green raw mangoes (kairi), with the peel
+ 8 chipotle peppers with the seeds
+ 1 tbs red chilli powder
+ 3 tbs organic jaggery or coconut sugar
+ 10 cloves
+ Salt

*Method*

+ Grate the mangoes and add some salt. Set aside for 10 minutes.
+ Transfer the grated mangoes into a pan, along with the rest of the ingredients.
+ Cook on medium heat, stirring continuously until it reaches a jam-like consistency, for 30–35 minutes.
+ Cool. Then pour into a glass jar and refrigerate.

• Keeps well for months under refrigeration.

*Nutritive value per serving*

• Energy: 12.79 kcal
• CHO: 2.57 gm
• Protein: 0.2 gm
• Fat: 0.19 gm
• Sodium: 3.19 mg
• Potassium: 39.65 mg
• Calcium: 5.83 mg
• Iron: 0.18 mg
• Vitamin A: 4.29 mcg
• Vitamin C: 6.78 mg

---

'I doubled the amount of this recipe because I felt it would taste awesome, and I was not wrong. I have already used it in so many preparations, from a dahi dip and a sandwich spread to even adding a punch to a dry chicken roast. Thanks, Savlyene'

—Raghav K., Mumbai

# ORANGE

This citrus fruit has many nutrients, such as carbohydrates, vitamins and minerals, which maintain good health. However, it is their rich content of bioactive plant compounds such as phenols and carotenoids that make oranges nutrient-dense. Its phenolic compounds include flavonoids such as hesperidin and anthocyanins, both good antioxidants that improve heart health, reduce blood pressure and have a blood-thinning effect. Its carotenoid, beta-cryptoxanthin, is a precursor to vitamin A and gets converted into the active form in the body. The other carotenoid lycopene helps in the removal of free radicals. The citric-acid content of oranges prevents the formation of kidney stones. Although oranges do not have large amounts of iron, they help protect against anaemia. This is because their citric acid and vitamin C content help increase the rate of absorption of iron from the digestive tract. Eating whole oranges is always a better option.

*Pro-tip:* Every bit of this fruit, including the seeds, can be used effectively. The fruit can be eaten as is. The peel can be sun-dried after removing the spidery white pith. These peels can be used to make marmalades, compotes, chutneys, etc. The dried peel powder also finds use in facial scrubs and skin cleansers. Bits of the dried peel can be used to make orange oils and orange vinegar by simple infusion. They also go into the making of eco-friendly disinfectants and kitchen cleaners. The essential oils extracted from the seeds provide the orange flavour to food and can also be used to condition hair.

## BALSAMIC ORANGE AND ONION CHUTNEY

Cranberry sauce is a staple accompaniment to Thanksgiving turkey. However, if the Pilgrims had access to oranges, I am sure this orange chutney would be the star at the Thanksgiving table. This simple chutney can be used as a sweet and tart side dish. The flavours of oranges, onions and vinegar are just made to go together. Go easy on the paprika if you do not want too much heat in the chutney or if you are going to eat it with spicy crackers.—*Charlyene*

*Preparation time* 10 minutes
*Cooking time* 20 minutes
*Serves* 4

*Ingredients*

- 6 oranges, peeled
- 1 tbs orange zest (save the rest of the peels for marmalade, candied orange peel or facial scrub)
- 3 onions, finely chopped
- 6 cloves
- 1 tsp paprika powder
- 1 tbs olive oil
- 2 tbs balsamic vinegar
- 1 tsp coconut sugar
- A pinch of salt

*Method*

- Cut each peeled orange across the grain into 3 slices.
- Heat the oil in a pan and cook the onions until translucent.

- Add the cloves, paprika powder and orange zest, and place the orange slices on it.
- Cover and cook for 10 minutes.
- Add the balsamic vinegar, coconut sugar and salt.
- Cook until the onions have softened and melded completely with the oranges.
- Cool and transfer to an airtight glass container, making sure you draw out all the pan juices.
- A teaspoon of the chutney will pep up any bland meal.

*Nutritive value per serving*

- Energy: 99.17 kcal
- CHO: 14.08 gm
- Protein: 1.87 gm
- Fat: 3.93 gm
- Sodium: 5.42 mg
- Potassium: 83.5 mg
- Calcium: 14.63 mg
- Iron: 0.23 mg
- Vitamin A: 0.06 mcg
- Vitamin C: 2.51 mg

'My husband tried out this recipe. We found it different and interesting. I feel it would be better to not add all the orange zest in one go, but to add it slowly and keep tasting, because sometimes the zest can give a bitter aftertaste'

—Alexandra Barry, Toronto, Canada

## CITRUS BHAPA DOI

There are times when I get the chance to travel with Mum when she conducts the GHA health workshops in different cities. I have just one condition—that I travel for food! Kolkata is a city known for its kathi rolls, kosha mangsho, mutton chops, chingri malai curry, macher jhol, ghugni chaat, singaras, puchkas, luchi alu dom, jhal muri and sweets. I've tasted them all and nothing, absolutely nothing, compares to the sweet undertones of that steamed pudding called bhapa doi. Our citrus version is a dessert you should add to your repertoire of desserts.—*Savlyene*

*Preparation time* 20 minutes
*Cooking time* 20 minutes
*Serves* 4

*Ingredients*

- 400 gm yoghurt (hung for 20 minutes in a muslin cloth potli). Use the whey water to knead roti dough or add it to your soups and gravies
- 1 cup orange juice, freshly squeezed
- 2 star anise
- 1 tbs orange zest
- 2 tbs jaggery or coconut sugar
- 2 tbs milk powder
- 2 tbs cornflour

*Method*

- Bring the orange juice to a boil with the star anise and the coconut sugar, and cook until it reduces to half the amount.

- Remove from the stovetop and let the star anise continue infusing in it. Keep aside to cool.
- In the meantime, mix the hung curd with the milk powder and cornflour, and stir well.
- Add the orange zest and reduced orange juice, which should be cool. Keep the star anise aside to garnish later.
- Transfer the mixture into 4 oven-proof bowls or ramekins.
- You can steam the citrus bhapa doi in the pressure cooker or in the oven (in a water bath) or even in a steamer on the stovetop.
- Use a knife or a toothpick to check if it is done in about 20 minutes.
- Cool in the refrigerator.
- Serve garnished with a few broken bits of the citrusy star anise.

*Nutritive value per serving*

- Energy: 206.84 kcal
- CHO: 22.89 gm
- Protein: 9.92 gm
- Fat: 8.4 gm
- Sodium: 74.06 mg
- Potassium: 54.61 mg
- Calcium: 278.22 mg
- Iron: 1.09 mg
- Vitamin A: 6.18 mcg
- Vitamin C: 24.56 mg

'I was born and brought up in Kolkata, so bhapa doi brings back fond memories of my childhood. The citrus twist added a new element. I plan to try variations with sweet lime and other seasonal fruits. Thanks, Savlyene'

—Meher B., Vadodara

# PAPAYA

Christopher Columbus referred to papayas as the fruit of the angels. It is a great fruit option to include in your daily diet and makes for a healthy breakfast snack. Zeaxanthin, a powerful antioxidant found in papayas, filters out the harmful rays of blue light and may help ward off macular degeneration. Its other antioxidant, beta-carotene, improves heart health, prevents asthma, enhances vision and may reduce the risk of cancer. Its proteolytic enzyme, papain, enhances digestion and prevents constipation. Its choline content reduces chronic inflammation. Green tea and fermented papaya, when consumed during the same meal, will prevent spikes in blood sugar levels. Slices of this fruit and its peel act as skin cleansers. Papaya-leaf juice helps boost platelet count in patients with dengue. The tender young papaya leaves can be steamed and consumed like you would any green leafy vegetable. The flowers can also be stir-fried and made into a crunchy snack. The seeds aren't without health benefits either. They contain antioxidants and fibre, and may be beneficial in keeping the gut healthy, lowering blood pressure, and easing muscle cramps and menstrual pain.

*Pro-tip:* Pregnant women should avoid the consumption of large amounts of raw papaya because of its enzyme papain. This enzyme, active in raw papayas, can cause uterine contractions and the softening of the cervix, which might lead to a miscarriage. Papain is more concentrated in raw green papaya and papaya latex. As the fruit ripens, its concentration decreases.

## RAW PAPAYA SALAD

For a few years, when my hubby would make back-to-back trips to Thailand for work, our pantry would look like a mini Thai supermarket. Packets of Thai rice, khanom jeen or fermented noodles, galangal root, kaffir limes and leaves, lemongrass, shrimp paste, fish sauce, oyster sauce, sriracha sauce, tins of coconut milk, red and green Thai curry pastes, Panang curry paste, Massaman curry paste, tom yum soup base and more lined the kitchen shelves. Could you blame my kids for thinking they were Thai? Anyway, here is a salad I quickly make to remind them of those days.—*Charmaine*

*Preparation time* 20 minutes
*Cooking time* 0 minutes
*Serves* 4

*Ingredients*

- 300 gm raw green papaya, shredded, with the inner peel
- 100 gm bean sprouts
- 1 large onion, sliced
- 50 gm carrots, shredded, with the peel
- 1/2 red bell pepper, finely sliced, with the peel and seeds
- 25 fresh mint leaves, with the stalks
- 4 tsp garlic, minced
- 1/2 tsp red chilli paste
- 1 tbs fish sauce or soya sauce (optional)
- 2 tbs sesame oil
- 4 tbs lime juice
- 1 tbs coconut sugar

## Method

- Put the ingredients for the Thai dressing (minced garlic, red chilli paste, soya/fish sauce, sesame oil, lime juice and coconut juice) in a tightly screwed glass bottle. Shake well to mix and set aside in the refrigerator.
- Toss the grated papaya and the salad veggies together in a large bowl.
- When ready to serve, add the dressing and give it a quick toss.
- Serve with sticky rice or as a side dish, garnished with roasted peanuts (optional).

## Nutritive value per serving

- Energy: 95.81 kcal
- CHO: 11.66 gm
- Protein: 2.82 gm
- Fat: 4.21 gm
- Sodium: 392.47 mg
- Potassium: 322.52 mg
- Calcium: 49.00 mg
- Iron: 0.74 mg
- Vitamin A: 154.06 mcg
- Vitamin C: 42.11 mg

'Refreshing, energizing and Thai-memory-evoking. Love it! I can eat it all'

—Shubham Kotnis, Pune

## SANTULA

Odisha, the city of Lord Jagannath, known for the Sun temple, the Jagannath temple, the Khandagiri caves, the Puri light house and the Konark beach, for starters, is also a foodies' paradise. From chenna poda (Odisha's cheesecake) to kanika (sweet pulao), rasabali (fried puris soaked in sweet, thickened milk), macha ghanta (fried-fish-head curry), chingdi malai (creamy prawn curry) to gupchup (pani puri), once you've feasted on all these delights, your gut will long for santula, a flavourful vegetable stew that is light and easy to digest. Try it soon.—*Charlyene*

*Preparation time* 10 minutes
*Cooking time* 25 minutes
*Serves* 4

*Ingredients*

- 150 gm raw papaya, cubed, with the inner peel
- 150 gm potato, cubed, with the peel
- 100 gm small brinjals, cubed, with the peel
- 2 onions, finely chopped
- 2 tsp ginger-garlic paste, home-made
- 1 tsp green chilli paste
- 1 tsp turmeric powder
- 1/4 tsp pepper powder
- 2 tsp mustard seeds
- 1/4 tsp asafoetida
- 2 tbs mustard oil
- 1 cup milk
- Salt to taste

*Method*

♦ Pressure-cook the cubes of papaya, potato and brinjal in 2 cups water, with some salt to taste.
♦ Heat oil in a pan and temper the mustard seeds and asafoetida.
♦ Sauté the chopped onions, along with the ginger-garlic and green-chilli paste, turmeric and pepper powders.
♦ Cook it for 5 minutes with some of the water from the cooked vegetables.
♦ When you get a thick gravy, add the pressure-cooked vegetables and the milk.
♦ Allow to simmer for 5 minutes.
♦ Add salt to taste.
♦ Serve hot.

*Nutritive value per serving*

♦ Energy: 148.63 kcal
♦ CHO: 12.84 gm
♦ Protein: 2.83 gm
♦ Fat: 9.55 gm
♦ Sodium: 16.24 mg
♦ Potassium: 440.76 mg
♦ Calcium: 66.45 mg
♦ Iron: 1.11 mg
♦ Vitamin A: 19.1 mcg
♦ Vitamin C: 20.24 mg

'I got my cook to make this for me. Very nice and light, though I love the salad more. Thank you, Charlyene'

—Shubham Kotnis, Pune

# PEAR

The Greek poet Homer called pears 'a gift from the gods'. At approximately 100 calories per medium-sized fruit, pears are a veritable storehouse of nutrients. They help prevent osteoporosis, improve energy levels, enhance digestion and facilitate proper bowel movement, all because of their dietary fibre, copper, potassium, iron, magnesium, and vitamins K and C content. Delicious when eaten ripe, they make for a healthy addition to fruit salads, pies, custards, cobblers, crumbles, chutneys, purees, juices and smoothies. Pears are so easy to digest that even babies can safely consume pureed pears. You will rarely get an upset stomach after eating pears, because their low acid level is gentle on the digestive system. Pear allergies are very rare. Be careful not to eat too many, though—they can lead to gas. You may also need to limit your pear intake if you have IBS. This is because of their higher fructose content, as compared to their glucose content.

*Pro-tip:* Pears ripen from the inside out. So a pear that looks perfect from the outside can be mushy on the inside. While buying pears, choose fruits without blemishes and dark spots. A ripe pear will be slightly soft near the stem area. If they are soft elsewhere, it is an indication that they are overripe. Pears give out ethylene gas, so be careful if you are storing them with other fruit. They will hasten the speed of ripening of those fruits and cause early rotting.

## PEAR FRANGIPANE TART

I wish every day was pie day or baking day, because I love to bake. Frangipane is a sweet filling for a pie or a tart that is normally made from ground almonds. It is named after the sixteenth-century Italian nobleman Marquis Muzio Frangipani, who invented a bitter almond fragrance. I have cut down on the number of almonds used, and incorporated cucumber and watermelon seeds in this recipe. Be sure to use the creamy white seeds without the outer hard peel. This tart looks prettier when topped with a pear fan.—*Savlyene*

*Preparation time* 1 hour, 10 minutes, plus 2 hours for pie-crust-resting time
*Baking time* 40 minutes
*Serves* 8

*Ingredients*

- 8-inch pie crust, blind-baked (use half the recipe of the apple pie crust on p. 240, as this tart will not have a pie-crust topping)
- 3 pears, with the peels (finely chop 2-1/2 pears and cut 1/2 pear into a fan to place on top of the tart)
- 50 gm almond meal
- 30 gm cucumber or watermelon seeds, peeled and coarsely ground
- 1 tbs oat flour
- 1 tbs wholewheat flour
- 2 eggs, or 2 tbs flax meal with 6 tbs water
- 100 gm coconut sugar
- 50 gm butter

- 50 ml vegetable oil
- 1 tsp vanilla extract

## Method

- Preheat the oven to 180 degrees.
- Cream the butter, oil and coconut sugar until light and fluffy.
- Add the eggs or flax eggs, and continue to whisk until well mixed.
- Add the almond meal, coarsely ground cucumber or watermelon seeds, oat flour, wheat flour and vanilla extract, and mix thoroughly.
- Add 2-1/2 finely chopped pears.
- If the batter is too thick, thin it with some milk.
- Put the 8-inch, previously blind-baked pie crust into the pie dish.
- Pour the frangipane batter into this.
- Gently place the pear fan at the centre.
- Bake for 35–40 minutes or until an inserted toothpick comes out clean.
- Serve warm.

## Nutritive value per serving

- Energy: 458.45 kcal
- CHO: 34.15 gm
- Protein: 7.05 gm
- Fat: 32.67 gm
- Sodium: 199.18 mg
- Potassium: 237.75 mg
- Calcium: 83.59 mg

- Iron: 2.06 mg
- Vitamin A: 17.88 mcg
- Vitamin C: 1.07 mg

---

'Decadently delicious, quick to make and looks so pretty when baked. I'm sharing this as my Instagram story today. Loved that the seeds blended so well with the almonds. Now all my friends will be jealous as hell that I got to make and eat this in quarantine time'

—Giselle Baretto, Mumbai

---

## POACHED PEARS

Pears are generally poached in wine. I've used beet juice instead. I just love the way the agave nectar, beet juice and ginger juice in this recipe combine to provide such an intriguing flavour to the pears. The citrus zest, cinnamon and star anise all add a tangy-spicy zing, and the poaching liquid gives the pears a striking burgundy hue. This dessert looks stunning and tastes so good.—*Charlyene*

*Preparation time* 10 minutes
*Cooking time* 30 minutes
*Serves* 4

*Ingredients*

- 4 pears (remove the peel and use in a chutney or a scrub)
- 2 cups beetroot juice
- 4 tbs ginger juice

- 4 tbs agave nectar or coconut sugar
- 1 tsp orange zest
- 1 tsp lime zest
- 2-inch stick of cinnamon
- 4 star anise

## Method

- Preheat the oven to 175 degrees.
- Mix the beet juice, ginger juice, agave nectar or coconut sugar with the orange and lime zest.
- Add 1 cup warm water and stir well.
- Take a small, deep baking dish in which the 4 pears will just fit.
- Place the 4 pears in the baking dish and add the poaching liquid.
- Add the star anise and cinnamon.
- The pears should be completely submerged in the poaching liquid, else add some more water to cover them.
- Cover the dish with parchment or butter paper, allowing the stems of the pears to pierce the paper.
- Cook for 25–30 minutes or until a knife slides out clean.
- Serve warm or cold.

## Nutritive value per serving

- Energy: 143.97 kcal
- CHO: 31.33 gm
- Protein: 2.66 gm
- Fat: 0.89 gm
- Sodium: 74.35 mg
- Potassium: 558.4 mg

- Calcium: 122.79 mg
- Iron: 2.22 mg
- Vitamin A: 5.76 mcg
- Vitamin C: 8.23 mg

'Years ago in catering college, I had made pears poached in red wine. This recipe took me back to that time. Since this has beet juice instead of wine, I could safely offer it to my two young grandsons. The poaching liquid and sauce leftover in the pan can be used separately on plain vanilla sponge cake'

—Vrinda Kolhatkar, Goa

# STRAWBERRY

What is the first thing that comes to mind when you see the silhouette of a strawberry? A mini heart! An omen of its heart-protective benefits. A member of the rose family, strawberries are not actually fruits or even berries, for that matter. They are actually the enlarged receptacle of a flower. Not only are they sweet and delicious, but are also filled with nutrients. Strawberries are a low-calorie food, packed with vitamins A and C and folate, minerals such as manganese and potassium, fibre, anthocyanin and polyphenol antioxidants, and are low in sodium and fat-free. They have been included as one of the top ten superfoods for a diabetic meal plan. Adding them to your meal plan whenever they are in season will help you stave off neurodegeneration and dementia in old age.

*Pro-tip:* Blend 2 tablespoons of pureed strawberries with a tablespoon of fresh cream if you have dry skin or a tablespoon of yoghurt if you have oily skin. Add a teaspoon of honey, a few drops of lime juice and 1/4 teaspoon lime zest. Apply this on you face and let it stay on for 15 minutes. Rinse off with cold water. It promotes blemish-free glowing skin.

## STRAWBERRY GRAPE AND CHIA SPREAD

This spread is extremely easy to make and a good way to use up fruits that are just lying around in the fruit basket. You do not need to limit to just grapes. We have made strawberry chia spreads with pears, peaches, apples, papayas and even avocado. The trick is to add more chia seeds if you feel it has not set to the level you would like. You may also choose to sweeten it with honey, agave nectar or date syrup. The sweetness in the recipe comes from natural fruit sugars and we chose to let it stay less sweet because we were going to serve it with biscotti.—*Charlyene*

*Preparation time* 15–20 minutes
*Cooking time* 0 minutes
*Serves* 10

*Ingredients*

- 200 gm strawberries
- 100 gm black grapes, seedless
- 4 tbs chia seeds

*Method*

- Hull and chop the strawberries.
- In a blender or a food processor, blend the chopped strawberries with the seedless black grapes.
- Add the chia seeds and mix well. Set aside.
- Within 15 minutes the chia seeds will swell and thicken the spread. If not, add more chia seeds.
- Transfer to a clean glass bottle and refrigerate.
- Will keep well under refrigeration for a week.

*Nutritive value per serving*

- Energy: 43.19 kcal
- CHO: 5.19 gm
- Protein: 1.13 gm
- Fat: 1.99 gm

- Sodium: 1.39 mg
- Potassium: 75.92 mg
- Calcium: 42.79 mg
- Iron: 0.57 mg
- Vitamin A: 0.41 mcg
- Vitamin C: 12.41 mg

'Loved the way it set. Didn't need to add more chia seeds. If eaten with a sweet biscuit, it doesn't need any additional sweetener, but I feel it would need more sweetness if you served it on a non-sweet slice of bread or toast. Excellent for diabetics too'

—Shobha Jain, Kuwait

## STRAWBERRY HUMMUS

When Mediterranean is on your mind and fresh Mahabaleshwar strawberries are poking out from your fruit tray, you do what any innovative, hungry person doing research for a cookbook does—you make strawberry hummus! Then you make it once more. Repeat again and again. Tweak the ratios of vinegar to agave nectar, etc., and finally come up with a dish that is fit to be presented in this cookbook.—*Savlyene*

*Preparation time* 15 minutes
*Cooking time* 0 minutes
*Serves* 10

*Ingredients*

- 250 gm chickpeas, boiled (save the cooking liquid for soups, etc., or for aqua faba)

- 250 gm fresh strawberries, hulled
- 2 tbs peanut butter
- 2 tbs agave nectar or honey
- 1/2 tsp apple cider vinegar
- 1 tsp ginger, freshly grated, with the peel
- 10 mint leaves, with the stalks

*Method*

- Put all the ingredients into a blender or a food processor, reserving 2 or 3 mint leaves for garnishing.
- Blend until smooth and creamy.
- Store in a clean glass jar in the refrigerator for 1 week.
- Serve with crackers, or wholewheat or oat rusks.

*Nutritive value per serving*

- Energy: 48.34 kcal
- CHO: 1.47 gm
- Protein: 4.57 gm
- Fat: 2.7 gm
- Sodium: 15.25 mg
- Potassium: 82.23 mg
- Calcium: 14.63 mg
- Iron: 0.89 mg
- Vitamin A: 3.23 mcg
- Vitamin C: 13.33 mg

'We love Middle Eastern food and dips. Chickpea hummus is our favourite. This is a nice twist. Since I did not have peanut butter, I made some at home. The small amount of apple cider vinegar made so much difference to this dish. Excellent idea, GHA!'

—Pooja D., Ahmedabad

# WATERMELON

Along with mangoes, this fruit, with its dark green exterior and deep red flesh, is synonymous with summer. The best time to eat it or drink its juice is in summer, when it is at its sweetest, when it effectively hydrates, detoxifies and cleanses the body on a cellular level. It is rich in fibre, choline, vitamins A and C, and lycopene, beta-carotene, lutein and zeaxanthin. These are excellent for providing protection from lung, mouth, pancreatic, breast, prostate, endometrial and colon cancers, reducing the risk of developing asthma and inflammation, flushing out edema, aiding in weight loss, improving vision, reducing blood pressure, alleviating depression, boosting the immune system, preventing insomnia, curbing sugar cravings, preventing constipation and improving memory. A glass of watermelon juice after a strenuous workout will ease muscle soreness and boost muscle-recovery time.

*Pro-tip:* Do not discard the rind and seeds. The light green inner rind of the watermelon is one of the best sources of chlorophyll. It can be grated and used in a salad or a dip, or it can be juiced for a delicious, healing drink. Watermelon seeds have an amazing effect on the nervous system, aiding in relaxing the body and lowering blood pressure. They contain iron, zinc and protein. Toast them and add to your salad, trail mixes, chutneys, raitas, etc.

## WATERMELON RIND SABJI

Whenever we buy watermelon, we make the most use of it. The sweet, red flesh is cut into cubes and eaten either as is, tossed into a salad or made into a cooling drink. We have even made chilled watermelon soups similar to tomato and cucumber gazpacho! The seeds are washed, sun-dried, oven-roasted and meticulously shelled, then tossed into a spice mix and toasted. What do we do with the whitish-green rind just below the dark green outer peel? Make sabji, of course!—*Savlyene*

*Preparation time* 10 minutes
*Cooking time* 10 minutes
*Serves* 4

*Ingredients*

- 4 cups watermelon rind, cubed (discard the dark green outer peel and use the whitish-green inner layer)
- 2 onions, finely chopped
- 2 tbs east Indian bottle masala (or 2 tbs mix of garam masala powder, turmeric powder, pepper powder, cumin powder, red chilli powder and coriander powder)
- 1 tsp saunf
- 1 tsp kalonji
- 2 tsp ginger-garlic paste, home-made
- 1 tbs vegetable oil
- 1 tbs coriander, freshly chopped
- 3 tbs lime juice
- Salt to taste

*Method*

◆ Heat oil in a pan and temper the saunf and kalonji.
◆ Add the chopped onions and sauté until translucent.
◆ Add the ginger-garlic paste and the east Indian bottle masala or the mix of spice powders.
◆ Cook for 1 minute, before adding the cubed watermelon rind.
◆ Add 1 cup warm water and cook for another 5 minutes.
◆ Add salt to taste and remove from the stovetop.
◆ Just before serving, add the chopped coriander and lemon juice.
◆ Serve hot with chapatis or parathas.

*Nutritive value per serving*

◆ Energy: 106.66 kcal
◆ CHO: 13.5 gm
◆ Protein: 2.32 gm
◆ Fat: 4.82 gm
◆ Sodium: 8.06 mg
◆ Potassium: 260.77 mg
◆ Calcium: 59.31 mg
◆ Iron: 22.45 mg
◆ Vitamin A: 23.85 mcg
◆ Vitamin C: 4.47 mg

'My sister-in-law just sent me the east Indian bottle masala, which came in really handy for this recipe. I love using every bit of food and have made #zeroediblefoodwaste my mantra. In the past, I had used watermelon rind in theplas and raitas, but not as sabji. Tastes like any gourd sabji. Hope readers stop wasting food peels, etc. Such a good idea'

—Suzie Thomas, Doha

## WATERMELON AND FETA SALAD

'It takes four men to dress a salad: a wise man for the salt, a mad man for the pepper, a miser for the vinegar and a spendthrift for the oil,' goes an anonymous saying. Our watermelon and feta salad has a unique flavour from the garlicky dressing and a lovely texture from the walnuts and figs. It is cool, refreshing, healthy and also fuss-free. —*Charlyene*

*Preparation time* 10 minutes
*Cooking time* 0 minutes
*Serves* 4

*Ingredients*

- 500 gm watermelon cubes, deseeded
- 200 gm feta cheese, tofu or paneer, crumbled
- 2 tbs walnuts, chopped
- 2 tbs figs, chopped, fresh or dried

*For the dressing*

- 4 tbs extra-virgin olive oil
- 4 tbs lime juice
- 1 tbs apple cider vinegar
- 1 tsp pepper, freshly ground
- 1 tsp garlic, minced
- Salt to taste

*Method*

- In a small bowl, whisk together extra-virgin olive oil, lime juice, vinegar, pepper and minced garlic.
- Add salt to taste and refrigerate.
- In a large salad bowl, combine the watermelon cubes, the crumbled feta, tofu or paneer, the chopped walnuts and the chopped figs.
- Cover and refrigerate.
- When ready to serve, gently drizzle the dressing over the salad.
- Serve chilled.

*Nutritive value per serving*

- Energy: 372.24 kcal
- CHO: 13.95 gm
- Protein: 9.54 gm
- Fat: 30.92 gm
- Sodium: 463.26 mg
- Potassium: 249.47 mg
- Calcium: 290.59 mg
- Iron: 1.28 mg

- ◆   Vitamin A: 71.2 mcg
- ◆   Vitamin C: 9.89 mg

'Sweet, salty, tangy and refreshing, this salad was a delight to our taste buds. I added more garlic because we always use more than what a recipe calls for. It keeps our cholesterol in check'

—Suzie Thomas, Doha

# MILK, MILK PRODUCTS

Despite being an extremely popular beverage, milk is one of the most controversial foods available. Whole milk, cow's milk, organic cow's milk, goat's milk, skimmed milk, A2 milk, lactose-free milk, flavoured milk—the list will leave you confused. Adding to the confusion are the thousands of debates on the health benefits and disadvantages of drinking milk, on whether humans should be drinking animal milk at all, on whether drinking large amounts of milk is linked to prostate and colorectal cancers, on whether women drinking cow's milk are at greater risk of bone fractures and death—the evidence is conflicting and the debates continue. Just as you read a scientific report on the health benefits of drinking milk, you get another report confirming the dangers of drinking it. The jury is still out, but if you do want to drink milk, please err on the side of caution and limit your intake to moderate amounts and choose organic alternatives over standard types of milk.

Milk alternatives are plant-based substitutes for animal milk. They may be produced from plant sources like oats, soy, hemp, rice, almonds, cashews and coconut. They may be called nut beverages or grain beverages or mylks to avoid confusion with regular milk. Irrespective of what they are called, these blended beverages can be a healthy addition to a balanced diet.

# MILK

Milk from bovine animals has a wide variety of nutrients, from protein and calcium to B-complex vitamins. Scientific studies show that while there should be concerns about the amount of hormones and antibiotics in cow's milk, they are still a small risk to overall human health. Milk is a good source of protein. The insoluble protein casein, which forms the bulk of milk proteins, helps in the absorption of calcium and phosphorus. Milk may not be the only source of calcium but it ranks as one of the best sources. Vitamin D is needed for your body to absorb the calcium available in milk. So opt to eat foods such as oily fish, liver, butter, mushrooms and egg yolks, which are precursors to vitamin D, or choose a vitamin D-fortified milk. The vitamin B12 in milk is an essential nutrient. It is only found in foods of animal origin, and milk is the only animal-origin food that vegetarians consume. While whole milk has nearly 8 grams of saturated fat, the skimmed or fat-free version has less than 1 gram fat. The combination of calcium, magnesium and potassium in milk is responsible for the decrease in hypertension.

Dairy cows are treated with hormones to increase milk production. This recombinant bovine growth hormone, or RBGH, can remain in milk but should not be of concern, as it cannot stay active in the human body. However, there is a risk of breast, prostate and colorectal cancers from the insulin-like growth factor-1, or IGF-1, hormone. All milk has to be tested and milk that has antibiotics in it has to be discarded and not used for human consumption, else it might lead to new bacteria that are resistant to antibiotics.

*Pro-tip:* Lactose, the carbohydrate sugar present in milk, requires the enzyme lactase for its digestion. In the absence of this enzyme, lactose does not get fully absorbed and bacteria in the colon start fermenting it, leading to gas, bloating, cramps, diarrhoea, nausea and vomiting. Milk allergies in young children can be attributed to the proteins in milk. People with lactose intolerance or those with milk allergies should opt for plant-based milks, or mylks, as mentioned earlier.

## CHOCOLATE SOIL POTS

'Hey, Mom, there is mint growing out of our dessert pots!' That is exactly the reaction I got from my girls the first time I made this dessert. I had refrigerated a tray of the pots to take to a potluck dinner and had promised to leave some for them. Both girls were thrilled to see the chocolate soil with the 'mini mint plants'! Ragi and carob chips give the base its dense chocolate colour and taste, while the 'soil' is a mix of almond meal, coarsely ground pumpkin seeds and cocoa powder.—*Charmaine*

*Preparation time* 10 minutes
*Cooking time* 20 minutes
*Serves* 8

*Ingredients*

*For the base*

♦   600 ml milk

- 150 gm finger millet (ragi) powder
- 150 gm carob chips or dark chocolate

*For the chocolate soil*

- 50 gm almonds, ground
- 50 gm pumpkin seeds, ground
- 50 gm cocoa powder
- A few sprigs of fresh mint

*Method*

- Mix the chocolate-soil ingredients well and set aside.
- Bring the milk to a gentle boil.
- Add the finger millet powder and keep stirring to mix thoroughly.
- Reduce the heat and simmer until the milk thickens, for 12–15 minutes.
- Remove from the stovetop and quickly add the carob chips or chopped dark chocolate.
- Stir until it dissolves.
- If you want it sweeter, you can add some agave nectar or jaggery sugar.
- Fill 8 shot glasses, pots or small dessert bowls with this mixture.
- Top with the chocolate soil.
- Stick some mint into each portion and refrigerate for a few hours to set it.
- Serve cold.

*Nutritive value per serving*

- Energy: 323.74 kcal
- CHO: 36.95 gm

- Protein: 9.29 gm
- Fat: 15.42 gm
- Sodium: 30.25 mg
- Potassium: 213 mg
- Calcium: 171.13 mg
- Iron: 1.57 mg
- Vitamin A: 1.75 mcg
- Vitamin C: 1.55 mg

> 'This was my first time making chocolate pots, and that, too, with ragi flour. It was very easy to make, but I did take some time stirring the ragi flour in so it did not turn out lumpy. The carob chips were a lovely addition. The pumpkin seeds in the chocolate soil were very nice too. I used tiny earthen pots to set the dessert and it really looked like mint pots'
>
> —Seema Rakesh Shah, Chicago, the US

## SAGO BERRY KHEER

On a trip to Leh, in Ladakh, we tried some of the locally available dried fruit, got hooked to their taste, bought some and now get them delivered to Mumbai. So there is always a stock of some Ladakhi sweet dried apricot, sea buckthorn or apricot kernels that come in handy when we are trying to add nutritive value and taste to our meals. This lot of berries added the element of sweetness, while the sweet apricot kernels added the pleasant crunch to this sago kheer.—*Charmaine*

*Preparation time* 10 minutes
*Cooking time* 25 minutes
*Serves* 4

*Ingredients*

- 500 ml cow's milk
- 100 ml coconut milk (save the coconut meal for a chutney or a facial scrub)
- 200 gm sago, soaked overnight
- 100 gm coconut sugar
- 100 gm blackberries
- 100 gm sweet apricot kernels (not the bitter ones)

*Method*

- Drain the water from the soaked sago and set aside.
- Bring the milk to a boil, add the soaked sago and 150 ml water.
- Allow it to cook, stirring regularly.
- The sago pearls will become translucent once they are cooked.
- Remove from the stovetop and add the coconut milk and coconut sugar.
- Mix well.
- Pour into serving bowls and top with the blackberries and the sweet apricot kernels.
- Alternatively, you can add the dried fruit to the sago mixture, stir it well and then portion out.
- Serve warm or cold.

*Nutritive value per serving*

- Energy: 483.62 kcal
- CHO: 73.32 gm

- Protein: 7.31 gm
- Fat: 17.9 gm
- Sodium: 69.81 mg
- Potassium: 501.12 mg
- Calcium: 280.95 mg
- Iron: 27.92 mg
- Vitamin A: 5.02 mcg
- Vitamin C: 7.46 mg

'The combination of coconut milk and sabudana is my favourite, because of my Karwari roots. I replaced the blackberries with black raisins, though. I preferred this kheer served warm but my daughter loved it chilled'

—Sushma Parab, Delhi

# CHEESE

A textbook definition of a 'whole food' is one that is good for you as long as you do not overdo its consumption. Cheese falls into the category of a 'whole food'. It is a good source of calcium, protein, fat, vitamins A, B2 and B12, phosphorus and zinc. This combination of nutrients can keep the teeth cavity-free for a longer time. High-fat cheese such as Brie and Cheddar have conjugated linoleic acid (CLA), which may prevent heart disease. Fermented cheese may help the heart function better. Parmesan cheese is low in lactose and can be tolerated by people with lactose intolerance. Since cheese is a calorie-dense food and some varieties are high in sodium, please limit your intake of this 'whole food'. Snacking occasionally on a small cube of cheese or adding a few sprinkles of it on to your veggies, soups or salads may not cause health issues and, instead, be beneficial.

*Pro-tip:*

- Mozzarella is a soft, white cheese with lesser sodium and calories.
- Parmesan is a hard, aged cheese rich in calcium.
- Cheddar is a semi-hard cheese high in vitamin K.
- Swiss cheese is a semi-hard cheese lower in sodium and fat.
- Feta from sheep or goat milk is high in sodium but low in calories.

- Goat cheese or chevre is a tangy, soft cheese with more MCT fatty acids.
- Cottage cheese is higher in protein.
- Ricotta is a lighter version of cottage cheese.
- Blue cheese, with its bluish-grey veins, has the highest amount of calcium.

## HASSELBACK POTATOES

A fancy variation of the simple baked potato, Hasselback potatoes may look extremely difficult to make, but looks can be deceptive. Ha ha! The trick to getting that perfectly fanned-out baked potato is in the chopping—or, rather, in the placing of two wooden pencils, previously cleaned, of course, on either side of the potato you are chopping. Then the chopping continues in regular intervals. The pencils will prevent you from accidentally chopping too far and ruining the potato.

The end result is a potato that is golden, crisp outside and soft, creamy and flavoursome inside.—*Charlyene*

*Preparation time* 10 minutes
*Cooking time* 30 minutes
*Serves* 4

*Ingredients*

- 4 large potatoes, with the peel (wash thoroughly to remove any soil or dirt, and dry with a kitchen towel)
- 2 tbs olive oil
- 2 spring onions, finely chopped (keep the chopped green stalks separately for the garnish)
- 2 tsp garlic powder or 3 tsp fresh garlic, minced

- 1 tsp paprika powder
- 1/2 tsp nutmeg, freshly ground
- 1 tsp lime zest
- 1 tsp pepper, freshly ground
- 4 tbs Cheddar cheese, grated (you can opt to use half the amount as well)
- Salt to taste

## Method

- Preheat the oven to 200 degrees.
- Place each potato lengthwise between two clean wooden pencils and slit the potatoes carefully at regular 1/4-inch intervals. The pencils will ensure that one side of the potato stays intact and that your knife does not cut through the potatoes.
- Place the potatoes, cut side up, on a greased baking tray.
- Drizzle the olive oil and add salt.
- Bake for about 20 minutes until the cut potato 'fans' just begin opening up.
- In a bowl, mix the finely chopped spring onions with the garlic powder or minced garlic, the paprika powder, the freshly ground nutmeg, the freshly ground pepper, the lime zest and a little more salt.
- Sprinkle the seasoning mix liberally on and in between the cuts of each potato.
- Top with 1 tablespoon of grated cheese per potato.
- Grill for 10 minutes or until golden and crisp.
- Garnish with the reserved chopped green stalks of the spring onions (optional).
- Serve hot.

*Nutritive value per serving*

- ✦  Energy: 205.47 kcal
- ✦  CHO: 16.99 gm
- ✦  Protein: 5.96 gm
- ✦  Fat: 12.63 gm
- ✦  Sodium: 103.3 mg
- ✦  Potassium: 614.78 mg
- ✦  Calcium: 135.66 mg
- ✦  Iron: 1.23 mg
- ✦  Vitamin A: 20.18 mcg
- ✦  Vitamin C: 27.02 mg

'I had been drooling over these potatoes every time I saw their pics on Instagram. When Charlyene sent me this recipe for the GHA trial, what I appreciated was the tip to use two pencils to help cut the potatoes. In my overenthusiasm, I used a lot more cheese, didn't grate it but used slices. Fantastic recipe. Thanks, Charlyene'

—Sakshi Arora, Madhya Pradesh

## TWICE-BAKED TOMATOES

The French classic uses breadcrumbs, garlic and lots of cheese. For our GHA twist on the French Provencal tomatoes, we stuff the tomato hollows with leftover rice, veggies and herbs, top it with a nut, seed and cheese crumb, and bake it until the top is a gratinated golden-brown. This side dish pairs with any main dish, and these are times when we make this the main dish served with a salad on the side.—*Savlyene*

*Preparation time* 20 minutes
*Cooking time* 15 minutes
*Serves* 4

## Ingredients

- 4 large, firm red tomatoes, with the peels and seeds
- 1 cup leftover cooked rice
- 4 tbs veggies such as corn, carrots, beans, peas, etc., boiled
- 1/2 tsp pepper powder
- 1/2 tsp paprika powder
- 2 tbs basil leaves, chopped
- 2 tbs onions, chopped
- 2 tsp garlic, minced
- 2 tbs vegetable oil
- Salt to taste

## For the crust

- 1 tbs almond meal
- 1 tbs pumpkin seeds, coarsely ground
- 2 tbs Cheddar or Parmesan cheese, grated

## Method

- Mix the crust ingredients and set aside.
- Cut the top end of each tomato (save the tops and finely chop them).
- Scoop out the inner pulp and seeds, and set aside along with the finely chopped tops of the tomatoes.
- Heat the oven to 180 degrees.

- Smear a little oil on the outer side of each tomato hollow and bake for 5 minutes.
- Keep warm in the oven.
- In the meantime, heat the oil in a pan and cook the onions.
- Add the garlic, cook for 2 minutes and add the tomato pulp seeds and finely chopped tomato tops. Cook for 2 minutes and add the basil, pepper and paprika.
- Add the veggies, the cooked rice, some salt to taste and mix well.
- Remove the warm tomato hollows from the oven and stuff the rice filling into each one.
- Top with the crust mixture.
- Bake for 5 minutes.
- Then grill for another 5 minutes or until the crust is golden brown and the cheese has melted.
- Serve hot.

*Nutritive value per serving*

- Energy: 217.37 kcal
- CHO: 17.14 gm
- Protein: 6.22 gm
- Fat: 13.77 gm
- Sodium: 58.51 mg
- Potassium: 231.13 mg
- Calcium: 99.69 mg
- Iron: 1.07 mg
- Vitamin A: 177.32 mcg
- Vitamin C: 19.88 mg

'I prepared two lots of this recipe. I added leftover rice to the filling of the second lot. Both variations earned me praise and I thank the GHA team for asking me to try out the recipe'

—Atul Sen, Delhi

# PANEER

This non-fermented, non-melting, mild-flavoured cheese, which finds its origins in the Persian 'panir', is an important part of Indian cuisine. Whether it is 'topli' paneer, made at home, purchased from the corner dairy or the commercial variety that is store-bought, paneer is the highlight of vegetarian meals. It is made by curdling boiling-hot milk using lime juice, sour yoghurt, vinegar or citric acid. The resulting curd is then separated from the liquid whey protein by using a muslin cloth. It is then pressed down with a weighted object for a couple of hours to obtain a slab of paneer. As a good source of protein for vegetarians, paneer contains nine essential amino acids. Its healthy MUFA fats help reduce LDL cholesterol when eaten in moderation in the raw form or when cooked in a gravy— but not when fried. As with other milk products, paneer is also a rich source of the vitamins and minerals needed for muscle and bone health—vitamin D, magnesium, calcium and phosphorus. It is a good protein source for diabetics. If small amounts of paneer are eaten at the start of a meal, the proteins in paneer prevent blood sugar spikes and promote a slow release of energy, thereby keeping the patient full for a longer period of time. Paneer is also low in the milk sugar lactose, so it can be eaten by people with lactose intolerance.

*Pro-tip:* Paneer has a high moisture and low sodium content, which makes it extremely perishable. If you want to make it at home, you must remember that it will stay fresh in your refrigerator for a maximum of four days. So make paneer in small amounts and more frequently.

## KASHMIRI LYODUR CHAMAN

Wazwan is a multicourse meal in Kashmir filled with gastronomical delights served in a *traem* or a copper platter. Almost all these dishes are meat-based, from the juicy kebabs to the tabak maaz, aab gosht, rogan josh, methi maaz, nate yakhni, goshtaba and rista. They have highly appealing flavour, texture and palatability. Holding its own when placed with these meaty heavyweights is the Kashmiri lyodur chaman, a creamy, aromatic fennel-, turmeric- and cardamom-infused yellow paneer gravy, cooked in milk. It is the favourite dish of Kashmiri Pandits. Try it once—it might just make you convert to vegetarianism!—*Savlyene*

*Preparation time* 10 minutes
*Cooking time* 20 minutes
*Serves* 4

*Ingredients*

- 300 gm paneer cubes
- 2 cups yoghurt, whisked
- 4 Kashmiri red chillies, dried
- 1 tsp turmeric powder
- 1 tsp white pepper powder
- 1 tsp cardamom powder
- 1 tbs fennel powder
- 1/4 tsp ginger powder, dried
- 1/4 tsp asafoetida powder

- 1 tbs vegetable oil (preferably mustard oil)
- 1 tbs fresh cream (optional)
- Salt to taste

## Method

- Heat the mustard oil in a pan until it reaches smoking point.
- Switch off flame and let the oil cool slightly.
- A few minutes later, while the oil is still warm, add the Kashmiri chillies, asafoetida, ginger powder, fennel powder, cardamom powder, white pepper powder and turmeric powder.
- Turn the flame back on and cook for only a few seconds so that the spices do not burn.
- Add the whisked yoghurt and stir continuously, so that it does not split or curdle on a low flame.
- Once it comes to a gentle boil, add the paneer cubes and stir well.
- Cook for 5 minutes on low flame.
- Add salt to taste. Mix well and cook for another 2 minutes on low flame.
- Ladle out on to a serving bowl and garnish with a swirl of fresh cream (optional).
- Serve hot with rotis or rice.

## Nutritive value per serving

- Energy: 317.25 kcal
- CHO: 17.5 gm
- Protein: 16.97 gm
- Fat: 19.93 gm

- Sodium: 68.52 mg
- Potassium: 124.27 mg
- Calcium: 526.92 mg
- Iron: 2.14 mg
- Vitamin A: 6.64 mcg
- Vitamin C: 0.29 mg

'Soft, creamy and delicious, this lyodur chaman tasted great with roomali roti. You have to take care while adding the dahi—stir carefully on a low flame and the gravy will not curdle, just as when making a kadhi. This is yummy and looks like a royal dish from Kashmir. I will try it once again with jeera pulao'

—Aruna Mehta, Mumbai

## LEHSUNI PANEER SAAGWALA

This one is for those times when you have an odd assortment of dark green leafy veggies—a small bunch of fenugreek leaves, a couple of spinach leaves, half a bunch of amaranth leaves, some fresh coriander, some fresh mint, some leftover arugula, a few kale leaves—and not even one of these veggies is sufficient to make a dish on its own. You cannot let them go to waste, so you innovate. When cooked with love, this results in a dish so flavoursome that your family will want you to add it to the weekly menu. Don't forget to add that squeeze of lime to reduce the oxalic acid content of the greens and to improve iron absorption.—*Charmaine*

*Preparation time* 10 minutes
*Cooking time* 20 minutes
*Serves* 4

*Ingredients*

+ 200 gm paneer cubes
+ 4 cups green leafy vegetables, chopped (a mix of spinach, fenugreek, amaranth, mint, coriander, kale, lettuce, arugula, radish greens, beet greens, etc., with their stalks)
+ 3 large onions, chopped
+ 8 cloves of garlic
+ 2 tsp garam masala
+ 2 tsp jeera powder
+ 1 tsp coriander powder
+ 1 tsp turmeric powder
+ 1/2 tsp pepper powder
+ 4 tbs lime juice
+ 1 tbs vegetable oil
+ Salt to taste
+ A couple of red chillies for tempering

*Method*

+ Place the green leafy vegetables in hot water and blanch them for 2 seconds.
+ Blend the chopped onion and the blanched green leafy vegetables in a blender (you may choose to add the garlic too, if you do not want to add it towards the end of the cooking process).
+ Heat the oil in a pan and fry the onion-leafy vegetable puree until it changes colour.

- Add the masala powders (and the garlic) and continue to fry for 2 minutes.
- Then add a cup or two of hot water and cook until the gravy reaches the desired consistency.
- Lower the flame, add the paneer cubes and cook for 2–3 minutes.
- Add salt to taste and remove from the stovetop.
- Just before serving, add the lime juice and the tempered red chillies.
- Serve hot with parathas or rotis.

*Nutritive value per serving*

- Energy: 242.5 kcal
- CHO: 18.47 gm
- Protein: 12.14 gm
- Fat: 13.34 gm
- Sodium: 79.78 mg
- Potassium: 1100.91 mg
- Calcium: 426.35 mg
- Iron: 6.70 mg
- Vitamin A: 652.82 mcg
- Vitamin C: 58.38 mg

'Paneer is a favourite food at home. Everyone loves paneer. But there's not as much love for leafy vegetables such as methi and kale. So I feel that this is the best way to get my folks to eat their greens. Loved it'

—Reena Patil, Pune

# KHOYA

When milk is subjected to high heat while being stirred constantly, the resultant evaporated mass is called khoya or mawa. It has an oily, grainy texture and a creamy colour. Most Indian sweets or mithais use khoya as the base. Hard khoya, or batti khoya, can be grated and is used to make barfis and ladoos. Granulated or grainy daanedar khoya is made by first curdling milk and then heating and evaporating it. This khoya is used to make Bengali sweetmeats such as kalakand. Any dessert with khoya is irresistible because of its rich, milky flavour and grainy texture, and is a treat for the palate. More importantly, because khoya is naturally sweet, you can get away with using less sugar in your dessert. Khoya is also used in savoury dishes and gravies to enhance the taste and nutritional value. Being a milk product, khoya has calcium, magnesium, phosphorus, and vitamins B, D and K. So it is good for the health of the bones, teeth, hair, skin and the immune system. It is also a good energizer and the vitamin K content helps in blood clotting. Being high in fat, it should be eaten occasionally and in limited amounts.

*Pro-tip:* Khoya can be used as an excellent skin exfoliator. Just cleanse your face well. Then apply a tablespoon of crumbled khoya gently to your skin with your fingers. Rub it around in small circular motions. Rinse off with warm or lukewarm water. Pat dry. You can also choose to leave the scrub on for 10 minutes before rinsing it off.

## KHOYA AMBA HALDI LADOOS

Amba haldi, or *curcuma amada*, is an Ayurvedic antioxidant spice used in the treatment of coughs and colds, asthma, joint and cartilage pain, skin wounds, intestinal worms and to settle indigestion. It is always better to use home-made khoya. It may take some time to make but the taste is so much better than the store-bought varieties. Heat whole milk in a pan, and when it comes to a boil, reduce the flame to minimum. Keep stirring continuously until the milk thickens and reduces to a quarter of the original amount. Once done, the khoya will leave the sides of the pan and form a thick mass at the centre. Cool, transfer to a clean glass container and refrigerate until you need to use it. It will solidify further in the refrigerator and will keep well for about a week.—*Charmaine*

*Preparation time* 15 minutes
*Cooking time* 10 minutes
*Serves* 20

*Ingredients*

- 150 gm fresh khoya
- 100 gm fresh amba haldi or 80 gm amba haldi powder
- 100 gm honey
- 1 tbs ghee
- 50 gm pumpkin seeds, coarsely ground
- 100 gm melon seeds, coarsely ground
- 100 gm white sesame seeds
- 50 gm almonds, coarsely ground
- 2 tbs fennel powder
- 1/2 tsp nutmeg, grated

*Method*

+ Dry-roast the nuts and seeds, and keep aside.
+ Heat the ghee in a pan and roast the crumbled khoya.
+ Mix the rest of the ingredients and form into equal-sized small balls.
+ If the ladoos are too soft, add some more coarsely ground almonds.
+ If you want the ladoos a bit sweeter, add more honey.
+ Place the ladoos in individual paper cases and refrigerate.
+ They will keep well for a week.

*Nutritive value per serving*

+ Energy: 139.84 kcal
+ CHO: 7.54 gm
+ Protein: 5.46 gm
+ Fat: 9.76 gm
+ Sodium: 6.76 mg
+ Potassium: 125.28 mg
+ Calcium: 139 mg
+ Iron: 1.96 mg
+ Vitamin A: 1.6 mcg
+ Vitamin C: 0.09 mg

'I made the khoya at home, so it was very fresh, and I needed to add only half the amount of honey. This has very good taste and nutrient value. My boys and my nieces loved these ladoos and finished them off in three days flat'

—Rochelle Mathias, Mumbai

## KHOYA DRY-FRUIT LADOOS

This traditional winter delicacy is very easy to put together and makes for a nourishing mid-morning or mid-evening snack. Use the tip to make home-made khoya from the recipe of Khoya Amba Haldi Ladoo. You can add any variety of nuts and seeds, or you may choose to omit nuts altogether and use only seeds—pumpkin, melon, watermelon, sunflower, flax, chia, etc. These khoya dry fruit ladoos keep well for a week in an airtight container under refrigeration.—*Charmaine*

*Preparation time* 10 minutes
*Cooking time* 5 minutes
*Serves* 20

*Ingredients*

- 100 gm fresh khoya
- 100 gm black or date palm jaggery, grated
- 80 gm ghee
- 50 gm almonds, chopped
- 50 gm walnuts, chopped
- 50 gm poppy seeds
- 50 gm black sesame seeds
- 50 gm soft black dates
- 1 tsp ginger powder, dried
- 1 tsp cardamom powder
- 1/2 tsp pepper powder

*Method*

- Dry-roast the chopped nuts and seeds, and set aside.

- Heat the ghee in a pan and roast the crumbled khoya.
- Mix the roasted crumbled khoya with the grated jaggery.
- Add the soft black dates and form a smooth mixture.
- Add the spice powders and the dried fruit, and mix well.
- Portion out into small equal-sized balls.
- If the ladoos are very soft, you can roll them in some toasted sesame seeds.
- Place in individual paper cases.
- Keeps well for a week under refrigeration.

*Nutritive value per serving*

- Energy: 123.75 kcal
- CHO: 8.36 gm
- Protein: 2.26 gm
- Fat: 9.03 gm
- Sodium: 1.37 mg
- Potassium: 6.46 mg
- Calcium: 132.63 mg
- Iron: 1.13 mg
- Vitamin A: 11.58 mcg
- Vitamin C: 0.13 mg

'I hand-pounded the dry fruit, because my daughter is a picky eater and is always looking to pull out bits from food. I am happy she likes the taste and has asked me to make more to be able to take to her friend's house once school reopens and play dates begin. So nice to be able to make healthy desserts at home that children eat without fuss'

—Mona Ahir, Nagpur

# YOGHURT

This popular fermented dairy product is made by adding live bacteria culture to warm milk. Scary? No, because the bacteria is the good kind, which has gut health benefits. Water-soluble milk proteins in yoghurt are called whey proteins, while the insoluble ones are caseins. These caseins make up most of the protein content of yoghurt and help increase the absorption of minerals such as calcium and phosphorus to enhance bone health. They also help improve blood pressure. Whey proteins are high in leucine, isoleucine and valine, which are all branched-chain amino acids (BCAAs) that promote weight loss and help muscle-building. Milk lactose breaks down during bacterial fermentation and forms glucose and galactose. Glucose gets converted to lactic acid, and this is what is responsible for the slightly sour taste of fresh yoghurt. Yoghurt has a similar vitamin and mineral profile to milk and other milk products, and only traces of lactose. Hence, it can be consumed by people with lactose intolerance. Lactic acid bacteria and bifidobacteria are the probiotics found in yoghurt that improve digestion, strengthen the immune system and lower cholesterol.

*Pro-tip:* You must have heard the nursery rhyme 'Little Miss Muffet, sat on a tuffet, eating her curd and whey . . .' Why am I taking you back to your kindergarten days? Well, because you may have often wondered what the clear liquid on top of a pot or yoghurt was—that's whey protein. It separates from yoghurt due to temperature fluctuations or when the yoghurt is being transferred from one place to another or even when your recipe calls for hung curd and you place it in a muslin cloth and need to keep a bowl below to collect the liquid that separates from it. That is whey protein, which you should never discard. Drink it as is or add it to soups, gravies, dressings or to knead the dough for rotis, etc.

## LEMON YOGHURT TART

The original recipe of a lemon curd tart, from where this lemon yoghurt tart draws inspiration, calls for a buttery-rich pie crust made from scratch and a lemon curd that comprises eggs, sugar and lots of butter. I've used a hung-curd filling, which tastes as good, is vegetarian and quick to make. To say that it is a whole lot healthier would be stating the obvious.—*Savlyene*

*Preparation time* 30 minutes, plus 2 hours to set
*Cooking time* 0 minutes
*Serves* 8

*Ingredients*

*For the pie crust (8-inch)*

- 300 gm Marie biscuit crumbs
- 50 gm jaggery, grated
- 50 gm butter

*For the lemon yoghurt filling*

- 1 kg yoghurt (hung for 2 hours; save the whey for beverages, soups, gravies, etc.)

- 100 ml milk
- 2 tbs milk powder
- 3 tbs agave nectar or any sweetener of your choice
- 30 gm gelatin
- 4 tbs lime juice
- 1 tsp lime zest
- A few drops of lemon yellow colour (optional)

## Method

### For the pie crust

- Melt the butter and set aside.
- Add the grated jaggery to the hot butter and stir well, until the jaggery dissolves.
- Place the biscuit crumbs in a bowl and gradually add the butter jaggery mixture.
- Lightly mix with your fingertips to resemble loose sand.
- Grease an 8-inch pie dish.
- Firmly press the biscuit mixture down the base, as well as the sides of the dish.
- Chill the pie crust in the freezer for 15 minutes.

### For the lemon yoghurt filling

- Dissolve the gelatin in 100 ml water and set aside.
- Place the milk and milk powder in a deep bowl and whisk well.
- Add the hung curd and whisk for 3 minutes, or until light and smooth.
- Add the sweetener and continue whisking for another 3 minutes.

- Add the lime juice and zest and mix well (you may want to add lesser lime juice if you prefer lesser tartness).
- Add the lemon yellow colour (optional).
- Warm the gelatin in a water bath to liquefy it and quickly mix it into the filling.
- Pour the filling into the prepared pie crust and chill to set.
- Garnish with toasted coconut and a drizzle of caramel (optional).
- Serve cold.

*Nutritive value per serving*

- Energy: 449.51 kcal
- CHO: 45.14 gm
- Protein: 16.95 gm
- Fat: 22.35 gm
- Sodium: 151.86 mg
- Potassium: 64.87 mg
- Calcium: 1429.78 mg
- Iron: 43.45 mg
- Vitamin A: 3.77 mcg
- Vitamin C: 5.21 mg

'When Savlyene sent the reference picture for this tart, I wondered if I would be able to make it. It looked store-bought. But it turned out to be easy to make, especially if the tart shell is made in advance. Scrumptious!'

—Jasmine Ling, Delhi

## YOGHURT BREAKFAST BOWL

The blue spirulina powder, along with the yoghurt, oats, almonds and raisins used here, provide iron, manganese, digestive enzymes, proteins and vitamins A, K and B12. You can use regular spirulina powder instead of the magical blue spirulina. This is easy to make, easy to digest and a great way to start your day.—*Charlyene*

*Preparation time* 5 minutes, plus overnight to soak the oats
*Cooking time* 0 minutes
*Serves* 1

*Ingredients*

- 150 gm yoghurt
- 80 gm steel-cut oats (avoid instant oats)
- 1/2 tsp blue spirulina powder
- 30 gm almond slivers
- 30 gm black raisins

*Method*

- Mix the oats, the black raisins and almonds in the yoghurt and soak overnight. You may need to add some water if you prefer a thinner consistency.
- In the morning, add the blue spirulina powder and stir well.
- The raisins provide sufficient sweetness but you may choose to add a healthier sweetener such as coconut sugar or date syrup for desired sweetness.
- Serve immediately.

*Nutritive value per serving*

- Energy: 400.92 kcal
- CHO: 40.75 gm
- Protein: 14.57 gm
- Fat: 19.96 gm
- Sodium: 52.68 mg
- Potassium: 726.87 mg
- Calcium: 301.67 mg
- Iron: 4.33 mg
- Vitamin A: 7.87 mcg
- Vitamin C: 2.07 mg

---

'My favourite meal is breakfast, and this bowl is simple to make, good to look at and good to taste'

—Warren D'Silva, Goa

# PLANT-BASED MILK/MYLK

A lactose intolerance, milk allergy, Crohn's disease, Ulcerative colitis, IBS and inflammation are some of the reasons why people opt for milk alternatives. They may also not like the taste of milk or maybe concerned about all the pesticide residues, antibiotics and hormones present in animal milk. The unethical practices in dairy farms also play a major role in people's decision to avoid animal milk. Another reason could be veganism.

Milk alternatives are plant-based substitutes for animal milk. They may be produced from plant sources like oats, soy, hemp, rice, almonds, cashews and coconut. They may be called nut beverages or grain beverages or mylks to avoid confusion with regular milk. Irrespective of what they are called, these blended beverages can be a healthy addition to a balanced diet.

# ALMOND MILK

As cases of lactose intolerance and dairy-milk sensitivity rise, and more and more people are opting for plant-based diets, there is an increase in the manufacture and consumption of plant-based milks. Almond milk is a top seller because of its creamy texture and good flavour. Almond milk is a good natural source of fat-soluble vitamin E, which is an antioxidant that protects the organs from free radical damage. Vitamin E combats stress and inflammation, protects against heart disease and cancer, enhances bone, brain and eye health, and may reduce the risk of Alzheimer's disease. Opt for unsweetened almond milk versions to limit your sugar intake. Avoid drinking almond milk if you are allergic to tree nuts. Almond milk is also not a good source of protein (1 gm), as compared to soya milk (7 gm) and cow's milk (8 gm). However, being low in digestible protein, almond milk is not suitable as a replacement for infants and young children with cow's milk allergies..

*Pro-tip:* Almond milk is easy to make at home and healthier too, because commercially made almond milk has thickeners, flavourings and preservatives that are added to enhance the texture, flavour and shelf life. Soak good-quality almonds overnight. In the morning, drain the almonds and remove the skin. Grind them fine and add water to form a smooth paste. Strain, add more water to adjust the consistency, and your almond milk is ready. It keeps well for four days if stored in the refrigerator. Home-made almond milk is not a good source of calcium and vitamin D. Please do not discard the almond meal. Use it to thicken gravies, make smoothies or chutneys, and also to bake almond-meal bread and cakes.

## DATE AND CINNAMON SMOOTHIE

A breakfast on the go, this is a smoothie you will love if you are always in a rush in the mornings. Moreover, it is filling and will keep you energized and satisfied well into lunchtime, provided you eat your lunch on time! The spiciness of the ginger, the iron from the dates, the fat-burning properties of the cinnamon powder, the sweetness and potassium from the banana, and the vitamin E from the almond milk make this a winning combination.—*Savlyene*

*Preparation time* 5 minutes
*Cooking time* 0 minutes
*Serves* 2

*Ingredients*

- 500 ml almond milk, chilled (save the almond meal for cookies, bread or a facial scrub)
- 2 bananas
- 4 dates, seedless
- 2 tbs ginger juice
- 1 tbs cinnamon powder
- A pinch of clove powder

*Method*

- Combine the chilled almond milk with the rest of the ingredients.

- Blend at high speed until smooth and creamy.
- Serve chilled.

*Nutritive value per serving*

- Energy: 183.49 kcal
- CHO: 36.02 gm
- Protein: 2.63 gm
- Fat: 3.21 gm
- Sodium: 3.3 mg
- Potassium: 423.37 mg
- Calcium: 522.18 mg
- Iron: 2.14 mg
- Vitamin A: 66.97 mcg
- Vitamin C: 5.22 mg

> 'I added lesser ginger juice because I am not too fond of ginger. This is very cool and refreshing'
>
> —Jayden Ling, Delhi

## DALGONA COFFEE

If you are feeling peckish mid-evening, having an energy slump midday or need something to awaken you in the morning, a chilled glass of Dalgona is what you need. Coffee and almond milk provide instant energy. Posts on regular Dalgona coffee went viral on social media during the lockdown, probably because people had the time to whip the coffee for hours. Here is our healthier and quicker version that makes use of a hand blender.—*Charlyene*

*Preparation time* 10 minutes
*Cooking time* 0 minutes
*Serves* 2

*Ingredients*

*   400 ml almond milk (save the almond meal to thicken soups and gravies)
*   2 tbs decaf coffee
*   1 tsp cinnamon powder
*   1-1/2 tbs coconut sugar
*   2 tbs hot water

*Method*

*   In a clean bowl mix the decaf coffee, cinnamon powder and coconut sugar.
*   Add 1 tablespoon hot water and blend with a hand blender.
*   Keep blending until the coffee lightens and you get soft peaks when you lift the blender away from the bowl.
*   If you want hot coffee, pour heated almond milk into two mugs. For a cold coffee, use chilled almond milk.
*   Divide the whipped coffee into two parts and gently spoon each part over each mug of almond milk.
*   Drink up!

*Nutritive value per serving*

*   Energy: 132.78 kcal
*   CHO: 25.56 gm
*   Protein: 2.55 gm
*   Fat: 2.26 gm

- Sodium: 19.55 mg
- Potassium: 637.27 mg
- Calcium: 457.45 mg
- Iron: 1.37 mg
- Vitamin A: 0.46 mcg
- Vitamin C: 0.09 mg

'We have been making Dalgona for years, even before it became a lockdown favourite viral on Instagram. I like the GHA coconut-sugar addition. Dalgona coffee transports you to another world. It is my go-to happy place'

—Arati Kejriwal, Mumbai

# CASHEW MILK

Another non-dairy, lactose-free, plant-based milk alternative to cow's milk, cashew milk has a rich, creamy consistency and a sweet, nutty taste. The antioxidants lutein and zeaxanthin present in cashews prevent ocular cellular damage and improve retinal health while preventing vision loss and the risk of developing age-related cataract. The iron content of cashews helps prevent iron-deficiency anaemia. Copper, a mineral in cashews, helps in the production of proteins such as collagen and elastin, which give your skin its elasticity and prevent premature ageing. Zinc, another mineral in cashews, may help increase immunity and decrease inflammation in the body. The magnesium and potassium content in home-made cashew milk, along with the high monounsaturated and polyunsaturated fatty acid content, is what makes this a good choice for decreasing the risk of cardiovascular disease. Cashew milk is also a good source of vitamin K, needed for the clotting of blood and the prevention of excessive loss of blood in an injury. However, if you are on blood thinners and vasodilators, please check with your nutritionist before you start consuming cashews or cashew milk. The vitamin K in them may decrease the effectiveness of your medication. Avoid cashew milk if you are allergic to tree nuts.

*Pro-tip:* When you make cashew milk at home, you need not strain it, thereby retaining its fibre content. When compared to cow's milk, home-made cashew milk, being unfortified, has lesser calcium, potassium and protein, but more iron, magnesium and heart-healthy unsaturated fats. Simply soak the cashews in hot water for about half an hour. Then drain them and blend on high speed with water until smooth and well combined. Adjust the consistency with more water if desired. Refrigerate in a clean glass jar, and it will last for about five days.

## THE GREEN LEAF SMOOTHIE

This one is green, really deeply green. Do not make a fuss to taste it because of its colour. A few sips down and you will realize that it is really sweet and flavourful. A few more sips, and you will never want this glass of deliciousness to end. Then your nutritionist will tell you that it is good for your skin, your eyes, your heart—well, your entire body—and you will be hooked to it for life. Cheers!—*Charlyene*

*Preparation time* 5 minutes
*Cooking time* 0 minutes
*Serves* 2

*Ingredients*

- 300 ml cashew milk
- 100 gm pineapple, chopped
- 1 apple, cored and chopped, with peel
- 4 tbs coriander, freshly chopped, with the stalks
- 2 tbs mint, freshly chopped, with the stalks
- 2 tbs basil leaves, freshly chopped
- 1 tsp moringa powder
- Ice cubes

*Method*

+ Blend all the ingredients on high speed until smooth.
+ Add the ice cubes and continue blending for another minute.
+ Pour into two tall glasses.
+ Serve chilled.

*Nutritive value per serving*

+ Energy: 58.58 kcal
+ CHO: 6.97 gm
+ Protein: 2.95 gm
+ Fat: 2.1 gm
+ Sodium: 14.94 mg
+ Potassium: 360.4 mg
+ Calcium: 384.04 mg
+ Iron: 3.86 mg
+ Vitamin A: 386.6 mcg
+ Vitamin C: 30.62 mg

'A delicious supermeal. Such a deliciously flavoured smoothie! The tropical taste of pineapple with a dash of mint, basil and coriander, among other ingredients, made it my absolute favourite. Having it chilled was really refreshing. I can't wait to have it again'

—Neev Vijay Kumar, Singapore

## CASHEW NOG SMOOTHIE

Every year at Christmas time, Dad makes us eggnog, and we love it. It is a decadent indulgence made of whipped eggs, sugar, milk, cream and lots of grated nutmeg. As teenagers, we were given a serving of this with a splash of bourbon on Christmas Eve. The eggs in an eggnog are raw but the alcohol that ages this drink preserves and sterilizes it. Do try our GHA take on this holiday tradition. No eggs, no sugar, no dairy milk, no cream and yet our cashew nog smoothie has all the creaminess and flavour of our Dad's traditional version!—*Savlyene*

*Preparation time* 5 minutes
*Cooking time* 0 minutes
*Serves* 4

*Ingredients*

* 750 ml cashew milk, home-made
* 100 gm cashews, soaked
* 150 gm date puree
* 2 tsp vanilla extract
* 2 tsp cinnamon powder
* 1/2 tsp nutmeg, freshly grated
* A pinch of star anise powder

*Method*

* Blend all the ingredients at high speed until smooth and creamy.
* Serve chilled.

*Nutritive value per serving*

- ◆ Energy: 309.73 kcal
- ◆ CHO: 41.69 gm
- ◆ Protein: 5.57 gm
- ◆ Fat: 13.41 gm
- ◆ Sodium: 21.75 mg
- ◆ Potassium: 191.07 mg
- ◆ Calcium: 430.52 mg
- ◆ Iron: 2.58 mg
- ◆ Vitamin A: 13.9 mcg
- ◆ Vitamin C: 0.28 mg

'Love the ease of preparing this smoothie. The deliciousness of this super meal is absolutely amazing, and the flavours are nutty, with a lovely hint of gentle spices. Such a delectable way to get my much-needed boost of energy, and it is nutritionally beneficial too. Was on the lookout for a satisfying and great-tasting super meal, and I have found it. No snacking in between meals for me from now on'

—Shamin Charles D'Souza, Singapore

# COCONUT MILK

Coconut milk has been used for years in the cuisines of people from south India, Sri Lanka, Thailand, Indonesia, Hawaii, South America and the Caribbean islands. It has recently found favour with those who want plant-based alternatives to cow's milk. Thick coconut milk is used in desserts and to thicken sauces. Thin coconut milk is used in gravies, soups and salad dressings. This high-calorie, high-saturated-fat milk is also rich in MCT (medium-chain triglyceride) fats, which may benefit weight loss. This is because MCTs go directly from the digestive tract to the liver to be used as a source of energy and are less likely stored as fat. MCTs also reduce appetite and effectively aid weight loss. The regular consumption of small amounts of coconut milk may help reduce inflammation in the body, decrease the size of a stomach ulcer and fight pathogens or disease-producing microorganisms that could have entered the body. Reduce your intake if you have a FODMAP intolerance.

*Pro-tip:* It is very easy to make coconut milk at home. Your grandmother, mother, aunts and older relatives have probably been making it for ages. So there is no need to buy commercially canned varieties that may contain bisphenol A (BPA). This chemical can leach directly into the food from the lining of the can used to pack food. It can cause cancer and reproductive health issues. Simply take freshly grated coconut meal and blend it with water to make a smooth paste. Sieve through a muslin cloth to get the first extract of thick coconut milk.

Then take the coconut meal residue and blend it again with some water. Sieve through a muslin cloth to get the second extract of thin coconut milk. Do not discard the coconut meal residue. Use it in your gravies, masala pastes, etc.

## CARDAMOM COCO SMOOTHIE

One of the reasons this smoothie tastes so good is because of the high fat content of the coconut milk. It is the perfectly spiced, nutritionally dense treat for festive holidays, family celebrations, graduation ceremonies, career promotions, engagement announcements, wedding anniversaries, baby showers, birthday parties, school reunions—for just about any joyous occasion, really.—*Charmaine*

*Preparation time* 5 minutes
*Cooking time* 0 minutes
*Serves* 4

*Ingredients*

- 750 ml thin coconut milk (not coconut cream)
- 4 bananas, frozen
- 3 tbs coconut sugar
- 1 tbs cardamom powder
- Ice cubes

*Method*

- Mix all the ingredients and blend on high speed until frothy.
- Add the ice cubes and continue blending for 2 minutes.

- Pour into chilled glasses.
- Serve immediately.

*Nutritive value per serving*

- Energy: 180.7 kcal
- CHO: 17.27 gm
- Protein: 1.45 gm
- Fat: 11.9 gm
- Sodium: 20.9 mg
- Potassium: 191.53 mg
- Calcium: 21.15 mg
- Iron: 0.52 mg
- Vitamin A: 4.46 mcg
- Vitamin C: 2.22 mg

'OMG! This is so easy to make and so delicious. A super-refreshing smoothie! Methinks its #instasmoothie #bestsmoothie'

—Ashish Kejriwal, Mumbai

## SPICED THAI SMOOTHIE

What started as a way to use up all those fresh kaffir lime leaves that Hubby would buy from Thailand ended up in this refreshing smoothie. As with Thai cuisine, where the flavour profiles are based around sweet, salty, hot and sour, the delicious blend of these very same flavours in your smoothie glass will excite your taste buds and those of your family.—*Charmaine*

*Preparation time* 5 minutes
*Cooking time* 0 minutes
*Serves* 4

## Ingredients

- 750 ml thin coconut milk (not coconut cream)
- 100 ml coconut water
- 200 gm papaya cubes
- 3 tbs chia seeds
- 3 tbs agave nectar
- 1 tbs lime juice
- 1 tbs ginger juice
- 1–2 kaffir lime leaves
- 1 pinch of coriander powder
- 1 pinch of pepper powder
- A pinch of salt

## Method

- Combine all the ingredients in a blender and blend on high speed for 2–3 minutes.
- Pour into glasses.
- Serve chilled.

## Nutritive value per serving

- Energy: 153.86 kcal
- CHO: 7.72 gm
- Protein: 1.59 gm
- Fat: 12.96 gm
- Sodium: 19.89 mg

- Potassium: 68.33 mg
- Calcium: 39.09 mg
- Iron: 0.72 mg
- Vitamin A: 19.56 mcg
- Vitamin C: 7.44 mg

'Tried out something similar in Penang. Super-duper refreshing. Absolutely love its refreshing taste. Serves as a meal'

—Roshni Jain, Jodhpur

# OAT MILK

This dairy-free, vegan substitute to cow's milk may not be as nutritious as whole oats but is a good choice for those with food allergies and intolerances. Oat milk is a popular choice for people who want a plant milk that is free of allergens such as nuts, lactose, soya and gluten—that is, as long as the oats are certified gluten-free. The beta-glucan soluble fibre in oat milk is good for lowering LDL cholesterol levels and for the overall health of the heart. Fortified commercially available oat milk has more calories, carbohydrates and fibre than almond milk, soya milk and cow's milk, but a lesser amount of protein. Vitamins B12 and B2 are added to commercial oat milk and the health benefits they provide are numerous and include optimizing the health of hair, skin and nails, alleviating mood, improving sleep patterns and decreasing stress. If you opt to buy commercially available oat milk, please choose an unsweetened variety. Commercial oat milk has phosphates to regulate the acidity of the product. Phosphates are a common additive in processed foods and are linked to kidney disease. If you are already consuming a high amount of processed foods, opt for any plant-based milk other than oat milk.

*Pro-tip:* Making oat milk at home is extremely easy. All you need to do is soak rolled oats (gluten-free, if you are allergic to gluten) in water for 1 hour. Rinse well and add more water. Then blend it well. Strain through a muslin cloth. Add a pinch of salt and pour the oat milk into a clean glass bottle. Store in the refrigerator.

## VITALITY GREEN BOOSTER

Here is a good way to get fussy eaters to eat their greens—or, rather, drink them. In fact, it is an easy way to guzzle four servings of greens and fruit in a matter of minutes. Use the freshest, crunchiest greens in your veggie basket. This booster provides an abundance of antioxidants and is perfect to sip on any time of the day.—*Charmaine*

*Preparation time* 15 minutes
*Cooking time* 0 minutes
*Serves* 4

*Ingredients*

- 600 ml oat milk
- 4 pears, chopped, with the peel
- 2 guavas, deseeded, with the peel
- 20 spinach leaves, blanched, with their stalks
- 20 kale leaves, blanched, with the stalks
- 150 ml coconut water

*Method*

- Blend all the ingredients at high speed until well blended.
- Taste. You may want to add a natural sweetener such as dates, and blend again.
- Serve immediately.

*Nutritive value per serving*

- Energy: 211.42 kcal
- CHO: 39.8 gm

- Protein: 6.35 gm
- Fat: 2.98 gm
- Sodium: 29.34 mg
- Potassium: 612.37 mg
- Calcium: 82.45 mg
- Iron: 2.4 mg
- Vitamin A: 111.31 mcg
- Vitamin C: 192.49 mg

'Since fresh kale was not available, we used mint. It tasted very good and the combination of pear and mint brought a touch of freshness to the recipe'

—Krishnakshi Ashar, Mumbai

## APPLE-OAT BLEND

If you are hoping for a particularly good start to your day, start it with this apple-oat blend. It will stand you in good stead, especially if you have risk factors for heart disease and type 2 diabetes. The liberal amounts of cinnamon used here will not only help lower blood pressure, blood cholesterol and blood sugar, but also act as a fat burner. Not forgetting that this blend smells like an apple pie!—*Savlyene*

*Preparation time* 5 minutes
*Cooking time* 0 minutes
*Serves* 4

*Ingredients*

- 500 ml oat milk
- 2 apples, chopped and cored with the peel

- 1 tbs coconut oil
- 2 tsp cinnamon powder
- 4 figs, dried
- A pinch of salt

*Method*

- Blend all the ingredients at high speed in a blender until smooth.
- Pour into 2 glasses.
- Serve cold.

*Nutritive value per serving*

- Energy: 185.06 kcal
- CHO: 29.47 gm
- Protein: 3.69 gm
- Fat: 5.82 gm
- Sodium: 1.75 mg
- Potassium: 73.27 mg
- Calcium: 48.3 mg
- Iron: 1.24 mg
- Vitamin A: 5.09 mcg
- Vitamin C: 2.68 mg

'The apple-oat blend is perfect when you have a sweet craving. It makes you feel full and energized after having it. It makes you feel extremely fresh too'

—Krina Ashar, Mumbai

# SOYA MILK

This delicious, inexpensive, easy-to-make vegan alternative to dairy milk is high in protein. It has nine essential amino acids and is a good balance of carbohydrates and fats. Its strong flavour may act as a deterrent for drinking as is, but it's a good choice for cooking and baking because of its higher fat content than other plant milks. It also has a texture and an overall nutritive profile that closely resembles cow's milk. Soya is rich in isoflavones, particularly genistein, and is heart-protective. Isoflavones are plant oestrogens, or phytoestrogens, which may reduce the risk of cancer and osteoporosis. Menopausal women will also benefit from its consumption. The recommended allowance for daily consumption is two servings of all soya foods, such as soya beans, soya milk and tofu. Limit your consumption if you have hypothyroidism or breast cancer. Avoid if you are allergic to soya and its products. It is better for your health, the planet and the animals.

*Pro-tip:* To make soya milk at home, soak soya beans in water overnight. In the morning, drain the beans and remove the outer skin. Blend well with water until light and creamy. Strain this blend through a muslin bag. Pour the soya milk into a vessel and bring it to a boil. Skim off the foam. Then add water according to the consistency you desire and cook on a low flame for 20 minutes. Cool and refrigerate. Soya is not a natural source of calcium, so up your calcium-rich food intake, else have calcium-fortified soya milk.

# SOYA-MILK CHOCOLATE PUDDING

Turning milk and eggs into a lovely pudding is easy. There are so many varieties that you can make, from the queen of puddings to bread-and-butter pudding, rice pudding, diplomat pudding and plum pudding. However, when your bestie has stopped eating the pudding basics of milk and eggs, and you want to treat her to dessert that is decadently delicious, you make her this yummy soya-milk chocolate pudding. Making it is super easy, but I cannot guarantee that there will be any leftovers for other friends to savour.—*Charlyene*

*Preparation time* 20 minutes
*Cooking time* 20 minutes, plus 2 hours to set
*Serves* 8

## Ingredients

- 300 ml soya milk
- 400 gm silken tofu
- 220 gm dark chocolate, chopped
- 60 gm gelatin
- 2 tbs black chia seeds
- 2 tbs agave nectar or honey

## Method

- Soak the gelatin in 100 ml water and set aside.
- Put the tofu in a blender and blend until smooth.
- Boil the soya milk, add the chia seeds and blend well.
- Lightly heat the gelatin in a water bath until it dissolves.
- Pour the dissolved gelatin into the soya milk-chia mixture and stir to mix well.

- Put the chopped dark chocolate into a large bowl and pour the hot soya milk mixture into this.
- Add the agave nectar or honey and whisk until smoothly blended.
- Add the blended tofu and continue to whisk until light and creamy.
- Add more agave nectar or honey if you want a sweeter pudding.
- Use swirls of melted white chocolate to decorate (optional).
- Pour into a springform pan and place in the refrigerator to set.
- Serve cold.

*Nutritive value per serving*

- Energy: 294.77 kcal
- CHO: 19.64 gm
- Protein: 16.68 gm
- Fat: 16.61 gm
- Sodium: 30.3 mg
- Potassium: 1569.88 mg
- Calcium: 2331.92 mg
- Iron: 89.77 mg
- Vitamin A: 1.03 mcg
- Vitamin C: 0.06 mg

'Looking at the perfection of the finished product, no one believed I made this soya-milk chocolate pudding myself. Everything about it is so perfect that I didn't even want to cut it. Simply out-of-the-world dreamy pudding!'

—Sangeeta L. Singh, Delhi

# AVOCADO SOYA SMOOTHIE

This creamy and surprisingly light smoothie takes just a few minutes to make, but will keep you satiated and energized for hours. This is a quick-fix meal for mornings when the family wants to drink breakfast, not eat it. It can also be a nutrient-dense post-workout meal, with all the healthy fats coming from avocado. Even your vegan friends can relish this smoothie and ask for more—a whole lot more.—*Savlyene*

*Preparation time* 5 minutes
*Cooking time* 0 minutes
*Serves* 4

## Ingredients

* 1 litre soya milk
* 2 firm avocados, deseeded and peeled
* 8 dates, seedless
* 1/4 tsp turmeric powder
* 1/8 tsp pepper powder
* 1 tsp lime juice
* Ice cubes

## Method

* Chop the avocados into bits.
* Combine the soya milk with the rest of the ingredients.
* Blend well.
* Add the ice cubes and continue to blend.
* Immediately pour into glasses.
* Served chilled.

*Nutritive value per serving*

- Energy: 276.04 kcal
- CHO: 13.35 gm
- Protein: 18.04 gm
- Fat: 16.72 gm
- Sodium: 2.09 mg
- Potassium: 254.93 mg
- Calcium: 23.56 mg
- Iron: 0.85 mg
- Vitamin A: 1.96 mcg
- Vitamin C: 6.69 mg

'I'm glad Dad delegated the making of this smoothie to me. Super-easy to make, delicious to taste. I added a bit more lemon juice, as it cuts down the richness of the creamy avocado and makes it even more delicious'

—Liam Fernandes, Toronto, Canada

# References

- Eds. Fortin, F. and Serge D. Amico. *The Visual Food Encyclopedia*, Macmillan, New York, 1996.
- Anderson, J., P. Baird, R. Davis, S. Ferreri, et al. 'Health Benefits of Dietary Fiber', *Nutrition Reviews*, 2009.
- Mitchell, D., F. Lawrence, T. Hartman and J. Curran. 'Consumption of Dry Beans, Peas and Lentils Could Improve Diet Quality in the US Population', *Journal of the American Dietetic Association*, 2009.
- Wood, R. *The New Whole Foods Encyclopedia*, Penguin Publishing Group, New York, 1988.
- Ensminger A.H., M.K.J. Ensminger et al. *Food for Health: A Nutrition Encyclopedia*, 1986.
- Margen, S. *Wellness Foods A to Z: An Indispensable Guide for Health-Conscious Food Lovers*, BASCO, 2002.
- Whitehair, K.J., L.A. Brannon and C.W. Shanklin. 'Written Messages Improve Edible Food Waste Behaviors in a University Dining Facility', *Journal of the Academy of Nutrition and Dietetics*, 2013.
- Thyberg, K.L. and David J. Tonjes. 'Drivers of Food Waste and Their Implications for Sustainable Policy Development', *Resources, Conservation and Recycling*, 2020.
- Yaffe-Bellany, David and Michael Corkery. 'Dumped Milk, Smashed Eggs, Plowed Vegetables: Food Waste of the Pandemic 2020', Nytimes.com, April 2020.
- Gerlock, G. 'To End Food Waste, Change Needs to Begin at Home', The Salt, NPR, 2014.

- Lehner, P. 'Tackling Food Waste at Home', NDRC, 2012.
- Antioxidants and Cancer Prevention, National Cancer Institute, 2017.
- Boyer, J. and R.H. Liu. 'Apple Phytochemicals and Their Health Benefits', *Nutrition Journal*, 2004.
- Haq, S.H. and A.A. AlAmro. 'Neuroprotective Effect of Quercetin in Murine Cortical Brain Tissue Cultures', *Clinical Nutrition Experimental*, 2019.
- Slavin, J.L. and B. Lloyd. 'Health Benefits of Fruits and Vegetables', *Advances in Nutrition*, 2012.

# Review

If you wish to use food as medicine to stave off disease, *The Good Health Always Cookbook* should earn a prized place on your kitchen shelf. In it, Charmaine D'Souza and her GHA team summarize the healing properties and ORAC values of different herbs and spices that are regularly used in different cuisines. They have worked on creating simple, primarily plant-based recipes, so you can easily incorporate superfoods into your daily diet. This cookbook is an ideal follow-up to her previous book, *Kitchen Clinic*, based on the therapeutic values of kitchen herbs and spices.

Neatly organized and easily approachable, *The Good Health Always Cookbook* is an enthusiastic introduction by a nutritionist to zero edible food waste. As a chef technologist, the most valuable lesson I teach my students is to never throw any edible food waste away. So no peels, seeds, skins and bones ever get thrown in the bin. This cookbook has recipes that incorporate the vegetable peels, seeds and even the cooking liquids into the main dish. It also has recipes that specifically make use of edible waste. My favourite is the banana-peel thoran!

The chapters review the different plant-based food groups and show how the nutrients in each food group impact our health. There are holistic recipes for each food item in the cereal, pulse, vegetable, fruit, dairy and non-dairy food groups. Interesting anecdotes, recipe variations, nutritive values, and luminous, home-clicked photographs document the different recipes. Each recipe also comes to you with honest feedback from a chosen few recipients who participated in the recipe trials.

The book has 120 recipes that are recommended for optimizing your health. Recipes from cuisines of countries such as Indonesia, Morocco, Italy, France, Germany, Great Britain and China, as well as from regional cuisines such as south Indian, Oriya, Andhra, Keralite, Bengali, Marwari, Rajasthani, east Indian, Goan, Kashmiri, Amritsari and Gujarati are listed and lucidly explained. Avid home cooks will find delight in delicious dishes, from smoothies to soups, salads, brownies, bowls, blends, cookies, crepes, curries, mousses, munchies and more—all tailored to improving physical and mental health.

With the focus on readily available and affordable ingredients, *The Good Health Always Cookbook* makes it easy to explore new ways of preventing and combating illness, all from the comfort of your kitchen.

—Chelston Fernandes
Chef technologist, George Brown College,
Toronto, Canada